HACCP

A Systematic Approach

to Food Safety

*A Comprehensive Manual for Developing
and Implementing a Hazard Analysis
and Critical Control Point Plan*

edited by

Kenneth E. Stevenson, Ph.D.

and

Dane T. Bernard

NATIONAL FOOD PROCESSORS ASSOCIATION

published by

The Food Processors Institute

1350 I Street, N.W., Suite 300
Washington, D.C. 20005-3305

THIRD EDITION
© 1999

THIRD EDITION, 1ˢᵗ Printing

©1999 The Food Processors Institute
Washington, D.C.

The Food Processors Institute
1350 I Street
Washington, D.C. 20005

Printed in the United States of America

LIBRARY OF CONGRESS
CATALOG CARD NO.: 99-62752

HACCP — A Systematic Approach to Food Safety: A Comprehensive Manual for Developing and Implementing a Hazard Analysis and Critical Control Point Plan.

Washington, D.C.: Food Processors Institute, The

196 p.

ISBN 0-937774-11-1

Allen M. Katsuyama
1938-1999

This HACCP Manual is dedicated to Allen Katsuyama. As a Principal Scientist of the National Food Processors Association's Center for Technical Assistance in Dublin, California, Allen's contributions to this manual are incalculable.

A Pioneer, who helped us understand the relationship between HACCP and sanitation/GMPs, and who helped shape the FPI Basic HACCP Workshop;

A Scientist, who provided excellent technical assistance and advice to the food industry;

A Teacher/Mentor, who left a valuable legacy of students and peers through his unselfish teaching and example;

A Colleague, who shared his expertise and vast experience with others; and, most of all,

A Friend.

ACKNOWLEDGMENTS

The Food Processors Institute (FPI) gratefully acknowledges the authors as well as the many people and organizations that have contributed material and direction to *HACCP: A Systematic Approach to Food Safety*, Third Edition.

This manual was designed to be used in conjunction with the Basic HACCP Course, sponsored by The Food Processors Institute. The contents of the manual have evolved primarily through the thoughtful insight of a variety of instructors; the valuable comments received from university and industry co-sponsors of FPI workshops; and the substantive feedback from participants of the workshops, which have been held over the past twelve years.

A special thanks to Lisa Weddig, National Food Processors Association, for coordinating the Third Edition; Margaret Hardin, National Pork Producers Council, and Robert Savage, The HACCP Consulting Group, for reviewing the manuscript; and Jon-Mikel Woody, FPI, for his many hours of formatting and proofreading.

LIST OF CONTRIBUTORS

Dane T. Bernard
Vice President, Office of Food Safety Programs
National Food Processors Association
1350 I Street, NW, Suite 300
Washington, DC 20005

David E. Gombas, Ph.D.
Acting Director, Center for Development of Research
  Policy and New Technologies
National Food Processors Association
1350 I Street, NW, Suite 300
Washington, DC 20005

Robert B. Gravani, Ph.D.
Professor of Food Science
Cornell University
Department of Food Science
11 Stocking Hall
Ithaca, NY 14853

Lloyd R. Hontz
Director, Food Inspection Issues—Technical
  Regulatory Affairs
National Food Processors Association
1350 I Street, NW, Suite 300
Washington, DC 20005

Michael Jantschke
Scientist, Center for Technical Assistance
National Food Processors Association
6363 Clark Avenue
Dublin, CA 94568

Allen M. Katsuyama, Ph.D.
Formerly with the National Food Processors
  Association

Nina G. Parkinson
Scientist, Center for Technical Assistance
National Food Processors Association
6363 Clark Avenue
Dublin, CA 94568

Virginia N. Scott
Senior Director, Office of Food Safety Programs
National Food Processors Association
1350 I Street, NW, Suite 300
Washington, DC 20005

Kenneth E. Stevenson, Ph.D.
Principal Scientist, Center for Technical Assistance
National Food Processors Association
6363 Clark Avenue
Dublin, CA 94568

Lisa M. Weddig
Scientist, Office of Food Safety Programs
National Food Processors Association
1350 I Street, NW, Suite 300
Washington, DC 20005

Jon-Mikel Woody
Program Manager
Food Processors Institute
1350 I Street, NW, Suite 300
Washington, DC 20005

FOREWORD TO THE THIRD EDITION

The revisions contained in the third edition of *HACCP—A Systematic Approach to Food Safety: A Comprehensive Manual for Developing and Implementing a Hazard Analysis and Critical Control Point Plan* reflect the continuing evolution of our understanding of Hazard Analysis and Critical Control Point (HACCP) plan development and implementation. The second edition of this manual was based on the National Advisory Committee on Microbiological Criteria for Foods (NACMCF) 1992 HACCP document. The Third Edition is based on the HACCP document adopted by NACMCF in 1997. This manual provides the most current description of HACCP principles now available. Changes have been made to many chapters, especially those describing hazard analysis, verification, and current regulatory requirements.

This manual provides a logical approach for introducing HACCP to workshop participants and for providing the information necessary for developing a model HACCP plan. The initial chapters provide the introduction, overview and background of HACCP as detailed by the NACMCF 1997 HACCP document. The succeeding chapters on biological, chemical and physical hazards provide the information necessary for identifying potential hazards that fall in those respective categories. These chapters also provide an overview of control mechanisms for each of the potential hazards. It is important to note that, depending on the outcome of the hazard analysis and identification of critical control points, many of the potential hazards under consideration may not be controlled within a HACCP plan. However, control measures discussed in these chapters are valuable for food establishments to adopt as part of their overall food management system.

Most HACCP experts now agree that the hazard analysis is probably the most difficult part of HACCP and the portion that is least understood. Thus, following the example of the NACMCF, this manual spends considerably more time in explaining current concepts on conducting a hazard analysis than the previous editions. Also, the manual chapter dealing with managing and organizing HACCP plans has been significantly modified from past versions and chapters on training and prerequisite programs have been added. These modifications reflect our realization of the importance of these various programs to the overall management of food safety. In light of the implementation of U.S. regulations based on HACCP principles, references to the current government requirements have been added to applicable chapters.

We trust that this manual will be of use in your own food safety management endeavors. We appreciate your comments and feedback on this manual. We also express our appreciation to the many contributors to this manual.

TABLE OF CONTENTS

Chapter 3: Prerequisites To HACCP 25

Chapter 4: Sanitation And Standard Operating Procedures 31

Chapter 5: Biological Hazards And Controls 39

Chapter 6: Chemical Hazards And Controls 53

Chapter 7: Physical Hazards And Controls 63

Chapter 1

INTRODUCTION TO HAZARD ANALYSIS AND CRITICAL CONTROL POINT SYSTEMS

K. E. Stevenson

HACCP CONCEPT

The **H**azard **A**nalysis and **C**ritical **C**ontrol **P**oint (HACCP) system is a management system focused on prevention of problems in order to assure the production of food products that are safe to consume. It is based on a common-sense application of technical and scientific principles to the food production process from field to table. The principles of HACCP are applicable to all phases of food production, including basic agriculture, food preparation and handling, food processing, food service, distribution systems and consumer handling and use.

The most basic concept underlying HACCP is that of prevention rather than inspection. A food grower, processor, handler, distributor or consumer should have sufficient information concerning the food and the related procedures they are using, so they will be able to identify where and how a food safety problem may occur. If the "where" and "how" are known, prevention becomes easy and obvious, and finished product inspection and testing becomes superfluous. A HACCP program deals with control of factors affecting the ingredients, product and process. The objective is to make the product safe to consume, *and* to be able to prove it. The where and how are the HA (hazard analysis) part of HACCP. The proof of the control of processes and conditions is the CCP (Critical Control Point) part. Flowing from this basic concept, HACCP is simply a methodical and systematic application of the appropriate science and technology to plan, control and document the safe production of foods.

By definition, the HACCP concept covers all types of potential food safety hazards—biological, chemical and physical—whether they are naturally occurring in the food, contributed by the environment or generated by a mistake in the manufacturing process. While chemical hazards are still feared by many consumers and physical hazards are the most commonly identified by consumers, microbiological hazards are the most serious from a public health perspective. For this reason, while HACCP systems address all three types of hazards, a majority of the emphasis is placed on microbiological issues. For example, a piece of metal (physical hazard) in a food product may result in a chipped tooth for one consumer, but contamination of a batch of milk with *Salmonella* may affect hundreds or even thousands of consumers.

1

ORIGIN OF HACCP

Development of Foods for the Space Program

The Pillsbury Company, the U. S. Army Natick Laboratories and NASA, developed the HACCP system in response to the food safety requirements imposed by NASA for "space foods" produced for manned space flights beginning in 1959. NASA had two principal safety issues. The first was related to potential problems with food particles—crumbs—and water in the space capsule under conditions of zero gravity. (They were concerned about potential problems of crumbs or water droplets interfering with electrical equipment.) The second issue was the need for absolute assurance of freedom from pathogens and biological toxins. A case of foodborne illness, e.g., staphylococcal food poisoning, in a space capsule, would have been catastrophic.

The first concern, food crumbs or liquid droplets in zero gravity, was addressed by developing bite-sized foods and by using specially formulated edible coatings to hold the food together. Also, highly specialized types of packaging were used to minimize the exposure of foods and liquids to the environment during storage, preparation and consumption. The second concern, microbiological safety was more difficult to address. Sampling of finished product, to establish microbiological safety of each batch of space food produced proved to be impractical, if not impossible. To quote Dr. Howard Bauman, who managed the development of HACCP at Pillsbury,

> We quickly found that by using standard methods of quality control there was absolutely no way we could be assured that there wouldn't be a problem. This brought into serious question the then prevailing system of quality control in our plants. . . If we had to do a great deal of destructive testing to come to a reasonable conclusion that the product was safe to eat, how much were we missing in the way of safety issues by principally testing only the end product and raw materials?

> We concluded after extensive evaluation that the only way we could succeed would be to establish control over the entire process, the raw materials, the processing environment and the people involved.

To help quantify the impracticality of attribute sampling and the resultant destructive testing of end product which would be necessary to assure microbiological safety, consider the following example. If *Salmonella* was present in a batch of product at the rate of 1 out of every 1000 units of product (defect rate = 0.1%), a sampling plan which analyzed 60 units from the batch would have >94% probability of approving the batch and missing the salmonella-contaminated product.

In addition to the statistical evidence that this sampling plan would be ineffective in detecting the contaminated product, there is the practical and economic reality that no company would be able to afford to destructively test 60 units out of every batch of product for the presence of *Salmonella*. Thus, an alternative approach had to be developed in order to obtain the level of assurance of product safety that NASA required for foods produced for the space program.

At first, they explored the use of NASA's "Zero Defects Program" which was designed for testing hardware intended for the space program. This program utilized a series of non-destructive tests of hardware for the purpose of assuring that the hardware functioned properly. While repeated, non-destructive testing could be used on every piece of hardware, this program was not appropriate for adaptation to foods.

Eventually, the "Modes of Failure" concept developed by the U.S. Army Natick Laboratories, was adapted to the production of foods. By gathering knowledge and experience concerning a food product/process, it was possible to predict what might go wrong (a "hazard"), how it would occur, and where it would occur in the process. Based on this type of analysis of the hazards associated with a specific product and process, it was possible to select points at which measurements and/or observations could be made that would demonstrate whether or not the process was being controlled. If the process was out of control, there was an increased probability that a food safety problem would occur. These points in the process were then, and are today, called critical control points (CCPs). Thus, HACCP was developed to target proper design of all of the factors associated with ingredients, processes and products in order to prevent hazards from occurring, and thereby ensure the safety of the products.

The Original HACCP System

The HACCP concept was first presented to the public at the 1971 National Conference on Food Protection (DHEW, 1971). This initial HACCP system consisted of three principles:

1. Identification and assessment of hazards associated with growing/harvesting to marketing/preparation.

2. Determination of the critical control points to control any identifiable hazard.

3. Establishment of systems to monitor critical control points.

Along with these principles, the system identified a CCP as a point in the manufacture of a product whose loss of control would result in an unacceptable food safety risk.

The preventive nature of the HACCP system is readily apparent when these principles are paraphrased, as follows:

1. Identify any safety-related problems associated with the ingredients, product and process.

2. Determine the specific factors that need to be controlled to prevent these problems from occurring.

3. Establish systems that can measure and document whether or not these factors are being controlled properly.

EARLY USES OF HACCP

At first, there was considerable interest in this new approach to food safety. The U.S. Food and Drug Administration (FDA) began training its inspectors in the elements of HACCP (Pillsbury, 1973), and they instituted special HACCP inspections of food plants. There were numerous conferences and sessions on HACCP, including a symposium at the 1974 Annual Meeting of the Institute of Food Technologists.

During the 1970's, FDA promulgated the low-acid and acidified canned food regulations—Title 21, *Code of Federal Regulations* Part 113 (originally 21 *CFR* 128b), "Thermally Processed Low-Acid Foods Packaged in Hermetically Sealed Containers," and 21 *CFR* 114, "Acidified Foods," respectively. While these regulations did not mention HACCP, their approach to controlling *Clostridium botulinum* certainly appears to be based upon HACCP concepts.

After this initial flurry of activity, interest in HACCP appeared to wane. While the description of the HACCP principles was relatively brief, developing a HACCP program is not a simple matter. It takes considerable time and expertise to set up a HACCP program. Therefore, except for use by a few large food companies and the required use of HACCP concepts for FDA-regulated thermally processed low-acid and acidified foods, HACCP was not widely used in the food industry.

1985 NAS REPORT

Interest in HACCP was rekindled in 1985 when a Subcommittee of the Food Protection Committee of the National Academy of Sciences (NAS) issued a report on microbiological criteria. This report (NAS, 1985) was the result of a study commissioned by several government agencies with responsibilities for food safety. While the objectives of the study were mainly related to establishing microbiological criteria for foods, the report included a particularly strong endorsement of HACCP. The report recommended that regulators and industry both utilize HACCP because it was the most effective and efficient means of assuring the safety of our food supply.

While the 1985 NAS report received mostly favorable responses, two areas elicited some unfavorable responses from industry:

1. The statement that HACCP would have to be required by regulation if it is to be widely utilized.

2. The apparent approval of regulatory access to a variety of records.

NATIONAL ADVISORY COMMITTEE ON MICROBIOLOGICAL CRITERIA FOR FOODS

Based upon recommendations in the 1985 NAS report, a committee, consisting primarily of food microbiologists, was appointed to serve as an expert scientific advisory panel to the Secretaries of Agriculture, Commerce, Defense, and Health and Human Services.

This committee held its first meetings in 1988, and was named the National Advisory Committee on Microbiological Criteria for Foods (NACMCF). Part of the mission of the NACMCF is to encourage adoption of the HACCP approach to food safety. In their initial meetings and discussions, it became obvious that there were several different opinions concerning the specifics associated with HACCP systems. Therefore, a HACCP group was appointed to study HACCP and make recommendations to NACMCF. In 1989, the NACMCF adopted a document (NACMCF, 1989) describing seven HACCP principles and a systematic approach for the application of HACCP to food production. Based upon additional information and experience in applying HACCP principles over the past decade, the NACMCF has adopted two revisions of its HACCP document (NACMCF, 1992 and 1997).

CODEX ALIMENTARIUS COMMITTEE ON FOOD HYGIENE

The Codex Alimentarius Committee on Food Hygiene (Codex) has been actively involved in the development of HACCP guidelines for use in international trade. This is a committee of the United Nations WHO/FAO Codex Alimentarius Commission, and they have worked in concert with the NACMCF to revise and refine explanations of the HACCP principles and guidelines for use in applying the HACCP principles to various food production operations. Recently, Codex adopted the latest version of the HACCP guidance document (Codex, 1997), and a copy of this document is reproduced in Appendix A.

SUMMARY

The HACCP system was developed originally by The Pillsbury Company, NASA and the U.S. Army Natick Laboratories to provide a system to produce safe foods for use in the space program. As designed, HACCP was a preventive and systematic approach to food safety. Substantial refinements and revisions by the NACMCF and Codex have provided a description of HACCP principles and their application which is recognized internationally as an efficient and effective system for use in managing food safety.

Note: The chapters which follow provide details concerning the HACCP Principles that were developed (and revised) by the NACMCF (1989, 1992, 1997), and additional information for use in applying the HACCP Principles to food processing operations.

REFERENCES

Codex. 1997. *Hazard Analysis and Critical Control Point (HACCP) System and Guidelines for Its Application.* Alinorm 97/13A. Codex Alimentarius Committee on Food Hygiene, Rome.

DHEW. 1971. *Proceedings of the 1971 National Conference on Food Protection.* U.S. Department of Health, Education and Welfare, Public Health Service, Washington, D.C.

FDA. 1999. Acidified foods. Title 21, *Code of Federal Regulations*, Part 114. U.S. Government Printing Office, Washington, D.C. (Issued annually.)

FDA. 1999. Thermally processed low-acid foods packaged in hermetically sealed containers. Title 21, *Code of Federal Regulations*, Part 113. U.S. Government Printing Office, Washington, D.C. (Issued annually.)

NACMCF. 1989. *HACCP principles for food production.* USDA, FSIS, Washington, D.C.

NACMCF. 1992. Hazard analysis and critical control point system. *Intl. J. Food Microbiol.* 16:1.

NACMCF. 1997. *Hazard analysis and critical control point principles and application guidelines.* USDA, FSIS, Washington, D.C. (Note: Subsequently published in 1998. *J. Food Protect. 61:762.*)

NAS. 1985. *An Evaluation of the Role of Microbiological Criteria for Foods and Food Ingredients.* National Academy Press, Washington, D.C.

Pillsbury Company. 1973. *Food Safety Through the Hazard Analysis Critical Control Point System.* Contract No. FDA 72-59. Research and Development Dept., The Pillsbury Company, Minneapolis, MN.

Chapter 2

HAZARD ANALYSIS AND CRITICAL CONTROL POINT PRINCIPLES AND APPLICATION GUIDELINES

National Advisory Committee on Microbiological Criteria for Foods

EDITORIAL NOTE

The National Advisory Committee on Microbiological Criteria for Foods (NACMCF) adopted a document entitled, "HACCP Principles for Food Production," in November, 1989. In that document, the NACMCF defined HACCP as "a systematic approach to be used in food production as a means to assure food safety," endorsed the use of HACCP by industry and regulators, described seven HACCP Principles, and provided a "guide for HACCP plan development for a specific food."

In 1992, the NACMCF adopted a revised document, "Hazard Analysis and Critical Control Point System," which included modifications to the seven HACCP principles. In comparison to the 1989 document, significant modifications were made to Principles 1 and 2 based upon information from a draft report of a Codex Food Hygiene Committee HACCP Working Group.

Similarly, the NACMCF adopted another revision of their HACCP document, "Hazard Analysis and Critical Control Point Principles and Application Guidelines," in 1997. Like the previous revision, many of the changes were patterned after changes which had been made in a Codex HACCP document. The Codex document, "Hazard Analysis and Critical Control Point (HACCP) System and Guidelines for Its Application," is reprinted in Appendix A of this manual.

In the 1997 NACMCF HACCP document, the NACMCF made the HACCP principles more concise; deleted, revised and added definitions; included new sections on prerequisite programs, education and training, and implementation and maintenance of the HACCP plan; and provided a revised and more detailed explanation of the HACCP principles. The order of the principles on record-keeping and verification was switched in order to coincide with that in Codex HACCP principles document. In addition, significant modifications were made to the explanations of the principles involving hazard analysis and verification. The 1997 NACMCF HACCP document is presented in its entirety in the remaining pages of this chapter.

EXECUTIVE SUMMARY

The National Advisory Committee on Microbiological Criteria for Foods (Committee) reconvened a Hazard Analysis and Critical Control Point (HACCP) Working Group in 1995. The primary goal was to review the Committee's November 1992 HACCP document,[1] comparing it to current HACCP guidance prepared by the Codex Committee on Food Hygiene. Based upon its review, the Committee made the HACCP principles more concise; revised and added definitions; included sections on prerequisite programs, education and training, and implementation and maintenance of the HACCP plan; revised and provided a more detailed explanation of the application of HACCP principles; and provided an additional decision tree for identifying critical control points (CCPs).

The Committee again endorses HACCP as an effective and rational means of assuring food safety from harvest to consumption. Preventing problems from occurring is the paramount goal underlying any HACCP system. Seven basic principles are employed in the development of HACCP plans that meet the stated goal. These principles include hazard analysis, CCP identification, establishing critical limits, monitoring procedures, corrective actions, verification procedures, and record-keeping and documentation. Under such systems, if a deviation occurs indicating that control has been lost, the deviation is detected and appropriate steps are taken to reestablish control in a timely manner to assure that potentially hazardous products do not reach the consumer.

In the application of HACCP, the use of microbiological testing is seldom an effective means of monitoring CCPs because of the time required to obtain results. In most instances, monitoring of CCPs can best be accomplished through the use of physical and chemical tests, and through visual observations. Microbiological criteria do, however, play a role in verifying that the overall HACCP system is working.

The Committee believes that the HACCP principles should be standardized to provide uniformity in training and applying the HACCP system by industry and government. In accordance with the National Academy of Sciences recommendation, the HACCP system must be developed by each food establishment and tailored to its individual product, processing and distribution conditions.

In keeping with the Committee's charge to provide recommendations to its sponsoring agencies regarding microbiological food safety issues, this document focuses on this area. The Committee recognizes that in order to assure food safety, properly designed HACCP systems must also consider chemical and physical hazards in addition to other biological hazards.

For a successful HACCP program to be properly implemented, management must be committed to a HACCP approach. A commitment by management will indicate an awareness of the benefits and costs of HACCP and include education and training of employees. Benefits, in addition to enhanced assurance of food safety, are better use of resources and timely response to problems.

The Committee designed this document to guide the food industry and advise its sponsoring agencies in the implementation of HACCP systems.

DEFINITIONS

CCP Decision Tree: A sequence of questions to assist in determining whether a control point is a CCP.

Control: (a) To manage the conditions of an operation to maintain compliance with established criteria. (b) The state where correct procedures are being followed and criteria are being met.

Control Measure: Any action or activity that can be used to prevent, eliminate or reduce a significant hazard.

Control Point: Any step at which biological, chemical, or physical factors can be controlled.

Corrective Action: Procedures followed when a deviation occurs.

Criterion: A requirement on which a judgment or decision can be based.

Critical Control Point: A step at which control can be applied and is essential to prevent or eliminate a food safety hazard or reduce it to an acceptable level.

Critical Limit: A maximum and/or minimum value to which a biological, chemical or physical parameter must be controlled at a CCP to prevent, eliminate or reduce to an acceptable level the occurrence of a food safety hazard.

Deviation: Failure to meet a critical limit.

HACCP: A systematic approach to the identification, evaluation, and control of food safety hazards.

HACCP Plan: The written document which is based upon the principles of HACCP and which delineates the procedures to be followed.

HACCP System: The result of the implementation of the HACCP Plan.

HACCP Team: The group of people who are responsible for developing, implementing and maintaining the HACCP system.

Hazard: A biological, chemical, or physical agent that is reasonably likely to cause illness or injury in the absence of its control.

Hazard Analysis: The process of collecting and evaluating information on hazards associated with the food under consideration to decide which are significant and must be addressed in the HACCP plan.

Monitor: To conduct a planned sequence of observations or measurements to assess whether a CCP is under control and to produce an accurate record for future use in verification.

Prerequisite Programs: Procedures, including Good Manufacturing Practices, that address operational conditions providing the foundation for the HACCP system.

Severity: The seriousness of the effect(s) of a hazard.

Step: A point, procedure, operation or stage in the food system from primary production to final consumption.

Validation: That element of verification focused on collecting and evaluating scientific and technical information to determine if the HACCP plan, when properly implemented, will effectively control the hazards.

Verification: Those activities, other than monitoring, that determine the validity of the HACCP plan and that the system is operating according to the plan.

HACCP PRINCIPLES

HACCP is a systematic approach to the identification, evaluation, and control of food safety hazards based on the following seven principles:

Principle 1: Conduct a hazard analysis.

Principle 2: Determine the critical control points (CCPs).

Principle 3: Establish critical limits.

Principle 4: Establish monitoring procedures.

Principle 5: Establish corrective actions.

Principle 6: Establish verification procedures.

Principle 7: Establish record-keeping and documentation procedures.

GUIDELINES FOR APPLICATION OF HACCP PRINCIPLES

Introduction

HACCP is a management system in which food safety is addressed through the analysis and control of biological, chemical, and physical hazards from raw material production, procurement and handling, to manufacturing, distribution and consumption of the finished product. For successful implementation of a HACCP plan, management must be strongly committed to the HACCP concept. A firm commitment to HACCP by top management provides company employees with a sense of the importance of producing safe food.

HACCP is designed for use in all segments of the food industry from growing, harvesting, processing, manufacturing, distributing, and merchandising to preparing food for consumption. Prerequisite programs such as current Good Manufacturing Practices (cGMPs) are an essential foundation for the development and implementation of successful HACCP plans. Food safety systems based on the HACCP principles have been successfully applied in food processing plants, retail food stores, and food service operations. The

seven principles of HACCP have been universally accepted by government agencies, trade associations and the food industry around the world.

The following guidelines will facilitate the development and implementation of effective HACCP plans. While the specific application of HACCP to manufacturing facilities is emphasized here, these guidelines should be applied as appropriate to each segment of the food industry under consideration.

Prerequisite Programs

The production of safe food products requires that the HACCP system be built upon a solid foundation of prerequisite programs. Examples of common prerequisite programs are listed in Appendix 2-A. Each segment of the food industry must provide the conditions necessary to protect food while it is under their control. This has traditionally been accomplished through the application of cGMPs. These conditions and practices are now considered to be prerequisite to the development and implementation of effective HACCP plans. Prerequisite programs provide the basic environmental and operating conditions that are necessary for the production of safe, wholesome food. Many of the conditions and practices are specified in federal, state and local regulations and guidelines (e.g., cGMPs and Food Code). The Codex Alimentarius General Principles of Food Hygiene describe the basic conditions and practices expected for foods intended for international trade. In addition to the requirements specified in regulations, industry often adopts policies and procedures that are specific to their operations. Many of these are proprietary. While prerequisite programs may impact upon the safety of a food, they also are concerned with ensuring that foods are wholesome and suitable for consumption (Appendix 2-A). HACCP plans are narrower in scope, being limited to ensuring food is safe to consume.

The existence and effectiveness of prerequisite programs should be assessed during the design and implementation of each HACCP plan. All prerequisite programs should be documented and regularly audited. Prerequisite programs are established and managed separately from the HACCP plan. Certain aspects, however, of a prerequisite program may be incorporated into a HACCP plan. For example, many establishments have preventive maintenance procedures for processing equipment to avoid unexpected equipment failure and loss of production. During the development of a HACCP plan, the HACCP team may decide that the routine maintenance and calibration of an oven should be included in the plan as an activity of verification. This would further ensure that all the food in the oven is cooked to the minimum internal temperature that is necessary for food safety.

Education and Training

The success of a HACCP system depends on educating and training management and employees in the importance of their role in producing safe foods. This should also include information on the control of foodborne hazards related to all stages of the food chain. It is important to recognize that employees must first understand what HACCP is and then learn the skills necessary to make it function properly. Specific training activities should include working instructions and procedures that outline the tasks of employees monitoring each CCP.

Management must provide adequate time for thorough education and training. Personnel must be given the materials and equipment necessary to perform these tasks. Effective training is an important prerequisite to successful implementation of a HACCP plan.

Developing a HACCP Plan

The format of HACCP plans will vary. In many cases the plans will be product and process specific. However, some plans may use a unit operations approach. Generic HACCP plans can serve as useful guides in the development of process and product HACCP plans; however, it is essential that the unique conditions within each facility be considered during the development of all components of the HACCP plan.

In the development of a HACCP plan, five preliminary tasks need to be accomplished before the application of the HACCP principles to a specific product and process. The five preliminary tasks are given in Figure 2-1.

Figure 2-1—Preliminary Tasks in the Development of the HACCP Plan

Assemble the HACCP Team
↓
Describe the Food and its Distribution
↓
Describe the Intended Use and
Consumers of the Food
↓
Develop a Flow Diagram Which
Describes the Process
↓
Verify the Flow Diagram

Assemble the HACCP Team

The first task in developing a HACCP plan is to assemble a HACCP team consisting of individuals who have specific knowledge and expertise appropriate to the product and process. It is the team's responsibility to develop the HACCP plan. The team should be multi-disciplinary and include individuals from areas such as engineering, production, sanitation, quality assurance, and food microbiology. The team should also include local personnel who are involved in the operation as they are more familiar with the variability and limitations of the operation. In addition, this fosters a sense

of ownership among those who must implement the plan. The HACCP team may need assistance from outside experts who are knowledgeable in the potential biological, chemical and/or physical hazards associated with the product and the process. However, a plan which is developed totally by outside sources may be erroneous, incomplete, and lacking in support at the local level.

Due to the technical nature of the information required for hazard analysis, it is recommended that experts who are knowledgeable in the food process should either participate in or verify the completeness of the hazard analysis and the HACCP plan. Such individuals should have the knowledge and experience to correctly: (a) conduct a hazard analysis; (b) identify potential hazards; (c) identify hazards which must be controlled; (d) recommend controls, critical limits, and procedures for monitoring and verification; (e) recommend appropriate corrective actions when a deviation occurs; (f) recommend research related to the HACCP plan if important information is not known; and (g) validate the HACCP plan.

Describe the Food and Its Distribution

The HACCP team first describes the food. This consists of a general description of the food, ingredients, and processing methods. The method of distribution should be described along with information on whether the food is to be distributed frozen, refrigerated, or at ambient temperature.

Describe the Intended Use and Consumers of the Food

Describe the normal expected use of the food. The intended consumers may be the general public or a particular segment of the population (e.g., infants, immunocompromised individuals, the elderly, etc.).

Develop a Flow Diagram Which Describes the Process

The purpose of a flow diagram is to provide a clear, simple outline of the steps involved in the process. The scope of the flow diagram must cover all the steps in the process which are directly under the control of the establishment. In addition, the flow diagram can include steps in the food chain which are before and after the processing that occurs in the establishment. The flow diagram need not be as complex as engineering drawings. A block type flow diagram is sufficiently descriptive (see Appendix 2-B). Also, a simple schematic of the facility is often useful in understanding and evaluating product and process flow.

Verify the Flow Diagram

The HACCP team should perform an on-site review of the operation to verify the accuracy and completeness of the flow diagram. Modifications should be made to the flow diagram as necessary and documented.

After these five preliminary tasks have been completed, the seven principles of HACCP are applied.

Conduct a Hazard Analysis (Principle 1)

After addressing the preliminary tasks discussed above, the HACCP team conducts a hazard analysis and identifies appropriate control measures. The purpose of the hazard analysis is to develop a list of hazards which are of such significance that they are reasonably likely to cause injury or illness if not effectively controlled. Hazards that are not reasonably likely to occur would not require further consideration within a HACCP plan. It is important to consider in the hazard analysis the ingredients and raw materials, each step in the process, product storage and distribution, and final preparation and use by the consumer. When conducting a hazard analysis, safety concerns must be differentiated from quality concerns. A hazard is defined as a biological, chemical or physical agent that is reasonably likely to cause illness or injury in the absence of its control. Thus, the word hazard as used in this document is limited to safety.

A thorough hazard analysis is the key to preparing an effective HACCP plan. If the hazard analysis is not done correctly and the hazards warranting control within the HACCP system are not identified, the plan will not be effective regardless of how well it is followed.

The hazard analysis and identification of associated control measures accomplish three objectives: Those hazards and associated control measures are identified. The analysis may identify needed modifications to a process or product so that product safety is further assured or improved. The analysis provides a basis for determining CCPs in Principle 2.

The process of conducting a hazard analysis involves two stages. The first, hazard identification, can be regarded as a brain storming session. During this stage, the HACCP team reviews the ingredients used in the product, the activities conducted at each step in the process and the equipment used, the final product and its method of storage and distribution, and the intended use and consumers of the product. Based on this review, the team develops a list of potential biological, chemical or physical hazards which may be introduced, increased, or controlled at each step in the production process. Appendix 2-C lists examples of questions that may be helpful to consider when identifying potential hazards. Hazard identification focuses on developing a list of potential hazards associated with each process

step under direct control of the food operation. A knowledge of any adverse health-related events historically associated with the product will be of value in this exercise.

After the list of potential hazards is assembled, stage two, the hazard evaluation, is conducted. In stage two of the hazard analysis, the HACCP team decides which potential hazards must be addressed in the HACCP plan. During this stage, each potential hazard is evaluated based on the severity of the potential hazard and its likely occurrence. Severity is the seriousness of the consequences of exposure to the hazard. Considerations of severity (e.g., impact of sequelae, and magnitude and duration of illness or injury) can be helpful in understanding the public health impact of the hazard. Consideration of the likely occurrence is usually based upon a combination of experience, epidemiological data, and information in the technical literature. When conducting the hazard evaluation, it is helpful to consider the likelihood of exposure and severity of the potential consequences if the hazard is not properly controlled. In addition, consideration should be given to the effects of short term as well as long term exposure to the potential hazard. Such considerations do not include common dietary choices which lie outside of HACCP. During the evaluation of each potential hazard, the food, its method of preparation, transportation, storage and persons likely to consume the product should be considered to determine how each of these factors may influence the likely occurrence and severity of the hazard being controlled. The team must consider the influence of likely procedures for food preparation and storage and whether the intended consumers are susceptible to a potential hazard. However, there may be differences of opinion, even among experts, as to the likely occurrence and severity of a hazard. The HACCP team may have to rely upon the opinion of experts who assist in the development of the HACCP plan.

Hazards identified in one operation or facility may not be significant in another operation producing the same or a similar product. For example, due to differences in equipment and/or an effective maintenance program, the probability of metal contamination may be significant in one facility but not in another. A summary of the HACCP team deliberations and the rationale developed during the hazard analysis should be kept for future reference. This information will be useful during future reviews and updates of the hazard analysis and the HACCP plan.

Appendix 2-D gives three examples of using a logic sequence in conducting a hazard analysis. While these examples relate to biological hazards, chemical and physical hazards are equally important to consider. Appendix 2-D is for illustration purposes to further explain the stages of hazard analysis for identifying hazards. Hazard identification and evaluation as outlined in Appendix 2-D may eventually be assisted by biological risk assessments as they become available.

While the process and output of a risk assessment (NACMCF, 1997)[2] is significantly different from a hazard analysis, the identification of hazards of concern and the hazard evaluation may be facilitated by information from risk assessments. Thus, as risk assessments addressing specific hazards or control factors become available, the HACCP team should take these into consideration.

Upon completion of the hazard analysis, the hazards associated with each step in the production of the food should be listed along with any measure(s) that are used to control the hazard(s). The term control measure is used because not all hazards can be prevented, but virtually all can be controlled. More than one control measure may be required for a specific hazard. On the other hand, more than one hazard may be addressed by a specific control measure (e.g. pasteurization of milk).

For example, if a HACCP team were to conduct a hazard analysis for the production of frozen cooked beef patties (Appendices 2-B and 2-D), enteric pathogens (e.g., *Salmonella* and verotoxin-producing *Escherichia coli*) in the raw meat would be identified as hazards. Cooking is a control measure which can be used to eliminate these hazards. Table 2-1 is an excerpt from a hazard analysis summary table for this product.

The hazard analysis summary could be presented in several different ways. One format is a table such as Table 2-1. Another could be a narrative summary of

the identification of each CCP is the use of a CCP decision tree (Examples of decision trees are given in Appendices 2-E and 2-F). Although application of the CCP decision tree can be useful in determining if a particular step is a CCP for a previously identified hazard, it is merely a tool and not a mandatory element of HACCP. A CCP decision tree is not a substitute for expert knowledge.

Critical control points are located at any step where hazards can be either prevented, eliminated, or reduced to acceptable levels. Examples of CCPs may include: thermal processing, chilling, testing ingredients for chemical residues, product formulation control, and testing product for metal contaminants. CCPs must be carefully developed and documented. In addition, they must be used only for purposes of product safety. For example, a specified heat process, at a given time and temperature designed to destroy a specific microbiological pathogen, could be a CCP. Likewise, refrigeration of a precooked food to prevent hazardous microorganisms from multiplying, or the adjustment of a food to a pH necessary to prevent toxin formation could also be CCPs. Different facilities preparing similar food items can differ in the hazards identified and the steps which are CCPs. This can be due to differences in each facility's layout, equipment, selection of ingredients, processes employed, etc.

Table 2-1—Excerpt from a hazard analysis summary table

Step	Potential Hazard(s)	Justification	Hazard to be addressed in plan? Y/N	Control Measure(s)
5. Cooking	Enteric pathogens: e.g., *Salmonella*, verotoxigenic *E. coli*	Enteric pathogens have been associated with outbreaks of foodborne illness from undercooked ground beef	Y	Cooking

the HACCP team's hazard analysis considerations and a summary table listing only the hazards and associated control measures.

Determine Critical Control Points (CCPs) (Principle 2)

A critical control point is defined as a step at which control can be applied and is essential to prevent or eliminate a food safety hazard or reduce it to an acceptable level. The potential hazards that are reasonably likely to cause illness or injury in the absence of their control must be addressed in determining CCPs.

Complete and accurate identification of CCPs is fundamental to controlling food safety hazards. The information developed during the hazard analysis is essential for the HACCP team in identifying which steps in the process are CCPs. One strategy to facilitate

Establish Critical Limits (Principle 3)

A critical limit is a maximum and/or minimum value to which a biological, chemical or physical parameter must be controlled at a CCP to prevent, eliminate or reduce to an acceptable level the occurrence of a food safety hazard. A critical limit is used to distinguish between safe and unsafe operating conditions at a CCP. Critical limits should not be confused with operational limits which are established for reasons other than food safety.

Each CCP will have one or more control measures to assure that the identified hazards are prevented, eliminated or reduced to acceptable levels. Each control measure has one or more associated critical limits. Critical limits may be based upon factors such as: temperature, time, physical dimensions, humidity, moisture level, water activity (a_w), pH, titratable acidity, salt concentration, available chlorine, viscosity, preservatives, or sensory information such as aroma and visual appearance. Critical limits must be scientifically based. For each CCP, there is at least one criterion for food safety that is to be met. An example of a criterion is a specific lethality of a cooking process such as a 5D reduction in *Salmonella*. The critical limits and criteria for food safety may be derived from sources such as regulatory standards and guidelines, literature surveys, experimental results, and experts.

An example is the cooking of beef patties (Appendix 2-B). The process should be designed to ensure the production of a safe product. The hazard analysis for cooked meat patties identified enteric pathogens (e.g., verotoxigenic *E. coli* such as *E. coli* O157:H7, and salmonellae) as significant biological hazards. Furthermore, cooking is the step in the process at which control can be applied to reduce the enteric pathogens to an acceptable level. To ensure that an acceptable level is consistently achieved, accurate information is needed on the probable number of the pathogens in the raw patties, their heat resistance, the factors that influence the heating of the patties, and the area of the patty which heats the slowest. Collectively, this information forms the scientific basis for the critical limits that are established. Some of the factors that may affect the thermal destruction of enteric pathogens are listed in Table 2-2. In this example, the HACCP team concluded that a thermal process equivalent to 155°F for 16 seconds would be necessary to assure the safety of this product. To ensure that this time and temperature are attained, the HACCP team for one facility determined that it would be necessary to establish critical limits for the oven temperature and humidity, belt speed (time in oven), patty thickness and composition (e.g., all beef, beef and other ingredients). Control of these factors enables the facility to produce a wide variety of cooked patties, all of which will be processed to a minimum internal temperature of 155°F for 16 seconds. In another facility, the HACCP team may conclude that the best approach is to use the internal patty temperature of 155°F and hold for 16 seconds as critical limits. In this second facility the internal temperature and hold time of the patties are monitored at a frequency to ensure that the critical limits are constantly met as they exit the oven. The example given in Table 2-2 applies to the first facility.

Table 2-2—Excerpt for a HACCP plan

Process Step	CCP	Critical Limits
5. Cooking	Yes	Oven temperature:____F Time; rate of heating and cooling (belt speed in ft/min): ____ft/min Patty thickness: ____in. Patty composition: e.g. all beef Oven humidity: ____% RH

Establish Monitoring Procedures (Principle 4)

Monitoring is a planned sequence of observations or measurements to assess whether a CCP is under control

and to produce an accurate record for future use in verification. Monitoring serves three main purposes. First, monitoring is essential to food safety management in that it facilitates tracking of the operation. If monitoring indicates that there is a trend towards loss of control, then action can be taken to bring the process back into control before a deviation from a critical limit occurs. Second, monitoring is used to determine when there is loss of control and a deviation occurs at a CCP, i.e., exceeding or not meeting a critical limit. When a deviation occurs, an appropriate corrective action must be taken. Third, it provides written documentation for use in verification.

An unsafe food may result if a process is not properly controlled and a deviation occurs. Because of the potentially serious consequences of a critical limit deviation, monitoring procedures must be effective. Ideally, monitoring should be continuous, which is possible with many types of physical and chemical methods. For example, the temperature and time for the scheduled thermal process of low-acid canned foods is recorded continuously on temperature recording charts. If the temperature falls below the scheduled temperature or the time is insufficient, as recorded on the chart, the product from the retort is retained and the disposition determined as in Principle 5. Likewise, pH measurement may be performed continually in fluids or by testing each batch before processing. There are many ways to monitor critical limits on a continuous or batch basis and record the data on charts. Continuous monitoring is always preferred when feasible. Monitoring equipment must be carefully calibrated for accuracy.

Assignment of the responsibility for monitoring is an important consideration for each CCP. Specific assignments will depend on the number of CCPs and control measures and the complexity of monitoring. Personnel who monitor CCPs are often associated with production (e.g., line supervisors, selected line workers and maintenance personnel) and, as required, quality control personnel. Those individuals must be trained in the monitoring technique for which they are responsible, fully understand the purpose and importance of monitoring, be unbiased in monitoring and reporting, and accurately report the results of monitoring. In addition, employees should be trained in procedures to follow when there is a trend towards loss of control so that adjustments can be made in a timely manner to assure that the process remains under control. The person responsible for monitoring must also immediately report a process or product that does not meet critical limits.

All records and documents associated with CCP monitoring should be dated and signed or initialed by the person doing the monitoring.

When it is not possible to monitor a CCP on a continuous basis, it is necessary to establish a monitoring frequency and procedure that will be reliable enough to indicate that the CCP is under control. Statistically designed data collection or sampling systems lend themselves to this purpose.

Most monitoring procedures need to be rapid because they relate to on-line, real-time processes and there will not be time for lengthy analytical testing. Examples of monitoring activities include: visual observations and measurement of temperature, time, pH, and moisture level.

Microbiological tests are seldom effective for monitoring due to their time-consuming nature and problems with assuring detection of contaminants. Physical and chemical measurements are often preferred because they are rapid and usually more effective for assuring control of microbiological hazards. For example, the safety of pasteurized milk is based upon measurements of time and temperature of heating rather than testing the heated milk to assure the absence of surviving pathogens.

With certain foods, processes, ingredients, or imports, there may be no alternative to microbiological testing. However, it is important to recognize that a sampling protocol that is adequate to reliably detect low levels of pathogens is seldom possible because of the large number of samples needed. This sampling limitation could result in a false sense of security by those who use an inadequate sampling protocol. In addition, there are technical limitations in many laboratory procedures for detecting and quantitating pathogens and/or their toxins.

Establish Corrective Actions (Principle 5)

The HACCP system for food safety management is designed to identify health hazards and to establish strategies to prevent, eliminate, or reduce their occurrence. However, ideal circumstances do not always prevail and deviations from established processes may occur. An important purpose of corrective actions is to prevent foods which may be hazardous from reaching consumers. Where there is a deviation from established critical limits, corrective actions are necessary. Therefore, corrective actions should include the following elements: (a) determine and correct the cause of non-compliance; (b) determine the disposition of non-compliant product; and (c) record the corrective actions that have been taken. Specific corrective actions should be developed in advance for each CCP and included in the HACCP plan. As a minimum, the HACCP plan should specify what is done when a deviation occurs, who is responsible for implementing the corrective actions, and that a record will be developed and maintained of the actions taken. Individuals who have a thorough understanding of the process, product and HACCP plan should be assigned the responsibility for oversight of corrective actions. As appropriate, experts may be consulted to review the information available and to assist in determining disposition of non-compliant product.

Establish Verification Procedures (Principle 6)

Verification is defined as those activities, other than monitoring, that determine the validity of the HACCP plan and that the system is operating according to the plan. The NAS (1985)[3] pointed out that the major infusion of science in a HACCP system centers on proper identification of the hazards, critical control points, critical limits, and instituting proper verification procedures. These processes should take place during the development and implementation of the HACCP plans and maintenance of the HACCP system. An example of a verification schedule is given in Table 2-3.

One aspect of verification is evaluating whether the facility's HACCP system is functioning according to the HACCP plan. An effective HACCP system requires little end-product testing, since sufficient validated

Table 2-3—Example of a Company Established HACCP Verification Schedule

ACTIVITY	FREQUENCY	RESPONSIBILITY	REVIEWER
Verification Activities Scheduling	Yearly or Upon HACCP System Change	HACCP Coordinator	Plant Manager
Initial Validation of HACCP Plan	Prior to and During Initial Implementation of Plan	Independent Expert(s)[a]	HACCP Team
Subsequent validation of HACCP Plan	When Critical Limits Changed, Significant Changes in Process, Equipment Changed, After System Failure, etc.	Independent Expert(s)[a]	HACCP Team
Verification of CCP Monitoring as Described in the Plan (e.g., monitoring of patty cooking temperature)	According to HACCP Plan (e.g., once per shift)	According to HACCP Plan (e.g., Line Supervisor)	According to HACCP Plan (e.g. Quality Control)
Review of Monitoring, Corrective Action Records to Show Compliance with the Plan	Monthly	Quality Assurance	HACCP Team
Comprehensive HACCP System Verification	Yearly	Independent Expert(s)[a]	Plant Manager

[a]Done by others than the team writing and implementing the plan. May require additional technical expertise as well as laboratory and plant test studies.

safeguards are built in early in the process. Therefore, rather than relying on end-product testing, firms should rely on frequent reviews of their HACCP plan, verification that the HACCP plan is being correctly followed, and review of CCP monitoring and corrective action records.

Another important aspect of verification is the initial validation of the HACCP plan to determine that the plan is scientifically and technically sound, that all hazards have been identified and that if the HACCP plan is properly implemented these hazards will be effectively controlled. Information needed to validate the HACCP plan often include (1) expert advice and scientific studies and (2) in-plant observations, measurements, and evaluations. For example, validation of the cooking process for beef patties should include the scientific justification of the heating times and temperatures needed to obtain an appropriate destruction of pathogenic microorganisms (i.e., enteric pathogens) and studies to confirm that the conditions of cooking will deliver the required time and temperature to each beef patty.

Subsequent validations are performed and documented by a HACCP team or an independent expert as needed. For example, validations are conducted when there is an unexplained system failure; a significant product, process or packaging change occurs; or new hazards are recognized.

In addition, a periodic comprehensive verification of the HACCP system should be conducted by an unbiased, independent authority. Such authorities can be internal or external to the food operation. This should include a technical evaluation of the hazard analysis and each element of the HACCP plan as well as onsite review of all flow diagrams and appropriate records from operation of the plan. A comprehensive verification is independent of other verification procedures and must be performed to ensure that the HACCP plan is resulting in the control of the hazards. If the results of the comprehensive verification identifies deficiencies, the HACCP team modifies the HACCP plan as necessary.

Verification activities are carried out by individuals within a company, third party experts, and regulatory agencies. It is important that individuals doing verification have appropriate technical expertise to perform this function. The role of regulatory and industry in HACCP was further described by the NACMCF (1994).[4]

Examples of verification activities are included as Appendix 2-G.

Establish Record-Keeping and Documentation Procedures (Principle 7)

Generally, the records maintained for the HACCP System should include the following:

1. A summary of the hazard analysis, including the rationale for determining hazards and control measures.

2. The HACCP Plan
   • Listing of the HACCP team and assigned responsibilities.
   • Description of the food, its distribution, intended use, and consumer.
   • Verified flow diagram.
   • HACCP Plan Summary Table that includes information for:
     —Steps in the process that are CCPs
     —The hazard(s) of concern.
     —Critical limits
     —Monitoring*
     —Corrective actions*
     —Verification procedures and schedule*
     —Record-keeping procedures*

   *A brief summary of position responsible for performing the activity and the procedures and frequency should be provided.

Table 2-4 is an example of a HACCP plan summary table:

3. Support documentation such as validation records.

4. Records that are generated during the operation of the plan.

Examples of HACCP records are given in Appendix 2-H.

Implementation and Maintenance of the HACCP Plan

The successful implementation of a HACCP plan is facilitated by commitment from top management. The next step is to establish a plan that describes the individuals responsible for developing, implementing and maintaining the HACCP system. Initially, the HACCP coordinator and team are selected and trained as necessary. The team is then responsible for developing the initial plan and coordinating its implementation. Product teams can be appointed to develop HACCP plans for specific products. An important aspect in develop-

Table 2-4—Example Format for a HACCP Plan Summary Table

CCP	Hazards	Critical limit(s)	Monitoring	Corrective Actions	Verification	Records

ing these teams is to assure that they have appropriate training. The workers who will be responsible for monitoring need to be adequately trained. Upon completion of the HACCP plan, operator procedures, forms and procedures for monitoring and corrective action are developed. Often it is a good idea to develop a timeline for the activities involved in the initial implementation of the HACCP plan. Implementation of the HACCP system involves the continual application of the monitoring, record-keeping, corrective action procedures and other activities as described in the HACCP plan.

Maintaining an effective HACCP system depends largely on regularly scheduled verification activities. The HACCP plan should be updated and revised as needed. An important aspect of maintaining the HACCP system is to assure that all individuals involved are properly trained so they understand their role and can effectively fulfill their responsibilities.

REFERENCES

[1]National Advisory Committee on Microbiological Criteria for Foods. 1992. Hazard analysis and critical control point system. *Int. J. Food Microbiol* 16:1–23.

[2]National Advisory Committee on Microbiological Criteria for Foods. 1997. The principles of risk assessment for illness caused by foodborne biological agents. Adopted April 4, 1997.

[3]National Academy of Sciences. 1985. *An Evaluation of the Role of Microbiological Criteria for Foods and Food Ingredients.* National Academy Press, Washington, DC.

[4]National Advisory Committee on Microbiological Criteria for Foods. 1994. The role of regulatory agencies and industry in HACCP. *Int. J. Food Microbiol.* 21:187–195.

APPENDIX 2-A
Examples of Common Prerequisite Programs

The production of safe food products requires that the HACCP system be built upon a solid foundation of prerequisite programs. Each segment of the food industry must provide the conditions necessary to protect food while it is under their control. This has traditionally been accomplished through the application of cGMPs. These conditions and practices are now considered to be prerequisite to the development and implementation of effective HACCP plans. Prerequisite programs provide the basic environmental and operating conditions that are necessary for the production of safe, wholesome food. Common prerequisite programs may include, but are not limited to:

Facilities. The establishment should be located, constructed and maintained according to sanitary design principles. There should be linear product flow and traffic control to minimize cross-contamination from raw to cooked materials.

Supplier Control. Each facility should assure that its suppliers have in place effective GMP and food safety programs. These may be the subject of continuing supplier guarantee and supplier HACCP system verification.

Specifications. There should be written specifications for all ingredients, products, and packaging materials.

Production Equipment. All equipment should be constructed and installed according to sanitary design principles. Preventive maintenance and calibration schedules should be established and documented.

Cleaning and Sanitation. All procedures for cleaning and sanitation of the equipment and the facility should be written and followed. A master sanitation schedule should be in place.

Personal Hygiene. All employees and other persons who enter the manufacturing plant should follow the requirements for personal hygiene.

Training. All employees should receive documented training in personal hygiene, GMP, cleaning and sanitation procedures, personal safety, and their role in the HACCP program.

Chemical Control. Documented procedures must be in place to assure the segregation and proper use of non-food chemicals in the plant. These include cleaning chemicals fumigants, and pesticides or baits used in or around the plant.

Receiving, Storage and Shipping. All raw materials and products should be stored under sanitary conditions and the proper environmental conditions such as temperature and humidity to assure their safety and wholesomeness.

Traceability and Recall. All raw materials and products should be lot-coded and a recall system in place so that rapid and complete traces and recalls can be done when a product retrieval is necessary.

Pest Control. Effective pest control programs should be in place.

Other examples of prerequisite programs might include quality assurance procedures; standard operating procedures for sanitation, processes, product formulations and recipes; glass control; procedures for receiving, storage and shipping; labeling; and employee food and ingredient handling practices.

APPENDIX 2-B
Example of a Flow Diagram for the Production of Frozen Cooked Beef Patties

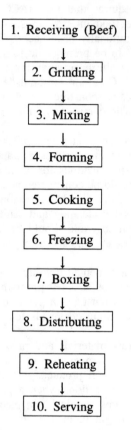

1. Receiving (Beef)
↓
2. Grinding
↓
3. Mixing
↓
4. Forming
↓
5. Cooking
↓
6. Freezing
↓
7. Boxing
↓
8. Distributing
↓
9. Reheating
↓
10. Serving

APPENDIX 2-C
Examples of Questions to be Considered When Conducting a Hazard Analysis

The hazard analysis consists of asking a series of questions which are appropriate to the process under consideration. The purpose of the questions is to assist in identifying potential hazards.

A. Ingredients
  1. Does the food contain any sensitive ingredients that may present microbiological hazards (e.g., *Salmonella, Staphylococcus aureus*); chemical hazards (e.g., aflatoxin, antibiotic or pesticide residues); or physical hazards (stones, glass, metal)?
  2. Are potable water, ice and steam used in formulating or in handling the food?
  3. What are the sources (e.g., geographical region, specific supplier)

B. Intrinsic Factors—Physical characteristics and composition (e.g., pH, type of acidulants, fermentable carbohydrate, water activity, preservatives) of the food during and after processing.
  1. What hazards may result if the food composition is not controlled?
  2. Does the food permit survival or multiplication of pathogens and/or toxin formation in the food during processing?
  3. Will the food permit survival or multiplication of pathogens and/or toxin formation during subsequent steps in the food chain?
  4. Are there other similar products in the market place? What has been the safety record for these products? What hazards have been associated with the products?

C. Procedures used for processing
  1. Does the process include a controllable processing step that destroys pathogens? If so, which pathogens? Consider both vegetative cells and spores.
  2. If the product is subject to recontamination between processing (e.g., cooking, pasteurizing) and packaging which biological, chemical or physical hazards are likely to occur?

D. Microbial content of the food
  1. What is the normal microbial content of the food?
  2. Does the microbial population change during the normal time the food is stored prior to consumption?
  3. Does the subsequent change in microbial population alter the safety of the food?
  4. Do the answers to the above questions indicate a high likelihood of certain biological hazards?

E. Facility design
  1. Does the layout of the facility provide an adequate separation of raw materials from ready-to-eat (RTE) foods if this is important to food safety? If not, what hazards should be considered as possible contaminants of the RTE products?
  2. Is positive air pressure maintained in product packaging areas? Is this essential for product safety?
  3. Is the traffic pattern for people and moving equipment a significant source of contamination?

F. Equipment design and use
  1. Will the equipment provide the time-temperature control that is necessary for safe food?
  2. Is the equipment properly sized for the volume of food that will be processed?
  3. Can the equipment be sufficiently controlled so that the variation in performance will be within the tolerances required to produce a safe food?
  4. Is the equipment reliable or is it prone to frequent breakdowns?
  5. Is the equipment designed so that it can be easily cleaned and sanitized?
  6. Is there a chance for product contamination with hazardous substances; e.g., glass?
  7. What product safety devices are used to enhance consumer safety?
       —metal detectors
       —magnets
       —sifters
       —filters
       —screens
       —thermometers
       —bone removal devices
       —dud detectors
  8. To what degree will normal equipment wear affect the likely occurrence of a physical hazard (e.g., metal) in the product?

9. Are allergen protocols needed in using equipment for different products?

G. Packaging

1. Does the method of packaging affect the multiplication of microbial pathogens and/or the formation of toxins?
2. Is the package clearly labeled "Keep Refrigerated" if this is required for safety?
3. Does the package include instructions for the safe handling and preparation of the food by the end user?
4. Is the packaging material resistant to damage thereby preventing the entrance of microbial contamination?
5. Are tamper-evident packaging features used?
6. Is each package and case legibly and accurately coded?
7. Does each package contain the proper label?
8. Are potential allergens in the ingredients included in the list of ingredients on the label?

H. Sanitation

1. Can sanitation have an impact upon the safety of the food that is being processed?
2. Can the facility and equipment be easily cleaned and sanitized to permit the safe handling of food?
3. Is it possible to provide sanitary conditions consistently and adequately to assure safe foods?

I. Employee health, hygiene and education

1. Can employee health or personal hygiene practices impact upon the safety of the food being processed?
2. Do the employees understand the process and the factors they must control to assure the preparation of safe foods?
3. Will the employees inform management of a problem which could impact upon safety of food?

J. Conditions of storage between packaging and the end user

1. What is the likelihood that the food will be improperly stored at the wrong temperature?
2. Would an error in improper storage lead to a microbiologically unsafe food?

K. Intended use

1. Will the food be heated by the consumer?
2. Will there likely be leftovers?

L. Intended consumer

1. Is the food intended for the general public?

Is the food intended for consumption by a population with increased susceptibility to illness (e.g., infants, the aged, the infirmed, immunocompromised individuals)?

APPENDIX 2-D
Example of How the Stages of Hazard Analysis are Used to Identify and Evaluate Hazards*

Hazard Analysis Stage		Frozen cooked beef patties produced in a manufacturing plant	Product containing eggs prepared for foodservice	Commercial frozen pre-cooked, boned chicken for further processing
Stage 1 Hazard Identification	Determine potential hazards associated with product.	Enteric pathogens (i.e., *Escherichia coli* O157:H7 and *Salmonella*)	Salmonella in finished product.	*Staphylococcus aureus* enterotoxin in finished product.
Stage 2 Hazard Evaluation	Assess severity of health consequences if potential hazard is not properly controlled.	Epidemiological evidence indicates that these pathogens cause severe health effects, including death, among children and elderly. Undercooked beef patties have been linked to disease from these pathogens.	Salmonellosis is a food-borne infection causing a moderate to severe illness that can be caused by ingestion of only a few cells of *Salmonella*.	Certain strains of *S. aureus* produce an enterotoxin which can cause a moderate food-borne illness.
	Determine likelihood of occurrence of potential hazard if not properly controlled.	*E. coli* O157:H7 is of very low probability, and salmonellae are of moderate probability in raw meat.	Product is made with liquid eggs which have been associated with past outbreaks of salmonellosis. Recent problems with *Salmonella* serotype Enteritidis in eggs cause increased concern. Probability of *Salmonella* in raw eggs cannot be ruled out. If not effectively controlled, some consumers are likely to be exposed to *Salmonella* from this food.	Product may be contaminated with *S. aureus* due to human handling during boning of cooked chicken. Enterotoxin capable of causing illness will only occur as *S. aureus* multiplies to about 1×10^6/g. Operating procedures during boning and subsequent freezing prevent growth of *S. aureus*, thus the potential for enterotoxin formation is very low.
	Using information above, determine whether this potential hazard is to be addressed in the HACCP plan.	The HACCP team decides that enteric pathogens are hazards for this product.	HACCP team determines that if the potential hazard is not properly controlled, consumption of product is likely to result in an unacceptable health risk.	The HACCP team determines that the potential for enterotoxin formation is very low. However, it is still desirable to keep the initial number of *S. aureus* organisms low. Employee practices that minimize contamination, rapid carbon dioxide freezing and handling instructions have been adequate to control this potential hazard.
		Hazards must be addressed in the plan.	**Hazard must be addressed in the plan.**	**Potential hazard does not need to be addressed in plan.**

*For illustrative purposes only. The potential hazards identified may not be the only hazards associated with the products listed. The responses may be different for different establishments.

APPENDIX 2-E
Example I of a CCP Decision Tree

Important considerations when using the decision tree:

The decision tree is used after the hazard analysis.

The decision tree then is used at the steps where a hazard that must be addressed in the HACCP plan has been identified.

A subsequent step in the process may be more effective for controlling a hazard and may be the preferred CCP.

More than one step in a process may be involved in controlling a hazard.

More than one hazard may be controlled by a specific control measure.

Q 1. Does this step involve a hazard of sufficient likelihood of occurrence and severity to warrant its control?

```
        ↓                    ↓
       YES                  NO → Not a CCP
        ↓
```

Q 2. Does a control measure for the hazard exist at this step?

```
        ↓             ↓             ↑
       YES           NO         Modify the step,
        |            ↓          process or product
        |                             ↑
        |      Is control at this step
        |      necessary for safety?  → YES
        |             ↓
        ↓      NO → Not a CCP → STOP*
```

Q 3. Is control at this step necessary to prevent, eliminate, or reduce the risk of the hazard to consumers?

```
        ↓                    ↓
       YES                  NO → Not a CCP → STOP*
        ↓
       CCP
```

*Proceed to next step in the process

APPENDIX 2-F
Example II of a CCP Decision Tree

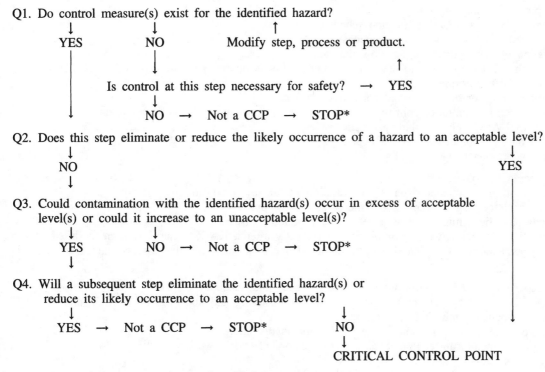

Q1. Do control measure(s) exist for the identified hazard?

    ↓   ↓   ↑

  YES   NO   Modify step, process or product.

                ↓   ↑

        Is control at this step necessary for safety? → YES

                ↓

             NO → Not a CCP → STOP*

Q2. Does this step eliminate or reduce the likely occurrence of a hazard to an acceptable level?

    ↓   ↓

  NO   YES

    ↓

Q3. Could contamination with the identified hazard(s) occur in excess of acceptable
    level(s) or could it increase to an unacceptable level(s)?

    ↓   ↓

  YES   NO → Not a CCP → STOP*

    ↓

Q4. Will a subsequent step eliminate the identified hazard(s) or
    reduce its likely occurrence to an acceptable level?

         ↓   ↓

  YES → Not a CCP → STOP*   NO

                                         ↓

                                  CRITICAL CONTROL POINT

*Proceed to next step in the described process

APPENDIX 2-G
Examples of Verification Activities

A. Verification procedures may include:
1. Establishment of appropriate verification schedules.
2. Review of the HACCP plan for completeness.
3. Confirmation of the accuracy of the flow diagram.
4. Review of the HACCP system to determine if the facility is operating according to the HACCP plan.
5. Review of CCP monitoring records.
6. Review of records for deviations and corrective actions.
7. Validation of critical limits to confirm that they are adequate to control significant hazards.
8. Validation of HACCP plan, including on-site review.
9. Review of modifications of the HACCP plan.
10. Sampling and testing to verify CCPs.

B. Verification should be conducted:
1. Routinely, or on an unannounced basis, to assure CCPs are under control.
2. When there are emerging concerns about the safety of the product.
3. When foods have been implicated as a vehicle of foodborne disease.
4. To confirm that changes have been implemented correctly after a HACCP plan has been modified.
5. To assess whether a HACCP plan should be modified due to a change in the process, equipment, ingredients, etc.

C. Verification reports may include information on the presence and adequacy of:
1. The HACCP plan and the person(s) responsible for administering and updating the HACCP plan.
2. The records associated with CCP monitoring.
3. Direct recording of monitoring data of the CCP while in operation.
4. Certification that monitoring equipment is properly calibrated and in working order.
5. Corrective actions for deviations.
6. Sampling and testing methods used to verify that CCPs are under control.
7. Modifications to the HACCP plan.
8. Training and knowledge of individuals responsible for monitoring CCPs.
9. Validation activities.

APPENDIX 2-H
Examples of HACCP Records

A. Ingredients for which critical limits have been established.
   1. Supplier certification records documenting compliance of an ingredient with a critical limit.
   2. Processor audit records verifying supplier compliance.
   3. Storage records (e.g., time, temperature) for when ingredient storage is a CCP.

B. Processing, storage and distribution records
   1. Information that establishes the efficacy of a CCP to maintain product safety.
   2. Data establishing the safe shelf life of the product; if age of product can affect safety.
   3. Records indicating compliance with critical limits when packaging materials, labeling or sealing specifications are necessary for food safety.
   4. Monitoring records.
   5. Verification records.

C. Deviation and corrective action records.

D. Employee training records that are pertinent to CCPs and the HACCP plan.

E. Documentation of the adequacy of the HACCP plan from a knowledgeable HACCP expert.

Chapter 3

PREREQUISITES TO HACCP

Dane T. Bernard and Nina G. Parkinson

INTRODUCTION

As the concept of HACCP evolves, increased emphasis is being placed on having a good foundation from which to develop a HACCP program. The phrase "prerequisite programs" is accepted as the appropriate term to describe a range of programs that are necessary to set the stage for HACCP-based systems and to provide on-going support for these systems. Food processors in the United States recognize that many of the prerequisite programs are based upon the current Good Manufacturing Practices (cGMPs) listed in the *Code of Federal Regulations* (FDA, 1999a). In addition to those related to the cGMPs, prerequisite programs can include other systems like ingredient specifications, consumer complaint management, ingredient-to-product traceability programs and supplier approval programs. Without these programs in place and performing effectively, HACCP may be ineffective in assuring the production of safe foods. Having adequate prerequisite programs in place simplifies the development and maintenance of a HACCP plan (Sperber et al., 1998). As noted earlier, the focus of HACCP is on those activities that have a direct and substantial impact on food safety.

Properly utilized, prerequisite programs will keep many things from becoming serious problems that could eventually have an impact on food safety. Prerequisite programs are an essential component of an establishment's operations and are intended to keep low-risk potential hazards from becoming serious enough to adversely impact the safety of foods produced.

HISTORY

The importance of support programs has been recognized by many organizations. Agriculture and Agri-Food Canada (AAFC) is credited with coining the term "prerequisite programs." and they incorporated the concept of prerequisite programs in the Canadian Food Safety Enhancement Program (CFIA, 1998).

In 1995, the U.S. Food and Drug Administration issued the Seafood HACCP Final Rule entitled "Procedures for the Safe and Sanitary Processing and Importing of Fish and Fishery Products" (FDA, 1995). This rule incorporated the concept of prerequisite programs by requiring that seafood processors address specific sanitation procedures. However, FDA did not require these processors to include written procedures for sanitation within the HACCP plan. The Food Safety and Inspection Service (FSIS) of the U.S. Department of Agriculture (USDA) issued a similar regulation for the meat and poultry industry, which also recognized the concept of prerequisite programs. This regulation, "Pathogen Reduction: Hazard Analysis and Critical Control Point (HACCP) Systems Final Rule" (USDA/FSIS, 1996), requires that "Each official establishment shall develop, implement and maintain written standard operating procedures for sanitation . . ." (also referred to as sanitation SOPs or SSOPs). Recently, a Proposed Rule was published for fruit and vegetable juice products (FDA, 1998) that is similar to the seafood HACCP regulation. Depending on which agency has jurisdiction over a particular food processing facility, it is imperative to know and follow the appropriate regulatory requirements

In 1997, the National Advisory Committee on Microbiological Criteria for Foods (NACMCF), issued a revision of their HACCP guidelines (see Chapter 2). At the request of USDA/FSIS, NACMCF provided greater focus to prerequisite programs than in their previous editions of the guidelines (NACMCF, 1998). The Codex Alimentarius Commission adopted a similar document in 1997, which addresses HACCP within the context of overall good hygienic practices. Although each group interprets prerequisite programs slightly differently, the basic concept—programs that are prerequisites to HACCP—is the same.

OVERVIEW OF PREREQUISITE PROGRAMS

Prerequisite programs provide the basic environmental and operating conditions that are necessary for the production of safe, wholesome food. Many of the conditions and practices are specified in federal, state and local regulations and guidelines (e.g., cGMPs and the Food Code). In many cases, the prerequisite programs for HACCP include programs and procedures that are already in place in a food processing establishment. Like HACCP plans, prerequisite programs should be well documented with written SOPs and should be adhered to by all employees. They should be reviewed and revised as needed to assure that they are being followed and that they are effective in accomplishing their objectives. Often, these procedures have been handed down through the years and are not always properly documented. Or, a program may have been written and validated, but never revised over time. In such instances, what is written in manuals may not reflect actual practices. These practices usually result in establishment procedures that are arbitrary, are difficult to monitor and control, or are ineffective.

Prerequisite Program or HACCP?

The determination of what is managed within a prerequisite program and what is included in a HACCP program is a key consideration, and it is often a difficult decision. The decision will hinge on the outcome of the hazard analysis and the HACCP team's assessment of potential risk of a hazard to consumers. This concept will be covered more thoroughly in the chapter on hazard analysis.

The basic differences between prerequisite programs and issues covered in a HACCP plan are:

- prerequisite programs deal only indirectly with food safety issues, while HACCP plans deal solely with food safety issues;
- prerequisite programs are more general and may be applicable throughout the plant crossing multiple product lines, while HACCP plans are based on hazard analyses that are product and line specific; and
- failures to meet a prerequisite program requirement seldom result in a food safety hazard or concern, while deviations from a HACCP plan critical limit typically result in action against the product.

Prerequisite programs include objectives other than food safety and it may not be easy to associate performance of a prerequisite program element with specific production lots or batches. Thus, usually it is more effective to manage prerequisite programs within a quality system rather than to include their performance and control as part of the HACCP plan. It is appropriate to control them in a prerequisite program provided that uninterrupted adherence to the prerequisite program is not essential for food safety. Occasional deviations from a prerequisite program requirement alone would not be expected to create a food safety hazard or concern.

In some cases, prerequisite programs can play an important role in controlling potential health hazards. For example, supplier control programs and chemical control programs can be used to minimize potential chronic health hazards such as those from mycotoxins or pesticides. Similarly, the potential for foreign material contamination in many food processes can be minimized by preventive maintenance programs and by upstream control devices such as sifters or magnets. Failure to conform to the requirements in a prerequisite program usually does not result in action against the product. Such non-conformances from prerequisite programs are not expected to result in production of product that presents an increased risk to consumers. In contrast, potential acute health hazards, such as the presence of *Salmonella* in a ready-to-eat product, are usually addressed in a HACCP plan where definitive critical control points (CCPs) are available to control the hazard. Deviations from compliance in a HACCP system normally result in corrective actions against the product because such deviations are presumed to result in production of product that represents an unacceptable risk to consumers.

This is a key consideration that can aid in distinguishing between control points within prerequisite programs and CCPs within a HACCP plan.

Certain activities that are normally addressed in prerequisite programs occasionally may be included in the HACCP plan. For example, while sanitation procedures are normally part of a prerequisite program, some manufacturers have chosen to manage selected sanitation procedures as CCPs in their HACCP systems. This decision, however, will depend on the results of the hazard analysis and the HACCP team's identification of the most effective measures that can be applied to control the specific hazards.

In addition, certain aspects of a prerequisite program may also be incorporated into a HACCP plan as verification procedures. For example, many establishments have preventive maintenance procedures for processing equipment to avoid unexpected equipment failure and loss of production. During the development of a HACCP plan, the HACCP team may decide that certain maintenance procedures, along with the calibration of an oven's temperature, should be included in the plan as verification activities. This would further ensure that all food in the oven is cooked to the minimum internal temperature that is necessary for food safety.

ESTABLISHING PREREQUISITE PROGRAMS

The first step in establishing effective prerequisite programs is to get commitment from management. As with HACCP plans, it is essential that management understand the importance of having well written prerequisite programs that are understood and carried out by operations and quality control personnel. It is also essential that management understand that this will take time and resources. Management commitment must be continuous to remain effective. A common misconception is that this commitment is a single action and they may not ''hang in there'' for the continuous changes that are necessary to keep the program in step with changes in the processes, products, and technology. Without management's support these programs may not be addressed effectively. Management should commit to providing resources to accomplish the following:

1. Documentation. A well written prerequisite program clearly communicates what procedures should be performed, at what frequency, who has responsibility and what actions should be taken if the procedures are not performed according to the written protocol, or if the procedures do not have the expected outcome. These written protocols should include SOPs addressing the objectives, procedures and practices and job descriptions for those individuals involved in carrying out the specific procedures outlined in the programs. If the prerequisite program is not documented properly, compliance will be very difficult to verify. If there are written protocols, then verification can be systematic and objective. Writing and/or revising prerequisite programs will take time and energy. Several individuals may need to devote time to prepare or review existing documents. These should be reviewed and revised by the people actually responsible for carrying out the different procedures. If no written protocols exist, the written SOPs should be prepared before attempting to write a HACCP program.

2. Employee Training. The success of prerequisite programs and a HACCP program, relies on a program that assures continuing education and training management and employees in the importance of understanding and following their assigned tasks. Without complete understanding of the purpose of the programs and each individual's role, the program is not likely to succeed. Management must provide adequate time for thorough education and training. Personnel must be given the materials and equipment necessary to perform the assigned tasks. Each individual's performance must be verified over time and reviewed when necessary.

3. Verification. Each SOP related to a prerequisite program should include procedures for routine verification. Verification activities should be carried out by someone other than the individual assigned to complete the primary task. This individual should verify that the SOP is being performed in the manner intended and that appropriate monitoring and record-keeping are completed. Periodically, the prerequisite programs should be independently audited, usually by QA, to verify and document that the overall program is being followed as intended, and that the prerequisite program is effective. Once the prerequisite programs are in place, they will need to be reviewed on a regular basis to assure that they are accomplishing their intended goal and that they are revised when necessary.

4. Resources. Management commitment of resources is also important for the successful maintenance of prerequisite programs. Through the course of implementing and verifying these programs, a firm may find it necessary to enhance their operation for example, by updating and adapting equipment, providing for additional personnel to work on new activities, or installing systems for monitoring and storing data. Many of these improvements would require an investment of additional capital or personnel.

PROGRAMS THAT MAY BE CONSIDERED AS PREREQUISITES

There are many activities within a processing facility that can be considered to be part of a prerequisite program. The following is a synopsis of programs that may be included as prerequisite programs and a description of the types of issues they should cover.

Facilities

The entire location, neighboring properties, surrounding areas, structure(s) and equipment need to be considered when planning a food processing facility. The main focus is to prevent potential contaminants from coming into contact with the food product. Contaminants may be airborne (bacteria, yeast, molds, dirt, insects, birds, etc.) as well as from overhead contaminants (condensate, chipping paint, rust, etc.). The facility should be designed so that product flows in one direction only. Again, the focus is to minimize the potential for cross-contamination of product in progress with material that is not clean. This includes raw ingredients and their containers, waste and other potential sources of contaminants. The building interior, equipment location and design, ventilation and lighting need to be considered from the standpoint of practical use, cleaning, sanitation and maintenance. Accessibility of these areas for the various activities must be considered when designing and renovating a facility. An adequate number of sanitary facilities and locations are also critical for all employees. Water used in production should be potable and testing records should be maintained. There must not be any cross-connections between potable and non-potable water lines. Plumbing should be appropriately equipped with vacuum breakers and other back flow protection devices as appropriate so that contamination of potable water supply lines is prevented.

Production Equipment

Sanitary design principles should be used in the design and manufacture of food production equipment, and establishments should verify that the appropriate design criteria have been applied before equipment purchases are made. The equipment should be designed to prevent the contamination of food, the accumulation of food residues that promote growth of microorganisms during production, and for accessibility and cleanability. There should be a predetermined schedule for the servicing of all equipment. This should include a scheduled replacement of worn parts and maintenance of equipment. Equipment also should be calibrated as necessary, and schedules should be established for this purpose.

Control of Raw Materials

Written specifications should be in place for all chemicals, pesticides, food ingredients and packaging materials associated with the processing facility. In addition, all suppliers should be scrutinized to assure that they are complying with all applicable laws, are using cGMPs (where applicable) and that they have food safety programs in place. In the case of some ingredients, it may be necessary to require proof of safety prior to acceptance. This may be achieved with a Certificate of Analysis (COA), a Letter of Guarantee, or other means of documentation that provide the buyer with assurance that the ingredient specifications are being met. An on-going audit program may be needed

to assure a supplier is complying with the established requirements. Upon receipt, all raw materials and packaging materials and their carriers should be inspected prior to acceptance and storage of the goods. All raw materials should be stored in appropriate temperature and relative humidity and kept away from finished products.

Sanitation

Written procedures and schedules should be in place for cleaning and sanitizing all food processing equipment. A master sanitation schedule should be developed and rigorously applied to assure good housekeeping and minimize product exposure to contaminants (Katsuyama, 1993). Written guidance should also be developed for personal hygiene standards for all plant workers. The guidance should include proper attire, handwashing, and personal health expectations. An environmental sampling program may be used to confirm the effectiveness of the establishment sanitation program. See Chapter 4 for more detailed information on sanitation and SSOPs.

Chemical Control

A control program for the storage and use of cleaning and sanitation chemicals, fumigants, pesticides, baits and all non-food chemicals used in or around the establishment must be in place to eliminate the possibility of cross-contamination to product, ingredients and/or packaging materials. All chemicals should be properly labeled and stored in an area separate from food storage areas, and the chemical storage area should be accessible to appropriate personnel only.

An effective program should be in place to discourage pest entry to the facility, including screens, air curtains, doors, etc. These should be monitored regularly to assure proper working condition. In addition, rodent bait stations, traps, insect electrocuters, etc. should be checked regularly and the date and findings documented along with any actions that were taken.

Production and Quality Controls

All areas where products are handled must be maintained at the proper temperature. The control of employee and equipment traffic and product flow may be necessary to minimize the contamination of finished products or product in progress. In some finished-product packaging rooms, positive air pressure is necessary to minimize product contamination. Sifters, screens, filters and magnets can be used to reduce or eliminate foreign material from a food process. Allergens are another type of contaminant, which must be controlled carefully within a food processing facility. Cross contamination of allergenic materials to foods that do not contain the allergen can result in serious problems (see

Chapter 6). Minimizing the potential for cross contamination is accomplished by rework control, production sequencing, cleaning equipment between products, and strict attention to product labeling.

Glass Control

Glass quality control programs are necessary to assure that glass packages can be adequately sealed and processed. These programs must manage glass breakage on the processing line and prevent or detect glass fragments that could occur through manufacturing defects or through distribution.

Receiving, Storage, and Distribution

If temperatures during storage and distribution are necessary for product quality and safety, they must be monitored and documented. In addition, vehicles used for the transportation of food, raw materials and packaging materials must be free of contaminants. This is especially important in bulk transportation by truck, rail car or ship; proper inspection, cleaning and sanitation procedures as well as temperature control when appropriate, must be followed and documented for these vessels.

Traceability and Recall

Each establishment must have the ability to trace all raw materials and finished products in order to conduct product retrieval. A crisis response plan and a crisis response team should be in place to handle such incidents. Proper lot coding of all materials along with appropriate records are necessary so that retrievals can be accomplished quickly and efficiently. Good record-keeping procedures may also limit the amount of material to be retrieved. Complete distribution records should be maintained so that the geographical extent of the retrieval is known. Once retrieved, the manner of product disposition should be determined.

Complaint Investigations

Consumer complaints should be reviewed carefully. Feedback from consumers may identify problem areas that can be corrected, leading to improved effectiveness of the affected prerequisite program.

Labeling

It is essential to have the correct label on each package for compliance with food-labeling regulations and for allergen control (see Chapter 6).

Training

All employees must receive training in areas that pertain to their jobs. If they don't understand the importance of their role in any program within the facility and its operations, the program is destined to fail. Written procedures should be in place and readily accessible, so that all employees can refer to them as needed. The types of training include personal safety, cGMPs, personal hygiene, employee practices, and other policies of the establishment, including the HACCP program, if it exists.

REGULATORY REQUIREMENTS

As was discussed earlier, FDA and USDA/FSIS have recognized the importance of prerequisite programs in their HACCP regulations. The regulatory requirements are covered in detail in Chapter 17. It is the responsibility of each food establishment to be aware of the regulations that they must follow.

SUMMARY

The development and execution of prerequisite programs is a critical step in the development of an effective HACCP program. Without adequate prerequisite programs, the HACCP program becomes complicated and impossible to manage. Determining which procedures in a processing facility are included in a prerequisite program as compared to the HACCP plan can be difficult. However, once this is accomplished, the development of the HACCP plan is clearer.

REFERENCES

1998. Food Safety Enhancement Program. Vol. 4, *Operational Guidelines*, 2nd ed., Appendix II. Canadian Food Inspection Agency, Ottawa, Canada.

FDA. 1995. Procedures for the safe and sanitary processing and importing of fish and fishery products; final rule. *Federal Register* 60 (242): 63096. (December 18).

FDA. 1999. Current Good Manufacturing Practices. Title 21, *Code of Federal Regulations*, Part 110. U.S. Government Printing Office, Washington, D.C. (Issued annually.)

FDA. 1998. Hazard Analysis and Critical Control Point (HACCP) Procedures for the safe and sanitary processing and importing of juice; proposed rule. *Federal Register* 63 (79) 20450. (April 24)

Katsuyama, A.M. (ed.) 1993. *Principles of Food Processing Sanitation*, 2nd ed. The Food Processors Institute, Washington, D.C.

NACMCF. 1998. Hazard analysis and critical control point principles and application guidelines. *J. Food Protect.* 61:762.

Sperber, W.H., K.E. Stevenson, D.T. Bernard, K.E. Deibel, L.J. Moberg, L.R. Hontz and V.N. Scott. 1998. The role of prerequisite programs in managing a HACCP system. *Dairy, Food Env. Sanit.* 18:418.

USDA/FSIS. 1996. Pathogen reduction; Hazard Analysis and Critical Control Point (HACCP) systems; final rule. *Federal Register* 61 (144) 38806. (July 25).

Chapter 4

SANITATION AND STANDARD OPERATING PROCEDURES

Allen M. Katsuyama and Michael Jantschke

INTRODUCTION

As mentioned in several previous discussions, sanitation is one of the essential prerequisite programs for the successful implementation and maintenance of a HACCP program. A good sanitation program will control many potential biological, chemical and physical hazards in a food operation that would otherwise have to be addressed in the HACCP system. Attempting to address all hygienic concerns in a HACCP program would overload the program and render it unmanageable. However, the exclusion of these lesser-risk hazards from a HACCP or food safety program is only justifiable if there is assurance that sanitation and other support programs are effective.

Besides the food safety aspects of sanitation, sanitary conditions also assure the production of unadulterated food that is wholesome and fit for human consumption. Good sanitation enhances product quality and shelf-life, reduces maintenance costs, and contributes to operational efficiencies. Modern food establishment operations would be impossible to sustain without effective sanitation programs in place.

GENERAL SANITATION

Contrary to popular perception, sanitation is not limited to the cleaning of equipment. Although clean equipment and a clean establishment environment are essential for producing safe and unadulterated foods, equally important are personnel practices, establishment facilities, properly designed equipment and operations, pest control measures, and warehousing practices. All of these components of a general sanitation program are addressed in regulations promulgated by the Food and Drug Administration (FDA) and by the U.S. Department of Agriculture's Food Safety and Inspection Service (FSIS). Written sanitation standard operating procedures (SSOPs) are recommended by FDA for all processors of fish and fishery products and are mandated by the USDA/FSIS for all meat and poultry processors. Detailed written procedures should be developed for all food establishments, especially for those operations where sanitation is identified as a prerequisite program for food safety.

The successful management of sanitation programs involves a pro-active approach and the participation of employees at every level of the decision-making process. Besides detailed procedures and SSOPs, the proper delegation of responsibilities and employee education are needed to make a sanitation program work effectively. Management must exercise a strong commitment of money, personnel, and materials to accomplish the task. Since personnel changes occur frequently in the industry, the training process must be an ongoing program requiring considerable commitment from everyone involved.

One aspect of a sanitation program that is often overlooked is the development of monitoring procedures. Without monitoring specific sanitation measures and keeping appropriate records, the assessment of the overall efficacy of the program will be difficult. Monitoring records also provide the basis for program verification through inspections and audits. Audits are a necessary tool to ensure that sanitary conditions are maintained over time.

REGULATORY REQUIREMENTS

Regulations for minimum sanitation requirements have been promulgated by FDA for food establishments generally (21 *CFR* 110) and for fish and fishery products (21 *CFR* 123), and by USDA/FSIS for meat and poultry products (9 *CFR* 308 and 381). On August 27, 1997, USDA/FSIS published a proposal to consolidate the sanitation regulations for meat and for poultry into a single regulation applicable to both types of establishments, to eliminate unnecessary differences between the meat and the poultry sanitation requirements, and to convert many of the highly prescriptive requirements into performance standards. These proposed regulations, which include a requirement for daily cleanup, are yet to be finalized. Although the current requirements for meat and poultry and for seafood are similar, there are some differences among the regulations.

Sanitation for Meat and Poultry Products—9 *CFR* 308 and 381

Sanitation requirements for meat processors (9 *CFR* 308) and for poultry processors (9 *CFR* 381, Subpart H) were promulgated to provide criteria for complying with provisions of the Federal Meat Inspection Act and the Poultry Products Inspection Act, respectively. Both acts mandate continuous inspection of all meat and poultry slaughter operations by USDA/FSIS. Processing establishments receive at least daily inspection. Processors must comply with the sanitation requirements, which are spelled out in considerable detail in the regulations. Although the two sets of regulations are organized quite differently, the provisions in each are very similar and prescribe sanitation requirements that parallel FDA's current Good Manufacturing Practices (cGMPs) described later.

Sanitation Standard Operating Procedures—9 *CFR* 416

In the process of developing its HACCP regulations, the USDA/FSIS considered various aspects of food safety in the processing of meat and poultry products. The following statement appeared in the preamble of the "mega-reg" publication in the Federal Register:

FSIS proposed that all meat and poultry establishments be required to develop, maintain, and adhere to written sanitation standard operating procedures (Sanitation SOPs). The proposal was based on FSIS's belief that effective establishment sanitation is essential for food safety and to successful implementation of HACCP (USDA/FSIS, 1996).

The SSOPs, for both meat and poultry are mandated by regulations that have been promulgated by USDA/FSIS (9 *CFR* 416). The sanitation requirements for meat products (9 *CFR* 308) and for poultry products (9 *CFR* 381, Subpart H) have been modified to reflect the additional requirement for written SSOPs. However, as noted previously, USDA/FSIS intends to replace all of the current sanitation regulations with a single set of consolidated performance standards in 9 *CFR* 416.

The regulations require that each official establishment develop, implement, and maintain written SSOPs. These SSOPs must include the following:

- The SSOPs must describe all procedures that will be conducted daily, before and during operations, that are sufficient to prevent direct contamination or adulteration of products. Each establishment must monitor daily the implementation of all SSOP procedures.
- The SSOPs must be initially signed and dated by the individual with overall on-site authority or by a higher level company official. The signature must signify that the establishment will implement and maintain the SSOPs. Subsequently modified SSOPs must likewise be signed and dated.
- Procedures that are to be conducted prior to operations must be identified as such and must, at a minimum, address the cleaning of food contact surfaces of facilities, equipment, and utensils. Each establishment must ensure that all pre-operational procedures are performed before the start of operations.
- The frequency with which each procedure in the SSOPs is to be conducted must be specified. The establishment employee(s) responsible for implementing and maintaining each procedure must be identified. Each establishment must ensure that all procedures are performed at the specified frequencies.

Maintenance of Sanitation SOPs

The SSOPs and the procedures identified within them must be evaluated routinely for effectiveness in preventing contamination or adulteration of products. The SSOPs and/or procedures must be revised as necessary to maintain their effectiveness and to keep them current to reflect changes in the facilities, equipment, operations, and personnel.

Corrective Actions

Appropriate corrective action must be taken whenever an SSOP, a specified procedure, or the implementation or maintenance of an SSOP fails to prevent product contamination or product adulteration. Corrective actions must include procedures for the appropriate disposition of affected product, means to re-establish sanitary conditions, and procedures to prevent the recurrence of direct product contamination or adulteration. The SSOP and specified procedure must be reevaluated and, if necessary, modified.

Recordkeeping Requirements

Daily records must be maintained to document the implementation and monitoring of the SSOPs and any corrective actions taken. These records must be initialed and dated by the individual(s) identified in the SSOP as being responsible for the implementation and monitoring of the specified procedure(s). The records must be kept at the establishment for at least 48 hours after completion, and may thereafter be kept off-site provided that the records can be made available to USDA/FSIS within 24 hours. All SSOP records must be maintained for at least six months.

Agency Verification

FSIS is required to verify the adequacy and effectiveness of the SSOPs and the specified procedures. Agency verification may include the following:

- Reviewing the SSOPs.
- Reviewing daily records.
- Direct observation of the implementation of SSOPs, the specified procedures, and/or corrective actions taken.
- Direct observation or testing to assess the sanitary conditions within the establishment.

Developing SSOPs for Meat and Poultry Establishments

Appendix A, Guidelines for Developing a Standard Operating Procedure for Sanitation (Sanitation SOPs) in Federally Inspected Meat and Poultry Establishments, and Appendix B, Model of a Standard Operating Procedure for Sanitation, were published in the *Federal Register* as a supplement to USDA/FSIS's final rule regarding pathogen reduction and hazard analysis and critical control point (HACCP) systems (USDA/FSIS, 1996). These guidelines, which are provided to assist companies in the development of written Sanitation

SOPs mandated by the regulations (9 *CFR* 416), are for (a) livestock slaughter and/or processing establishments; (b) poultry slaughter and/or processing establishments; (c) import inspection establishments; and (d) identification warehouses. The established sanitary procedures should be tailored to the conditions and situations existing at the establishment. Emphasis must be placed not only on the prevention of contamination or adulteration, but also on the prevention of cross contamination.

Pre-Operational Sanitation

Establish procedures for pre-operational sanitation that will ensure prior to starting production that the facilities, equipment and utensils are free of any soil, tissue debris, chemical or other injurious substance that could contaminate a meat or poultry food product.

1. Develop detailed procedures for daily, routine pre-operational sanitation, including the cleaning of product contact surfaces of facilities, equipment and utensils.

2. Develop details as appropriate to describe equipment disassembly, re-assembly after cleaning, use of acceptable chemicals according to label directions, and cleaning techniques.

3. If appropriate, describe in detail the application of sanitizers to product contact surfaces after cleaning.

Operational Sanitation

Establish procedures to be conducted during operations to ensure that a sanitary environment is maintained wherever any meat or poultry food product is prepared, stored, or handled.

1. Develop details for the daily, routine sanitary procedures that will be conducted during operations to prevent direct product contamination or adulteration.

2. Describe in detail how equipment and utensils will be cleaned and sanitized or disinfected during production, at breaks, between shifts, and at midshift cleanup.

3. Describe the company's employee hygiene program, including rules for personal hygiene, cleanliness of outer garments and gloves, hair restraints, hand washing, health, etc.

4. Develop detailed procedures for the handling of product in raw and in cooked product areas.

Implementation and Monitoring of the Sanitation SOPs

The SSOPs must identify the position of the employee(s) responsible for implementing and maintaining the

SSOP, as well as the employee(s) responsible for monitoring and evaluating the effectiveness of the SSOP and for taking corrective actions as needed.

1. Develop detailed procedures for evaluating the effectiveness of the SSOP. One or more of the following methods may be employed:
   * Organoleptic/sensory (e.g., sight, feel, smell).
   * Chemical (e.g., checking the chlorine level).
   * Microbiological (e.g., microbial swabbing and culturing of product contact surfaces of equipment or utensils).

2. Specify the method, frequency, and recordkeeping processes associated with monitoring.
   * For pre-operational monitoring, describe how the effectiveness of cleaning of all direct product contact surfaces, including the facility, equipment, and/or utensils, will be evaluated and documented.
   * For operational sanitation monitoring, describe how to evaluate and document adherence to the SSOP. Include descriptions of actions that identify and correct instances of direct product contamination from environmental sources (facilities, equipment, pests, etc.) or employee practices (personal hygiene, product handling, etc.).
   * All establishment records of pre-operational and operational sanitation monitoring, including corrective actions to prevent direct contamination, must be retained at the official establishment for 48 hours. Thereafter, the records may be held off-site. The records must be retained for at least six months and be made available to USDA/FSIS program employees within 24 hours of request.

Corrective Actions

Whenever deviations occur from the procedures set forth in the SSOPs, corrective actions must be taken to prevent direct product contamination or adulteration.

1. Develop procedures for documenting corrective actions. Provide instructions on the procedures to both employees and management.

2. Ensure that all actions are recorded.

SSOP Details

While it may appear from the above description that the development of written SSOPs is a mammoth task, the Agency does not expect companies to develop extensive and detailed manuals. Moreover, companies should bear in mind that failure to comply with the SSOP requirements they design and implement can, under worst case scenarios, lead to administrative, criminal, civil or other actions by the Agency.

This is one reason for exercising caution in the level of detail incorporated into the SSOPs. For instance, most companies would specify in their SSOPs the use of an approved sanitizer for a particular purpose, rather than specifying the manufacturer and brand name of the sanitizer currently in use. Otherwise a switch to a different but equally effective compound would either require an amendment to the SSOPs or would in fact be a technical violation. (This is not meant to suggest that the Agency would take action against a relatively minor issue such as this, but an accumulation of similar issues would be viewed with some concern.) In a similar vein, many processors would elect to include in their SSOPs the fact that a particular piece of equipment is to be broken down, cleaned and sanitized daily, rather than including the step-by-step detail of procedures for disassembling and reassembling each piece of equipment. Detailed sanitation procedures could still be developed to assist in training employees, but these procedures would only enhance and not be a part of the SSOPs required by the Agency.

Current Good Manufacturing Practices—21 *CFR* 110

The cGMPs which were revised in 1986, were promulgated by FDA to provide criteria for complying with provisions of the Federal Food, Drug, and Cosmetic Act (FD&C Act) requiring that all human foods be free from adulteration. Since food adulteration, as defined in the FD&C Act, includes aesthetic and economic considerations, several specific details of the cGMPs do not deal directly with food safety. However, many of the requirements have some direct or indirect influence on the biological, chemical, or physical safety of the finished products.

The cGMP regulations are divided into several subparts, each containing detailed requirements pertaining to various operations or groups of operations in food processing facilities. Emphasis is placed on the prevention of product contamination from direct and indirect sources.

Personnel

The cGMPs charge establishment management with responsibilities for establishment personnel. Criteria for disease control, cleanliness (personal hygiene and dress codes), education and training are described. These requirements are designed to prevent the spread of disease from worker to worker, from workers to the food processing area and from workers to the food itself. Also included is the requirement that a competent supervisory person be assigned the responsibility for assuring compliance by all personnel.

Buildings and Facilities

The general principles of establishment design and construction necessary to protect food from insanitary conditions are described. The methods for adequate maintenance of grounds are enumerated. To reduce food contamination, several design mechanisms for the separation of various operations are recommended. Adequate working space, lighting, and ventilation are required.

Basic rules for food establishment sanitation are also established. The rules describe general requirements for (a) maintenance of physical facilities (building and fixtures), (b) pest controls, (c) cleaning and sanitizing of equipment and utensils, and (d) storage and handling of cleaned equipment and utensils. The proper use and storage of cleaning chemicals, sanitizing agents, and pesticides are emphasized.

Minimum requirements for sanitary facilities and accommodations are also described, including requirements for (a) water used for various purposes, (b) plumbing for both water and wastewater, including a rule specifically prohibiting backflows and cross-connections, (c) sewage disposal, (d) toilet facilities, (e) hand-washing facilities and supplies, and (f) rubbish and offal disposal.

Equipment and Utensils

General principles of design, construction, and maintenance of processing equipment and utensils are described. Cleanability is emphasized. Since precluding microbial contamination is crucial, requirements for equipment used to control or prevent growth of microorganisms are listed. This includes cooling equipment (freezers and cold storage) and other instruments and devices for measuring and/or controlling pH, acidity, water activity, etc. Requirements for compressed air and other gases used in food processing are also set forth. The use of polychlorinated biphenyls (PCBs) as a component in equipment is now virtually prohibited in food and feed processing establishments.

Production and Process Controls

This subpart imposes requirements on food establishments to assure the suitability of raw materials and ingredients, to maintain the integrity of processed foods, and to protect finished foods from deterioration. Among the requirements is the need for all operations involving foods to "be conducted in accordance with adequate sanitation principles," and that establishment sanitation "be under the supervision of one or more individuals assigned responsibility for this function." Quality control programs, including appropriate testing procedures where necessary, are required to insure compliance with sanitation principles and with the FD&C Act.

Methods and procedures for handling raw materials and ingredients are articulated and include inspection, segregation, and washing or cleaning to insure the cleanliness and fitness of these materials. These materials must not contain levels of microorganisms that can produce food poisoning or other disease in humans or they must be properly treated to destroy such microorganisms. Compliance with regulations related to natural toxins and extraneous materials is stressed.

The need to protect foods from contamination is also emphasized. Required conditions are listed for holding foods that support the rapid growth of microorganisms which cause foodborne disease, or those that can spoil foods as a result of multiplication. Requirements to insure freedom from adulteration are stated for several types of foods (batters and other preparations, intermediate moisture and dehydrated foods, and acidified foods), and for various operations (mechanical processing steps, heat blanching, and filling/packaging).

Warehousing and Distribution

Storage and transportation of finished foods must be conducted under conditions preventing physical, chemical, and microbiological contamination. Although permanently legible code marks on all food packages are no longer generally required, the use of printed codes is highly recommended in the event that a recall becomes necessary to remove products from distribution channels. FDA has published guidelines for policies and procedures of the agency and steps that firms should follow during product recalls (21 *CFR* 7, Subpart C).

Defect Action Levels

FDA recognizes that "natural or unavoidable defects" which present no human health hazard occur in some foods, such as raw agricultural commodities, and carry through to the finished product. The current level of defects permitted is based largely on the industry's ability to reduce the levels occurring in the raw product through cGMPs. The "action" levels represent the limits at or above which FDA may take legal action to remove the commodities from the consumer market.

These defect action levels cannot be used as an excuse for poor manufacturing practices. FDA clearly advises that failure to operate under cGMPs will leave a firm liable to legal sanctions even though products might contain natural and unavoidable defects at levels lower than the currently established action levels. Additionally, the mixing of food with defects above the action level and foods with defects below the action level to produce a product with an acceptable defect level is prohibited. The "blended" lot is unlawful regardless of the defect level in the finished product.

Sanitation for Fish and Fishery Products—21 *CFR* 123

Sanitation Standard Operating Procedures

FDA promulgated regulations describing procedures for the safe and sanitary processing and importing of fish and fishery products. Although the primary purpose of the regulations is to require all processors of fish and fishery products to develop HACCP programs, incorporated within these regulations is an emphasis on the need to comply with the cGMPs discussed above. The FDA recommends that each processor develop and implement written SSOPs for each facility where fish and fishery products are produced. SSOPs are expected to delineate how the processor will ensure that certain minimum sanitation conditions and practices are to be met and how those conditions and practices will be monitored.

Monitoring

The following provisions addressed in the cGMPs are specifically identified as concerns in the processing of fish and fishery products; the regulations suggest that these be addressed in written SSOPs, however written SSOPs are not required. Nevertheless, each processor is required to develop detailed monitoring procedures for the following concerns:

- Safety of the water that comes into contact with food or food contact surfaces, or is used in the manufacture of ice.
- Condition and cleanliness of food contact surfaces, including utensils, gloves, and outer garments.
- Prevention of cross-contamination from insanitary objects to food, food packaging material, and other food contact surfaces, including utensils, gloves, and outer garments, and from raw product to cooked product.
- Maintenance of hand washing, hand sanitizing, and toilet facilities.
- Protection of food, food packaging material, and food contact surfaces from adulteration with lubricants, fuel, pesticides, cleaning compounds, sanitizing agents, condensate, and other chemical, physical, and biological contaminants.
- Proper labeling, storage, and use of toxic compounds.
- Control of employee health conditions that could result in the microbiological contamination of food, food packaging materials, and food contact surfaces.
- Exclusion of pests from the food establishment.

The regulation states that "sanitation controls may be included in the HACCP plan." If a processor determines through a hazard analysis that any of these items are sufficiently significant food safety hazards, those items should be included in the HACCP plan. Otherwise, these concerns may be addressed with SSOPs and monitored appropriately.

Recordkeeping Requirements

Sanitation control records must be maintained to document the monitoring of those items listed above and corrective actions that were taken for any noted deficiencies. These records, which are subject to regulatory inspection, must include the following information:

- The name and location of the processor or importer.
- The date and time of the activity that the record reflects.
- The signature or initials of the person performing the operation.
- Where appropriate, the identity of the product and the production code, if any.

These records must be retained for at least one year for refrigerated products and for at least two years for frozen, preserved, or shelf-stable products.

SUMMARY

Since a good sanitation program will control many potential biological, chemical and physical hazards in a food operation, sanitation is one of the essential prerequisite programs necessary for the successful implementation and maintenance of a HACCP program, as well as to provide for product quality and establishment operational efficiencies. However, sanitation is not limited solely to the cleaning of equipment. Instead, a general sanitation program also must address personnel practices, establishment facilities, properly designed equipment and operations, pest control measures, and warehousing practices, consideration of which are mandated by FDA and USDA/FSIS regulations.

The importance of good sanitation to food safety also is emphasized in regulatory HACCP programs. FDA *recommends* that written SSOPs be developed by processors of fish and fishery products, while USDA/FSIS *requires* written SSOPs for meat and poultry processors.

Written SSOPs should include at least the following:

- Detailed descriptions of all procedures that are to be conducted daily— before, during and after operation—that will prevent direct contamination or adulteration of products. The frequency of each procedure must be specified. The employee(s) responsible for each procedure must be identified.
- Detailed descriptions of appropriate corrective actions that are to be taken whenever there is a failure to prevent product contamination. The corrective actions must include procedures for the disposition of affected product.
- Daily records that are to be maintained to document the implementation and monitoring of the SSOPs and any corrective actions taken.

REFERENCES

FDA. 1999. Current Good Manufacturing Practices. Title 21, *Code of Federal Regulations*, Part 110. U.S. Government Printing Office, Washington, DC. (Issued annually)

FDA. 1999. Procedures for the Safe and Sanitary Processing and Importing of Fish and Fishery Products. Title 21, *Code of Federal Regulations*, Part 123. U.S. Government Printing Office, Washington, DC. (Issued annually)

USDA/FSIS. 1996. Final Rule: Pathogen Reduction; Hazard Analysis and Critical Control Point (HACCP) Systems. *Federal Register*, Vol. 61 (144) 38806.(July 25)

USDA/FSIS. 1999. Sanitation. Title 9, *Code of Federal Regulations*, Part 308. U.S. Government Printing Office, Washington, DC. (Issued annually)

USDA/FSIS. 1999. Sanitation. Title 9, *Code of Federal Regulations*, Part 381, Subpart H. U.S. Government Printing Office, Washington, DC. (Issued annually)

USDA/FSIS. 1999. Sanitation. Title 9, *Code of Federal Regulations*, Part 416. U.S. Government Printing Office, Washington, DC. (Issued annually)

CHAPTER 5

BIOLOGICAL HAZARDS AND CONTROLS

Virginia N. Scott

INTRODUCTION

It is not within the scope of this chapter to provide in-depth coverage of microbiology or microbial food safety, nor even to list all of the biological hazards that may need to be considered in developing a HACCP plan. This chapter is designed to raise the awareness of the reader about the types of biological hazards that should be considered for specific types of foods and the potential control measures that may be applied. For more information about specific microorganisms in foods consult the list of references, especially the International Commission on Microbiological Specifications for Foods (ICMSF) texts (ICMSF, 1986; 1996; 1998).

FOODBORNE DISEASE IN THE UNITED STATES

While the food supply in the U.S., and in most other developed countries, is considered to be safe, we have to recognize that we cannot make food absolutely safe.

The greatest risk for illness or injury from food comes from biological hazards.

Incidence and Impact of Foodborne Disease

There are many limitations in the data available on the incidence and impact of foodborne disease. A task force convened by the Council of Agricultural Science and Technology to study the risk of foodborne disease concluded that the range of 6.5 to 33 million cases of foodborne disease with 9000 fatalities annually in the United States was based on defensible assumptions. The total yearly cost attributed to foodborne illness in the U.S. was estimated to be in the billions (CAST, 1994). Although some people may take issue with the magnitude of the numbers, there is no doubt that foodborne illness is a problem that warrants attention.

Foodborne Disease Reported to CDC

The "official" reporting of foodborne disease statistics in the United States began in 1923 with the publication by the Public Health Service of summaries of outbreaks of gastrointestinal illness attributed to milk. In 1938, summaries of outbreaks caused by all foods were added. The Centers for Disease Control and Prevention (CDC—then the Communicable Disease Center) assumed responsibility for publishing reports on foodborne illness in 1961. Reports on outbreaks of foodborne and waterborne disease come to CDC primarily from state and local health departments. They are also received from federal agencies such as the U.S. Food and Drug Administration (FDA), the U.S. Department of Agriculture (USDA), the armed forces and occasionally from private physicians. This type of reporting is called "passive surveillance."

Early surveillance efforts revealed an association of infant diarrhea and typhoid fever with milk and water, resulting in the requirements for milk pasteurization and chlorination of municipal water supplies (Todd, 1990). This resulted in significant decreases of illness from these sources. While waterborne illness will not be considered further here, water can be a source of food contamination. The number of outbreaks of foodborne disease (Table 5-1) remained relatively constant from 1988 to 1992 (the last year for which published data are available) and are comparable to the numbers reported between 1983 and 1987 (Bean et al., 1990). The data reported for foodborne disease outbreaks do not include sporadic cases, which are far more common than cases associated with large outbreaks.

Foodborne Disease Outbreaks

CDC defines a foodborne disease outbreak as the occurrence of two or more cases of a similar illness from the ingestion of a common food. Note that before 1992 one case of botulism or marine-toxin or chemical intoxication constituted an outbreak if the etiology was confirmed (CDC, 1996).

Outbreaks are classified by etiologic agent if laboratory evidence of a specific agent is obtained and specified criteria are met. If a food source is implicated epidemiologically but adequate laboratory confirmation of an agent is not obtained, the outbreak is classified as unknown etiology. The etiologic agent was not confirmed in 60% of outbreaks from 1983 to 1987 (Bean et al., 1990) and in 59% of outbreaks from 1988 to 1992 (CDC, 1996), indicating the need for improved investigative techniques to identify known pathogens

more frequently and recognize currently unidentified pathogens.

Actual vs. Reported Foodborne Disease Outbreaks

The reported outbreaks of foodborne disease represent only the "tip of the iceberg." It is estimated that only a small fraction of foodborne disease cases are reported to CDC. The likelihood of an outbreak being recognized and reported to health authorities depends on, among other factors, consumer awareness, physician awareness, disease surveillance activities of state and local health departments, etc. Large outbreaks are more likely to be reported than small ones. Foodborne disease outbreaks associated with food prepared and/or served at restaurants, hospitals and nursing homes are more likely to be recognized than those from family meals at home. Outbreaks involving serious illness, hospitalization or deaths are also more likely to be recognized and reported than those due to pathogens causing mild illness. Foodborne diseases characterized by short incubation periods, such as staphylococcal intoxication, are more likely to be recognized as common source foodborne disease outbreaks than those involving longer incubation periods, such as hepatitis A. Outbreaks involving more common foodborne pathogens are also more likely to be confirmed than those involving less common pathogens, in part because the laboratory may not be knowledgeable in the detection of all foodborne pathogens.

Some states may have better surveillance for foodborne illness than others, either because of interest, expertise or resources. This can result in a further underestimation of the size of the foodborne disease problem. CDC, USDA and FDA began a project in 1995 to conduct active surveillance on diarrheal illnesses (FSIS, 1997). Such data could eventually result in better estimations of the amount and sources of foodborne illness.

Foods Frequently Involved in Outbreaks

The foods most frequently involved in outbreaks are foods of animal origin, although outbreaks from contaminated fruits and vegetables have become more common in recent years. Beef, poultry, pork, fish, and eggs have been commonly involved (Bean and Griffin, 1990; CDC, 1996; Potter, et al., 1997).

Steps Necessary to Cause Foodborne Illness

For a foodborne illness to occur the pathogen or its toxin(s) must be present in the food. In most cases the mere presence of the pathogen is not sufficient for it to cause a foodborne disease; the pathogen must grow

Table 5-1—Outbreaks and Cases of Foodborne Disease[a]

	Outbreaks	Cases
1988	451	15,732
1989	505	15,867
1990	532	19,883
1991	528	14,876
1992	407	11,015

[a]CDC, 1996

to high enough numbers to cause an infection or to produce toxin. Thus, in most instances the food must be capable of supporting growth of the pathogen and the food must remain in the growth temperature range long enough for the organism to multiply and/or produce toxin. (However, some foodborne disease organisms, such as *E. coli* O157:H7, have a very low infectious dose, and their presence alone constitutes a hazard.) Finally, enough of the food must be ingested to exceed the threshold of susceptibility of the person ingesting the food (Riemann and Bryan, 1979).

Place Where Illness Acquired

In outbreaks where the place in which the food was eaten was known, the data reported to CDC indicate that food service establishments and group-feeding situations are the most common sites where foodborne illness is acquired (Table 5-2). This implies that foodborne disease is primarily a problem associated with food preparation and storage, which is supported by the data on the factors contributing to foodborne disease outbreaks (CDC, 1996).

Types of Foodborne Disease

Foodborne disease can be classified as either infections or intoxications. Infections are caused by viable pathogenic microorganisms entering the body and colonizing, and the body's reacting to the organism and/or its toxins (Riemann and Bryan, 1979). There are two types of foodborne infections (Riemann and Bryan, 1979). One type results from penetration of the intestinal mucosa by the infecting organism and its subsequent multiplication therein (*Salmonella, Shigella*), or its multiplication in other tissues (hepatitis A, *Trichinella spiralis*). A second type results from release of enterotoxins by an infecting organism as it multiplies, lyses (breaks apart), or sporulates (makes a resistant form called a spore) in the intestinal tract (*Vibrio cholerae, Clostridium perfringens*).

An intoxication is caused by the ingestion of toxins. These may be found naturally in certain plants and animals (e.g., poisonous mushrooms), or may be metabolic products of certain bacteria (botulinal toxin, staphylococcal enterotoxin), molds (mycotoxins) or algae/dinoflagellates (saxitoxin).

The CDC classifies foodborne disease outbreaks as bacterial, viral, parasitic, or chemical. The vast majority of cases of foodborne disease are caused by bacterial agents (Table 5-3).

Bacterial Agents

In foodborne disease outbreaks in which the etiologic agent was identified, bacteria accounted for approximately 80% of the outbreaks and 90% of the cases between 1988 and 1992 (CDC, 1996). In the United States, the most common bacterial agents of outbreak–associated foodborne illness include *Salmonella, Staphylococcus. aureus, C. perfringens, Clostridium botulinum* and, to a lesser degree, *Bacillus cereus, Shigella,* and *Campylobacter. Salmonella* caused 69% of the bacterial foodborne disease outbreaks between 1988 and 1992 (CDC, 1996), and 60% of these were caused by *Salmonella* serotype Enteritidis; outbreaks from *S.* Enteritidis rose significantly during this period, from 47% of the *Salmonella* outbreaks in 1988 to 75% of the *Salmonella* outbreaks in 1992. The primary source of *S.* Enteritidis is eggs.

Campylobacter, Escherichia coli O157:H7 and *Listeria monocytogenes* have only recently been recognized as foodborne disease organisms. Since *Campylobacter* outbreaks were first reported to the CDC system in 1980, *Campylobacter* has accounted for up to 6% of outbreaks and outbreak–associated cases annually (Bean and Griffin, 1990). However, active surveillance through FoodNet (see above) has indicated that *Campylobacter* is the most frequently isolated bacterium from persons with diarrhea (45%), followed by *Salmonella* (30%), *Shigella* (17%) and *E. coli* O157:H7 (5%).

In addition to the agents listed above, other bacteria that warrant consideration, depending on the food, include vibrios (such as *V. parahaemolyticus, V. cholerae, V. vulnificus*), other pathogenic *E. coli* (enterotoxigenic, enteropathogenic, and enterohemorrhagic strains other than O157:H7), and *Y. enterocolitica..*

Viral Agents

Hepatitis A and Norwalk viruses account for most foodborne illness from viruses (Cliver, 1997a). Although viruses have accounted for less than 10% of foodborne disease outbreaks and cases, they are undoubtedly a much more important cause of foodborne disease than the data suggest. The low number of reported outbreaks probably reflects the limitations of current laboratory techniques for detecting viruses

---

Table 5-2—Where Foodborne Illness is Acquired

	Restaurants, Cafeterias, Delicatessens	School, Picnics, Churches, Camps	Private Residences
1983–1987[a]	44%	11%	23%
1988–1992[b]	42%	9%	19%

[a]Bean et al., 1990; [b]CDC, 1996

Table 5-3—Etiologic Agents of Foodborne Disease

Agent	1973–1987[a]		1988–1992[b]	
	Outbreaks (%)	Cases (%)	Outbreaks (%)	Cases (%)
Bacteria	66	87	80	90
Viruses	5	9	4	6
Parasites	5	1	2	1
Chemicals	25	4	14	2

[a]Bean and Griffin (1990), [b]CDC, 1996

and viral infections. As diagnostic capabilities for viruses increase, the proportion of foodborne disease attributed to them will also increase.

Since viruses are obligate intracellular parasites, they cannot multiply in food. Foodborne viral disease results from fecal contamination of food, generally due to poor personal hygiene of a food handler, although shellfish can also be a source as the result of fecal pollution of growing waters (Cliver, 1997b).

Concerns About Aids

The Human Immunodeficiency Virus (HIV) which causes the disease AIDS (Acquired Immune Deficiency Syndrome) is a severe public health problem. AIDS has never been shown to be transmitted by food or drink (Khan, 1988; Cliver, 1988). Individuals who are known to be infected with the virus can handle food safely if they observe basic sanitation precautions for food handling and take care to avoid injury when preparing food. As with any food handler, should an injury occur, food contaminated with blood should be discarded for aesthetic as well as safety reasons. Employees should be restricted from handling food if they have evidence of infection or illness that would otherwise require that they not handle food (CDC, 1985).

Parasitic Agents

The most common foodborne parasites are *Trichinella spiralis* and *Giardia lamblia*. However, recently *Cryptosporidium parvum* and *Cyclospora cayetanensis* have emerged as increasing problems. *Giardia* and *Cryptosporidium* are more frequently associated with waterborne transmission, but have also been transmitted through foods. Waterborne parasites such as *Giardia* and *Cryptosporidium* may become foodborne when contaminated water is used to wash foods such as fruits and vegetables. In addition, poor personal hygiene by an infected food handler can result in transmission of these parasites.

Toxoplasma gondii is another parasite often transmitted through foods (Speer, 1997). *Toxoplasma gondii* and *T. spiralis* infections result from consumption of uncooked or undercooked meats, primarily pork (Speer, 1997; Kim, 1997).

In seafood, helminths (worm-like parasites) such as nematodes or roundworms (e.g., *Anisakis*), cestodes or tapeworms (e.g., *Diphyllobothrium*) and trematodes or flukes (e.g., *Chlonorchis*) may be a concern (Hayunga, 1997). Relatively few cases are reported in the U.S., probably because of good sanitation and food handling practices and relatively low consumption of raw or undercooked seafood. Generally most fishery products consumed in the U.S. are effectively processed or cooked. However, changing dietary habits incorporating ethnic and natural foods and a tendency to reduce cooking times for seafoods increase the chances for parasitic infection.

Factors Contributing to Foodborne Disease Outbreaks

While the vast majority of foodborne illness outbreaks are directly related to conditions or improper controls during food preparation and serving, the role of the food industry in presenting foods which minimize consumer risk cannot be overstated. Although the factors related below apply more to the foodservice situation, they should be considered during the hazard analysis.

Improper Storage/Holding Temperature

Improper storage or holding temperature in food service establishments, in homes, or during "events" where food is served outside the home, is the most common factor contributing to bacterial foodborne illness. Foodborne disease organisms will grow in foods held at temperatures between 5°C and 55°C; most bacterial pathogens grow very rapidly at temperatures between 25°C and 40°C. Thus, hot foods that are not rapidly cooled for storage or not held hot enough prior to consumption may be at temperatures in the "danger zone" (allowing bacterial growth) for sufficient time to produce enough organisms or toxin to cause illness. Foods prepared several hours ahead of time and in large quantities are sometimes improperly cooled (e.g., refrigerated in large, deep containers) or held at improper temperatures (e.g., on steam–tables or in ovens that are not kept warm enough), resulting in outbreaks of foodborne disease. Improper holding temperature is a frequent contributing factor in outbreaks attributed to *C. perfringens*, *B. cereus*, *S. aureus* and *Salmonella*. Improper holding of certain species of raw seafood is responsible for the formation of histamine (see chapter 6 for more discussion on histamine). To the extent possible, establishments should consider how their products are likely to be used (abused?) when conducting the hazard analysis.

Inadequate Cooking

Inadequate cooking represents a hazard since cooking is relied upon to destroy many foodborne disease organisms and toxins. Undercooking poultry can lead to illness from *Salmonella* or *Campylobacter*, and improperly processing canned food can result in botulism (the latter is primarily a problem with home-canned or home–prepared foods). Similarly, undercooked seafood can result in illness from *Vibrio parahaemolyticus*, *V. vulnificus* or, rarely, *V. cholerae*, and undercooked pork or bear meat can result in trichinosis.

Poor Personal Hygiene

Many foodborne disease organisms are transferred by the fecal–oral route. Infected food handlers with poor personal hygiene transfer organisms to the food. This is a major contributing factor in foodborne outbreaks due to viruses (hepatitis A, Norwalk), bacteria such as *Shigella*, or parasites such as *Giardia*. *Staphylococcus aureus* may be transferred from the skin or nares of food handlers and, if given sufficient time and temperature conditions to grow, may produce enterotoxin in the food.

Cross–contamination

Foodborne pathogens can be transferred from raw product to utensils and equipment, which, if then used for cooked or other ready–to–eat foods, can transfer the pathogens and lead to illness. Cutting boards, slicers, mixers, saws, and grinders with hard–to–clean areas are particular challenges. Utensils and equipment used in the preparation of raw products should never be used for cooked products without thorough cleaning and sanitizing. Cross–contamination can also occur when cooked foods are stored with raw product, particularly raw foods of animal origin. Thus it is important to separate raw foods from ready–to–eat foods. This separation should include storage, preparation areas, personnel and utensils.

Improper Reheating

If pathogens survive the cooking process or cross contamination occurs followed by temperature abuse, the number of organisms present may survive reheating the food. This is particularly of concern when leftovers are warmed rather than thoroughly reheated.

Poor Storage Practices

If cooked product is stored with raw product or ingredients, contamination may occur. For example, when frozen raw meats are thawed in a refrigerator containing other foods, drip from the thawing meat can potentially contaminate cooked or ready–to–eat foods; this may cause illness when the contaminated foods are consumed. Also, storing chemicals and foods together can result in contamination of foods that may cause illness.

MICROBIAL HAZARDS: CHARACTERISTICS & CONTROLS

The remaining sections of this chapter will discuss the microbiological hazards that are responsible for foodborne illness and what can be done to ensure their control. To establish a comprehensive HACCP program, microbiological hazards need to be carefully identified and evaluated to determine the likelihood of occurrence, severity of the hazard, and potential control measures that can be put in place.

This material on microbiological hazards provides only a fraction of the information needed to develop an acceptable HACCP program. A microbiologist who is knowledgeable about the particular industry, product(s), and manufacturing process should be part of the HACCP team that establishes the HACCP program.

Potential for Microorganisms to Cause Illness

Not all microorganisms are created equally when one measures the potential for causing foodborne illness. The potential for causing illness, or the type of hazard a microbe presents, ranges from severe to none, with every variation between these extremes. Microbes which do not present a direct health hazard can still be important in the general contamination of a product, causing reduced shelf–life and spoilage.

As with most situations, there is usually more than one factor that may influence a particular risk. The type of hazard that a foodborne microorganism may present is further influenced by handling conditions to which the food is subjected. Food that is handled in a manner that destroys the microorganisms (i.e., cooking) reduces the potential for foodborne illness. Food that is maintained in a steady state (i.e., frozen) where the microbes cannot grow generally does not change the potential for causing illness. Food that is handled such that the microorganisms are allowed to proliferate (i.e., improper thawing) may result in an increased potential for the microorganism to cause illness.

Infectious Dose

The numbers of microorganisms needed to cause illness varies with the specific strain of the microorganism and the susceptibility of the host. A child may be more susceptible and therefore fewer numbers will be required to cause illness than for an adult. Likewise, hosts that are elderly, debilitated, suffering from other illnesses or injuries, immunocompromised, or somehow less resistant, also may become ill when exposed to fewer pathogenic microorganisms than would be required to cause illness in a healthy adult. With toxigenic microorganisms, the level of toxin needed to cause the disease is more important than the level of the microorganism. Although with organisms such as enterotoxin-producing *S. aureus*, the two may be very closely related.

Table 5-4 provides examples of the varying doses of microorganisms needed to cause disease. With many organisms, such as *C. perfringens* and most strains of *Salmonella*, the infective dose is rather high. However, remember that contamination of a food with a very low level of these microbes can still cause illness, if the food is subsequently mishandled. Other organisms,

Table 5-4—Infectious Dose of Foodborne Pathogens[a]

Organism	Approximate Infectious Dose (Cells)
Bacillus cereus	$10^5 - 10^{11}$
Campylobacter jejuni	500
Clostridium perfringens	$10^6 - 10^{10}$
Cryptosporidium	30
Escherichia coli (pathogenic types)	$10^6 - 10^{10}$
E. coli O157:H7	$10^1 - 10^3$
Listeria monocytogenes	?
Salmonella species (non-typhi)	$10^5 - 10^{10}$
Salmonella typhi	$<10^3 - 10^9$
Shigella species	$10^1 - 10^6$
Vibrio cholerae	10^6
Yersinia enterocolitica	?

[a]CAST, 1994

such as *E. coli* O157:H7, cause illness at very low doses.

Prevention of Foodborne Illness

There are three major ways of preventing foodborne disease: prevent contamination of foods; destroy foodborne disease agents that may be present in foods; and/or prevent foodborne disease agents from growing in foods (for more information see section on Control of Microorganisms).

Prevent Contamination of Foods

It should be assumed that raw foods may contain pathogens (e.g., *Salmonella* on poultry, *C. botulinum* on vegetables). While many new controls are being implemented during harvesting, slaughter, and processing, we cannot entirely prevent the contamination of raw foods. However, it is possible to minimize or prevent contamination of many of the foods we eat. Shellfish should only be harvested from approved growing waters. The use of good personal hygiene practices in food preparation will help prevent foodborne disease from organisms such as viruses, *Salmonella*, *Shigella* and *S. aureus*.

Raw foods should be handled separately from cooked and ready–to–eat foods to avoid cross contamination. Utensils, equipment and work surfaces used for raw foods should be thoroughly cleaned and sanitized prior to using for cooked or ready–to–eat foods.

Destroy or Remove Foodborne Disease Agents

Many foodborne disease organisms will be destroyed by proper cooking. In general, raw animal products such as eggs, fish, poultry, and meat should be cooked to 63°C or above for 15 seconds to destroy pathogens (FDA, 1999). The Food Safety and Inspection Service (FSIS) of the USDA has published cooking guidelines that the Agency accepts as meeting the newly mandated lethality performance standards for the reduction of

Salmonella in certain ready-to-eat meat and poultry products (USDA/FSIS, 1999a and 1999b). One option in these guidelines is to cook poultry products until an internal temperature of at least 160°F is met. An establishment has the option of developing equivalent cooking procedures to meet the lethality performance standard.

Freezing ($-20°C$ for 7 days, or $-35°C$ for 15 hours) can be used to destroy parasites in fish and meat, but it has little effect on bacterial pathogens in food. Irradiation can also be used in some cases to destroy pathogens (e.g., on raw poultry and ground beef depending on current government approvals). New technologies for inactivation of microorganisms, such as high pressure, pulsed light, pulsed electric fields, etc. are being developed but are not yet widely used. Acids and preservatives sometimes kill certain microorganisms, however, in most cases they are used to prevent growth rather than to kill. Chemical rinses (e.g., acid wash; TSP, or trisodium phosphate, dips), hot water, and steam treatments of animal carcasses and chlorine washes of fruits and vegetables can be used to reduce levels of microorganisms, including pathogens, but not to eliminate them.

Prevent Multiplication of Foodborne Disease Agents

As indicated previously, the presence of certain foodborne disease agents at any level is a hazard, e.g., *E. coli* O157:H7. However, many other organisms must multiply to large numbers to cause disease. For example, *S. aureus* must reach levels of about 10^6 to produce enough toxin to cause disease. *Clostridium perfringens* and *V. cholerae* must also be present in high numbers (approximately 10^6/g) to cause illness. Thus, storing and preparing foods under conditions that prevent growth (multiplication) is a primary means of preventing foodborne disease.

Although *Y. enterocolitica* can grow at temperatures as low as $-1.3°C$, freezing generally prevents growth of all foodborne disease organisms. Proper refrigeration temperatures ($\leq 5°C$) will prevent multiplication of most foodborne disease organisms and slow the multiplication of others; the lower the temperature, the slower the growth rate (see Control of Microorganisms).

It is important to lower the temperature of foods rapidly to keep microorganisms from growing. A good rule of thumb is to reduce the temperature from 60°C to 5°C (140°F to 41°F; the "danger zone" for microbial growth) in ≤ 4 hours. USDA/FSIS has published guidelines that the Agency accepts as meeting the newly mandated stabilization (cooling) performance standards for preventing the growth of spore-forming bacteria in certain heat-treated meat and poultry products. (USDA/FSIS, 1999b and 1999c). One option in these guidelines is to rapidly cool products from 130°F to 80°F (54.4°C to 26.7°C) in 1.5 hours and from 80°F to 40°F (26.7°C to 4.4°C) in 5 hours. An establishment has the option of developing equivalent cooling rates to meet the stabilization performance standard.

Decreasing the pH (by increasing the acidity using vinegar, etc.) and/or the water activity (by drying or adding humectants like sugar, etc.) of a food or judicious use of preservatives can prevent or retard the growth of foodborne pathogens. Combining sub–inhibitory levels of several factors can be used effectively to control pathogens, particularly under refrigeration conditions.

Holding foods at elevated temperatures can also prevent growth of foodborne pathogens. Care should be taken to see that all parts of the food are above 60°C (>140°F). For example, on steam trays where the heat source is beneath the trays, the temperature at the surface should be kept at 60°C or above.

Sources and Characteristics of Common Foodborne Pathogens

It is important to emphasize at this point that it is only those organisms known to cause illness in humans that we refer to as pathogens. While many organisms are capable of spoiling foods, the pathogens are limited to a relatively few types of microorganisms.

Presentation of detailed information concerning the characteristics, properties and diseases caused by all of the foodborne pathogens is beyond the scope of this manual. Furthermore, due to the similar nature of many of the non–sporeforming bacterial foodborne pathogens, control of the more common types of foodborne disease agents will also control vegetative cells of other bacterial pathogens. Table 5-5 presents an overview of the pathogens of particular concern for specific food categories.

The most common source of a number of pathogens is an infected food handler. Pathogens commonly transmitted in this manner include viruses (especially hepatitis A), parasites (e.g., *Giardia*) and bacteria such as *S. aureus* and *Shigella*. The source of other pathogens

is the environment. Viruses in water may contaminate shellfish, which "filter feed" and concentrate microorganisms from the water. Parasites such as *Cryptosporidium* and *Giardia* in water can contaminate fruits and vegetables during irrigation or washing. *Listeria monocytogenes* is a common environmental contaminant. It is found on many raw products, including meats, poultry, and vegetables. When these products are brought into the plant, the organism can contaminate the plant. The organism can also be carried in on the shoes of workers. Thus, it is impossible to keep the organism out of the plant. Even with frequent cleaning and sanitizing of the environment, it is not possible to completely prevent contamination of foods by *L. monocytogenes*.

Tables appended to the end of this chapter present information on a number of pathogens that are common causes of foodborne disease, or of the most concern, from the standpoint of control in the food processing industry. Each of these microorganisms are discussed from the standpoint of the following:

- The disease caused by the microorganism or its toxin(s).
- The source (reservoir) of the microorganism.
- The most common method(s) of transmission.
- The characteristics of the microorganism; and
- Selected control procedures.

Additional information on hazardous microorganisms can be found in cited references (ICMSF, 1996; ICMSF, 1998; NAS/NRC, 1985).

Indicator and Simulator Organisms

Indicator organisms do not represent a direct health hazard in a food product. However, in some cases they do serve to indicate that the potential is present for a health hazard to exist. Generally, these organisms may signal:

- The possible presence of a pathogen or toxin; or
- The possibility that faulty practices (ineffective process, poor sanitation, etc.) occurred during production, processing, storage and distribution (NAS/NRC, 1985).

Common indicator organisms include the following:

- Aerobic Plate Count (APC).
- Coliforms.
- Fecal Coliforms.
- Enterobacteriaceae (used more in Europe).
- *E. coli* (non–pathogenic types).
- *Listeria* (for *L. monocytogenes*).

Simulator organisms are those organisms that are used as substitutes for pathogenic organisms in testing protocols. For example, *Clostridium sporogenes*, due to its similarity to proteolytic strains of *C. botulinum*,

Table 5-5—Pathogens of Concern in Particular Foods

Food Type	Pathogens of Most Concern
Beef	*Salmonella*, *E. coli* O157:H7, *C. perfringens*
Pork	*Salmonella*, *Y. enterocolitica*, *C. perfringens*, *T. gondii*, *T. spiralis*
Poultry	*Salmonella*, *Campylobacter*, *C. perfringens*
Fish	Vibrios, *C. botulinum* (especially non-proteolytic types) helminths, viruses
Vegetables	*Salmonella*, *E. coli* O157:H7, *L. monocytogenes*, *C. botulinum*
Fruits	*E. coli* O157:H7, *Salmonella*, *Cyclospora*
Eggs	*Salmonella*
Milk/Dairy	*Salmonella*, *Campylobacter*, *L. monocytogenes*, *Y. enterocolitica*

has been used in thermal process establishment protocols for canned foods as a substitute for *C. botulinum*. *Enterococcus faecalis* has served as a substitute for *L. monocytogenes* in determining the appropriate heat process for extended shelf life refrigerated foods, and *Listeria innocua* has been used in place of *L. monocytogenes* in a variety of in–plant challenge tests. Simulator organisms can play an important role in validating a process for HACCP plans; pathogens should not be intentionally taken into a plant to validate processes.

Spoilage Microorganisms

Spoilage microorganisms do not represent a health hazard. They are associated with spoilage and the economic loss associated with an ingredient or food. Spoilage organisms affect the quality of the food product, not the safety of a food.

Spoilage organisms represent a broad group of microbes. Generally, they are specific to the type of food and the technology of processing. Examples of food groups and their related spoilage microorganisms include the following:

- Refrigerated foods – psychrotrophs.
- Juice concentrates – osmophilic yeasts.
- Fermented foods – acid tolerant lactic acid bacteria and yeast.
- Meat products – psychrotrophic pseudomonads.
- Hot–filled juices – heat resistant molds.

Microorganisms that spoil foods can do so at various times in the process: before and during preparation or processing; under normal conditions of intended use; under unusual circumstances, i.e., if present, and not destroyed or controlled by normal processing techniques.

Spoilage microorganisms do not represent a hazard and thus are not of immediate concern when setting up a HACCP program. While they may cause economic loss, they are not a threat to the health of a consumer.

Control of Microorganisms

It was noted previously that the three major ways of preventing foodborne illness are to prevent contamination, destroy or remove microorganisms on foods, and/or to prevent organisms from growing. To determine the best means to control microorganisms and microbial toxins, one must first understand the characteristics of the microorganisms that may be amenable to some form of control (Tompkin and Keuper, 1982). Thus, determine what allows them to be present or survive in a food. Various factors that influence the presence and/or level of microbes include:

- Source of microbe: naturally occurring on ingredient, in–process contaminant from equipment, food handlers, etc;

- Temperature of growth: optimum and range; growth rate at low temperatures.
- Heat resistance: vegetative cells, spores, toxins.
- Sensitivity to acidity: pH limits for growth, optimum and range.
- Sensitivity to low moisture: a_w limit for growth, optimum and minimum.
- Sensitivity to preservatives.
- Influence of oxygen: aerobic, anaerobic, facultative, microaerophilic.
- Sensitivity to unique conditions: radiation, sanitizers, high salt concentration.

Remember, by knowing how the organisms first get into the food, and any unusual characteristics that may permit them to multiply, one can identify potential means to control these microbes. Controls are the keys to prevention of hazards. For microorganisms, the controls simply are the means to reduce, eliminate or prevent the growth of these pathogens.

As noted previously, in most cases pathogens must grow (multiply) in foods to appropriate levels to cause foodborne disease. Thus, the food must contain the nutrients required by the organism to grow. The organism must have water, i.e., the available water, or water activity, must be high enough to permit growth. The pH must be in the favorable range and the amount of oxygen must be such that growth can be initiated. The food must be free from substances that prevent growth of the pathogen (preservatives, etc.). The food must be at a temperature allowing growth and the organism must be given time to multiply.

Effect of Temperature on Growth of Pathogens

Although most pathogenic organisms are mesophilic, a number of foodborne pathogens are psychrotrophic, i.e., they are capable of growth at refrigeration temperatures. Table 5-6 shows the minimum temperature for growth of a variety of foodborne pathogens. Most of the organisms capable of growth at refrigeration tem-

Table 5-6—Minimum Growth Temperatures for Foodborne Pathogens[a]

Microorganism	Minimum Temperature (°C)
Bacillus cereus	4 (most strains 6–10)
Campylobacter jejuni	32
Clostridium botulinum (non-proteolytic)	3.3
Clostridium botulinum (proteolytic)	10
Clostridium perfringens	12
Escherichia coli (pathogenic)	7–8
Listeria monocytogenes	− 0.4
Salmonella	5 (most strains 7–10)
Shigella	6
Staphylococcus aureus	7 (10 for toxin)
Vibrio cholerae	10
Vibrio parahaemolyticus	5
Vibrio vulnificus	8
Yersinia enterocolitica	− 1.3

[a]ICMSF, 1996

peratures grow slowly at low temperatures, requiring extended time to reach high numbers (Table 5-7).

Effect of pH on Growth of Pathogens

Foods can be divided into two major categories: low–acid (pH > 4.6) and acid (pH ≤4.6). These categories were established based upon the growth of *C. botulinum*. The minimum pH for growth of *C. botulinum* in foods is generally accepted as 4.8, although it has been shown to grow as low as pH 4.0 in strictly controlled laboratory environments (Raatjes and Smelt, 1979; Smelt at al., 1982; Tanaka, 1982; Young–Perkins and Merson, 1986). The minimum pH for growth of *Salmonella* in laboratory media is 4.0 (Chung and Goepfert, 1970). The minimum pH for growth of *Listeria monocytogenes* in laboratory media is between 4.5 and 5.0, depending on the acidulant (Conner et al., 1990; Sorrells et al., 1989). The minimum pH for growth in specific foods may differ and will increase when other conditions, such as temperature and water activity, are not optimum.

Controls

Within any operation there may be many control points (CPs) for potential biological hazards. Many of these controls will be implemented through prerequisite programs (Chapter 3). Chapter 9 on hazard analysis and Chapter 10 on critical control points (CCPs) will address determining whether CCPs are warranted for certain hazards. The most common controls for biological hazards include the following:

- Microbiological or other specifications for raw materials or ingredient (dependent on intended use, process requirements, etc.).
- Time/temperature applications (thawing/tempering, cooking, freezing, holding, cooling rates, refrigerating, storing, etc.).
- Preservative factors for the food (pH, a_w, etc.).
- Prevention of cross contamination.
- Food handling practices.
- Employee hygiene.
- Packaging integrity.
- Storage, distribution display practices.
- Consumer directions for use (to prevent abuse).
- Equipment/environmental sanitation.

It is not possible to provide details on all possible controls for various pathogens in individual products. However, Table 5-8 provides examples of controls that may be considered.

Table 5-8—Examples of Controls for Biological Hazards

Biological Hazard	Food	Control Measures
L. monocytogenes	Sliced luncheon meat	Cook to inactivate *L. monocytogenes*; prevent recontamination prior to packaging (especially at slicer)
Salmonella; pathogenic sporeformers	Chocolate syrup	Pasteurize to destroy *Salmonella*; formulate to ensure low a_w to prevent sporeformers from growing
C. botulinum	Pasteurized cheese spread	Formulate (NaCl, nisin, phosphates, moisture, pH, amount of cheese) to control *C. botulinum*; pasteurize to destroy vegetative cells
S. aureus, Salmonella, E. coli O157:H7, pathogenic sporeformers	Dry fermented sausage	Use starter culture to ensure pH drop prevents growth of *S. aureus* and inactivates *Salmonella* and some *E. coli* O157:H7; dry to reduce a_w and prevent sporeformers from growing; heat post-drying to inactivate additional *E. coli* O157:H7
Parasites	Sushi	Freeze fish to kill parasites or select species not known to have parasite hazard (e.g., large species tuna)

SUMMARY

Foodborne illness can result when biological hazards in foods are not properly controlled. HACCP requires an understanding of the types of biological hazards important in a specific food. The characteristics of the microorganism(s) must be examined to determine the appropriate controls.

Table 5-7—Lag Time and Generation Time for *Listeria Monocytogenes* in Fluid Dairy Products[a]

Temperature (°C)	Lag Time (h)	Generation Time (h)
21	5	1.7–1.9
13	10	5.8–6.0
8	24–48	10.6–13.1
4	120–144	33.3–36.3

[a]Marth, 1998

REFERENCES

Bean, N. H. and P. M. Griffin. 1990. Foodborne disease outbreaks in the United States, 1973–1987: pathogens, vehicles and trends. *J. Food Protect.* 53:804.

Bean, N. H., P. M. Griffin, J. S. Goulding and C. B. Ivey. 1990. Foodborne disease outbreaks, 5-year summary, 1983–1987. *J. Food Protect.* 53:711.

CAST. 1994. *Foodborne Pathogens: Risks and Consequences.* Task Force Report No. 122. Council for Agricultural Science and Technology, Ames, IA.

CDC. 1985. Recommendations for preventing transmission of infection with human T-lymphotropic virus type III/lymphadenopathy-associated virus in the work place. *Morbid. Mortal. Weekly Rep.* 34(45):682.

CDC. 1996. Surveillance for foodborne-disease outbreaks – United States, 1988–1992. *Morbid. Mortal. Weekly Rep.* 45 (No. SS-5), October 25.

Chung, K. C., and J. M. Goepfert. 1970. Growth of *Salmonella* at low pH. *J. Food Sci.* 35:326.

Cliver, D.O. 1988. Virus transmission via foods (IFT Scientific Status Summary). *Food Technol.* 42(10):241.

Cliver, D.O. 1997a. Foodborne viruses. Chapter 24, In *Food Microbiology, Fundamentals and Frontiers*, ASM Press, Washington, D.C.

Cliver, D.O. 1997b. Virus transmission via food (IFT Scientific Status Summary). *Food Technol.* 51(4):71.

Conner, D. E., V. N. Scott and D. T. Bernard. 1990. Growth, inhibition and survival of *Listeria monocytogenes* as affected by acidic conditions. *J. Food Protect.* 53:652.

FDA. 1999. *Food Code.* Food and Drug Administration, U.S. Department of Health and Human Services, Washington, D.C.

Hayunga, E. G. 1997. Helminths acquired from finfish, shellfish and other food sources. Chapter 26, In *Food Microbiology, Fundamentals and Frontiers*, ASM Press, Washington, D.C.

ICMSF. 1986. *Microorganisms in Foods 2—Sampling for Microbiological Analysis: Principles and Specific Applications*, 2nd. Ed., The International Commission on Microbiological Specifications for Foods. Univ. Toronto Press, Toronto, Canada.

ICMSF. 1996. *Microorganisms in Foods 5—Microbiological Specifications of Food Pathogns*, The International Commission on Microbiological Specifications for Foods. Blackie Academic & Professional, London.

ICMSF. 1998. *Microorganisms in Foods 6—Microbial Ecology of Food Commodities.* The International Commission on Microbiological Specifications for Foods. Blackie Academic & Professional, London.

Khan, P. 1988. AIDS and the food worker. *Food Eng.* (January):79.

Kim, C. W. 1997. Helminths in Meat. Chapter 25, In *Food Microbiology, Fundamentals and Frontiers*, ASM Press, Washington, D.C.

Marth, E.H. 1998. Extended shelf life refrigerated foods. *Food Technol.* 52(2): 57.

NAS/NRC. 1985. *An Evaluation of the Role of Microbiological Criteria For Foods and Food Ingredients.* National Academy Press, Washington, D.C.

Potter, M. E., S. G. Ayala, and N. Silarug. 1997. Epidemiology of foodborne disease. Chapter 20, In *Food Microbiology, Fundamentals and Frontiers*, ASM Press, Washington, D.C.

Raatjes, G. J. M. and J. P. P. M. Smelt. 1979. *Clostridium botulinum* can grow and form toxin at pH values lower than 4.6. *Nature, London* 281:398.

Riemann, H. and F. L. Bryan. 1979. *Food-borne Infections and Intoxications*, 2nd ed. Academic Press, N.Y.

Smelt, J. P. P. M., G. J. M. Raatjes, J. S. Crowther and C. T. Verrips. 1982. Growth and toxin formation by *Clostridium botulinum* at low pH values. *J. Appl. Bacteriol.* 52:75.

Sorrells, K. M., D. C. Enigl and J. R. Hatfield. 1989. Effect of pH, acidulant, time and temperature on the growth and survival of *Listeria monocytogenes.* *J. Food Protect.* 52:571.

Speer, C.A. 1997. Protozoan parasites acquired from food and water. Chapter 27, In *Food Microbiology, Fundamentals and Frontiers*, ASM Press, Washington, D.C.

Tanaka, N. 1982. Toxin production by *Clostridium botulinum* in media at pH lower than 4.6. *J. Food Protect.* 45:234.

Todd, E. 1990. Epidemiology of foodborne illness: North America. *The Lancet* 336:788.

Tompkin, R. B. and T. V. Keuper. 1982. How factors other than temperature can be used to prevent microbiological problems. In, *Microbiological Safety of Foods in Feeding Systems*, ABMPS Report No. 125, National Research Council, National Academy Press, Washington, D.C.

USDA/FSIS. 1997. FSIS/CDC/FDA Sentinel Site Study: The Establishment and Implementation of an Active Surveillance System for Bacterial Foodborne Diseases in the United States. (USDA Report to Congress). Food Safety and Inspection Service, U.S. Department of Agriculture, Washington, D.C.

USDA/FSIS. 1999a. *Appendix A, Compliance Guidelines for Meeting Lethality Performance Standards for Certain Meat and Poultry Products.* Food Safety and Inspection Service, Washington, D.C. (Issued January 1999, updated May 1999). (This document is available on the FSIS website at www.fsis.usda.gov/OA/fr/95033F-a.htm)

USDA/FSIS. 1999b. Performance standards for the production of certain meat and poultry products; final rule. *Federal Register.* 64(3):732. (January 6)

USDA/FSIS. 1999c. *Appendix B, Compliance Guidelines for Cooling Heat-Treated Meat and Poultry Products (Stabilization).* Food Safety and Inspection Service, Washington, D.C. (Issued January 1999, updated May 1999). (This document is available on the FSIS website at www.fsis.usda.gov/OA/fr/95033F-b.htm)

Young-Perkins, K. E. and R. L. Merson. 1986. *Clostridium botulinum* germination, outgrowth and toxin production below pH 4.6; Interactions between pH total, acidity and buffering capacity. *J. Food Sci.* 52:1084.

Table 5-9—*Campylobacter*

Disease, Symptoms and Onset	Campylobacteriosis. Abdominal pain, fever, diarrhea (profuse, watery, frequent; or alternatively bloody), sometimes accompanied by vomiting. Onset time and duration 2–7 days.
Source	Intestinal tract of wild and domestic warm-blooded animals. Most common contaminated foods are raw milk and poultry.
Transmission	Direct contact with animals or via contaminated water, milk or meat.
Characteristics of Microorganism	• Non-sporeforming, Gram —, small, vibroid or spiral-shaped cells. • Microaerophilic ($5\%O_2$ + 10% CO_2 optimum). • Grows between 32–45°C (optimum 42–43°C). • Grows at pH 4.9–9; rapid death below pH 4.0. • Sensitive to heat and to drying. • Food type influences survival to refrigerated and frozen conditions.
Control	• Chlorination of water. • Pasteurization of milk. • Thorough cooking of poultry. • Avoid cross-contamination from raw poultry.

Table 5-10—*Clostridium botulinum*

Disease, Symptoms and Onset	Botulism. A severe intoxication resulting from the ingestion of pre-formed toxin. Blurred or double vision, dry mouth, difficulty swallowing, paralysis of respiratory muscles. Vomiting and diarrhea may be initially present. Symptoms develop 12–36 hrs after eating contaminated food (sometimes days). Unless adequately treated (antitoxin, respiratory support), fatality rate high. Recovery may be slow (months, rarely years).
Source	Soil, marine sediment, and the intestinal tract of animals, including fish. Vegetables and grains will contain *C. botulinum* spores.
Transmission	Toxin must be ingested to cause disease. Spores are ubiquitous. Spores must be assumed to be present on all foods, including frozen and refrigerated foods. Spores must germinate and grow to vegetative cells to produce toxin.
Characteristics of Microorganism	• Sporeforming, Gram + rods. Spores are extremely heat resistant; controlled retort processing is necessary to destroy. Toxin is destroyed by heat (boiling for 5 min.). • Organism grows best under anaerobic or reduced oxygen conditions. Non-proteolytic types can grow at low temperatures (to 3°C; 38°F); most proteolytic types can grow above 10°C (50°F). • Low pH ($\leq$ 4.6) prevents growth of microbe; $a_w \leq$ 0.91 prevents growth. • Spores can germinate and grow in most low-acid foods under anaerobic conditions. Primarily associated with underprocessed home-prepared foods. Note: Also can cause problems if competitive microbes are destroyed and then the product is subjected to temperature abuse, e.g., frozen pot pies, baked potatoes.
Control	Retort product to destroy spores, add inhibitor to spore germination, low pH, low a_w (water activity), temperature control, proper heating of food.

Table 5-11—*Clostridium perfringens*

Disease, Symptoms and Onset	Perfringens food poisoning. A gastroenteritis characterized by abdominal pain, diarrhea and nausea. Vomiting and fever are usually absent. Mild disease of short duration (one day). Incubation period from 6 to 24 hours, usually from 10 to 12 hr.
Source	Soil. Intestinal tract of healthy persons and animals (cattle, pigs, poultry, fish).
Transmission	Ingestion of food, contaminated by soil or feces, which had been held under conditions permitting growth of organisms. Usually inadequately heated or reheated meats, stews or gravies. Spores survive normal cooking temperatures and germinate and grow during mishandling after cooking. Dose causing disease generally >500,000 cells per gram. Enterotoxin is produced in the gut resulting in symptoms. Common in cafeterias, food service establishments that have inadequate facilities for cooking and refrigeration of large amounts of food, or inadequate hot holding and reheating of food.
Characteristics of Microorganism	• Sporeforming, Gram + rods. Spores survive normal cooking procedures, including boiling. • Grows well anaerobically and in reduced oxygen conditions. Temperature range for growth is 12° to 50°C. Optimum growth temperature is 43° to 45°C. • Slow cooling and non-refrigerated storage of cooked meat and poultry permit growth to high numbers needed for infection. Can grow in foods placed on steam tables if food is not adequately heated ($\geq$60°C). Inadequate reheating allows organisms to survive.
Control	• Proper heating reheating, and cooling of cooked, perishable foods. Large quantities of food should be distributed in shallow pans for proper cooling during refrigeration.

Table 5-12—*Escherichia coli*—Pathogenic Types, Including O157:H7

Disease, Symptoms and Onset	Gastroenteritis. Diarrhea, may be bloody, and fever. Strains that cause diarrhea may be invasive, enteropathogenic, or enterotoxigenic. Incubation period is generally 12 to 72 hr after ingestion of food. Infection with enterohemmorhagic strains may result in HUS (hemolytic uremic syndrome) and renal failure, especially in young children
Source	Intestinal tract of humans and animals. Infected persons are often asymptomatic.
Transmission	Major mode of transmission is fecal contamination of food or water. Cross contamination. Person-to-person spread has been demonstrated. Poor handwashing in day care and nursery after patient contact has contributed to spread of disease. Infectious dose is very low for *E. coli* O157:H7. Carriers shed large numbers of microorganisms. Transmission of *E. coli* O157:H7 primarily associated with undercooked ground beef.
Characteristics of Microorganism	• Non-sporeforming, Gram — rods, killed by mild heat (above 60°C). • Grows under aerobic or anaerobic conditions. Grows well in moist, low-acid foods at temperatures >7°C. Optimum temperature for growth 35–37°C. • Low pH (<4.6) will prevent growth; but O157 can survive.
Table 5-12 (cont.)	• Difficult to differentiate pathogenic from non-pathogenic *E. coli* in usual microbiological testing. *E. coli* O157:H7 not detected by standard *E. coli* methodology.
Control	• Proper cooking and reheating of foods. • Proper refrigeration (≤4 C). • Good sanitation and personal hygiene. • Low pH, low a_w.

Table 5-13—Listeria monocytogenes

Disease, Symptoms and Onset	Listeriosis. An acute meningoencephalitis with or without associated septicemia. Characterized by sudden fever, intense headache, nausea, vomiting, delirium and coma (in elderly, immunocompromised, infants). May cause abortion in pregnant women. Fatality rate about 30%. In normal host, may cause few symptoms to an acute, mild, febrile illness with flu-like symptoms; very large numbers (10^9/ml) have been shown to cause gastroenteritis. Incubation period is generally one to several weeks.
Source	Animals, humans, the environment. Found in water and mud. Assume foods of animal origin, agricultural commodities contaminated.
Transmission	Associated with the consumption of contaminated vegetables and dairy products. In neonates, transmission from mother to fetus *in utero*.
Characteristics of Microorganism	• Non-sporeforming, Gram + rods, killed by pasteurization temperatures (71.7°C for 15 sec). • Grows under aerobic and anaerobic conditions. Able to grow at refrigeration temperatures (−0.4°C; 31°F). • Low pH (< 4.6) prevents growth of organism. • Extremely hardy in comparison to most vegetative cells. Withstands repeated freezing and thawing. Survives for prolonged periods in dry conditions. • Live organisms must be ingested to cause disease. Infectious dose related to susceptibility of host. Susceptible hosts may succumb to as few as 100 cells; healthy, non-susceptible hosts may withstand 10,000,000 cells.
Control	• Proper heat treatment. • Low pH. • Avoidance of recontamination. • Proper temperature control. • Low a_w.

Table 5-14—*Salmonella*

Disease, Symptoms and Onset	Salmonellosis. An acute gastroenteritis characterized by sudden onset of headache, abdominal pain, mild fever, diarrhea, nausea and vomiting. Dehydration may be severe. In some instances may cause death. Incubation period is 6 to 72 hours, usually about 12 to 36 hours.
Source	Intestinal tract of domestic and wild animals, and humans.
Transmission	Ingestion of the organism in food from infected animals or in food contaminated by the feces of an infected animal or person. Primarily from consumption of raw or undercooked eggs, milk, meat and poultry. Infectious dose may be only a few cells (100 to 1000), but generally is much higher.
Characteristics of Microorganism	• Non-sporeforming, Gram — rods, killed by mild heat (above 60°C). • Grows under aerobic and anaerobic conditions. Grows in a temperature range of 5.2 to 47°C. Optimum temperature for growth is 35 to 37°C. • Low pH (usually < 4.6 in foods) prevents growth; optimum pH for growth is 6.5 to 7.5. • Survives well in frozen or dry state. Organisms in dry state (and in foods with relatively low water activities) are more resistant to heat. • Over 2000 serovars of salmonellae are known.
Control	• Thorough cooking of food. • Avoid recontamination. • Low pH. • Proper hygiene of food handlers.

Table 5-15—*Staphylococcus aureus*

Disease, Symptoms and Onset	Staphylococcal food poisoning. An intoxication of abrupt onset characterized by severe nausea, cramps and vomiting. Often accompanied by diarrhea. Deaths rare. Duration of illness one to two days. Onset of symptoms between 1 and 6 hours after consumption of food; generally, 2 to 4 hours.
Source	Usually humans; organism harbored in nasal passages and on skin. Occasionally from cows with infected udders.
Transmission	Ingestion of food containing staphylococcal enterotoxin. Microbe multiplies in food to high level and produces a heat-stable enterotoxin. Food handlers commonly contaminate foods that do not undergo adequate heating to kill the organism or refrigeration to prevent growth of microbe (e.g., sandwiches, custards, salad dressings, pastries, sliced meats). As little as 2 hours at unrefrigerated temperatures may allow sufficient growth and toxin production.
Characteristics of Microorganism	• Non-sporeforming, Gram + cocci, killed by mild heat (above 60°C). Enterotoxins are very heat stable, and will withstand boiling for prolonged periods. May not be inactivated during normal retorting process. • Grows in either aerobic or anaerobic conditions. Temperature growth range is 7 to 48°C; toxin produced between 10 and 48°C. Optimum growth temperature is 37°C. • pH growth range 4 to 10. Enterotoxin generally not produced below pH 4.5 (aerobic) or 5.0 (anaerobic). • Grows at low water activities down to 0.85; toxin generally not produced below a_w 0.90. • Organisms resistant to high salt (up to 15%). • Large numbers of cells (>500,000) per gram food needed in order to produce sufficient amounts of enterotoxin to result in illness.
Control	• Proper hygiene. • Proper refrigeration of foods (<4°C). • Proper holding of perishable foods when hot (>60°C). • Exclusion of food handlers with boils, sores, abscesses.

Table 5-16—*Vibrio parahaemolyticus*

Disease, Symptoms and Onset	Gastroenteritis. Diarrhea, abdominal cramps, nausea, vomiting, headache, and (rarely) fever and chills. Onset time 4–96 hours, duration 3 days.
Source	Inshore marine waters; seafood
Transmission	Consumption of raw, underprocessed or recontaminated seafood, primarily shrimp, crab or molluscan shellfish
Characteristics of Microorganism	• Non-sporeforming, Gram +, curved rods; Grows aerobically or anaerobically. • Grows between 5 and 43°C (optimum 37°C). • Grows at pH 4.8 to 11. • Grows in 0.5–10% NaCl (optimun 3%). • Destroyed by mild heat. • Large numbers generally required to cause illness. • Pathogenicity associated with a thermostable hemolysin (Kanagawa +).
Control	• Prevent multiplication of organism after harvest by chilling seafoods to <5°C. • Cook to internal temperature ≥65°C. • Avoid cross contamination of cooked or other ready-to-eat foods.

Table 5-17—Hepatitis A Virus

Disease, Symptoms and Onset	Hepatitis. Fever, malaise, nausea, abdominal discomfort, often followed by jaundice. Severity tends to increase with age, ranging from inapparent infection to weeks of debility. Onset time 15–50 days (average 4 weeks), generally lasting until 7 days after the onset of jaundice. Permanent loss of liver function may occur. Shedding of virus occurs for 10–14 days before symptoms become apparent.
Source	Intestinal tract of humans.
Transmission	Human to human; spread by fecal to oral route. Water contaminated with sewage can contaminate foods such as shellfish and fresh produce. Consumption of foods contaminated by infected food handler or contaminated raw shellfish are primary sources of hepatitis from foods.
Characteristics of Microorganism	• Virus particles: featureless spheres 28 nm in diameter; single-stranded RNA coated with protein. • Cannot replicate in food. • Heat sensitive: killed instantaneously at 85°C (185°F). • Resistant to acid, freezing, drying and ionizing radiation. • Inactivated by oxidizing agents such as chlorine, ozone, and hydrogen peroxide.
Control	• Proper employee hygiene. • Harvest shellfish from approved growing water. • Heat treatment. • Vaccination.

Chapter 6

CHEMICAL HAZARDS AND CONTROLS

Allen M. Katsuyama, Michael Jantschke and David E. Gombas

INTRODUCTION

Although biological hazards are of greatest concern because they are capable of causing widespread foodborne illnesses, chemical hazards also have been associated with foodborne illness or injury, albeit generally affecting fewer individuals. Therefore, a well designed HACCP program requires consideration of potential chemical hazards and implementation of appropriate control measures. While consideration must be given to potential chemical hazards, there is substantial controversy regarding the actual risk of illness or injury to consumers from many of the chemicals that are used in food production and processing. Thus, there is a diversity of opinions regarding whether most potential chemical hazards warrant inclusion within a HACCP plan or whether these potential hazards should be managed within a prerequisite program. The answer to this question is that it depends on the results of the hazard analysis, which will be discussed in chapter 9. This chapter, as the chapters before and after it, presents information needed for the identification of potential hazards during the first stage of the hazard analysis.

A wide variety of chemicals are routinely used in the production and processing of foods. The use of some chemicals, like agricultural pesticides and growth regulators, may not be under the direct control of the establishment. In contrast, some chemicals such as equipment lubricants, sanitizers, and additives for treating water used in processing may be present or used throughout the facility. Other chemicals may be present or used specifically for particular processes; for example, antimicrobial solutions used at a step in a slaughtering line, or nitrite used in a sausage formulation. While these chemicals do not present significant hazards when used properly, some of them are capable of causing severe health effects or even death if misused. Therefore, during the hazard analysis the HACCP team must determine if any of these chemicals are reasonably likely to be used in a manner that will result in illness or injury to consumers.

LAWS AND REGULATIONS

Whether or not a chemical is allowed in food is the decision of the agency, the U.S. Food and Drug

53

Administration (FDA) or the U.S. Department of Agriculture (USDA), responsible for enforcing the provisions of pertinent laws. The primary goal of such laws is to ensure that the foods available to the public are safe and free of adulterants.

The Federal Meat Inspection Act, the Poultry Products Inspection Act, and the Egg Products Inspection Act give USDA regulatory authority over all operations of processing establishments that produce these products. These acts and the Federal Food, Drug, and Cosmetic Act (FD&C Act) define several conditions that determine when a food is adulterated. Two of these conditions relate directly to chemical hazards: a food is considered to be adulterated (1) if it bears or contains any poisonous or deleterious substance which may render it injurious to health, or (2) if it bears or contains any added poisonous or deleterious substance. HACCP does not change or alter these legal definitions—food operations are responsible for complying with all applicable laws regarding adulteration. If a food contains a substance not approved for that food, or contains a substance at levels in excess of approved use, the food is considered adulterated. These acts (laws) expressly prohibit knowingly shipping or marketing foods that are adulterated. However, since adulteration per-se includes non-safety concerns, everything that may constitute adulteration does not necessarily need to be addressed in a HACCP plan, and, by the same logic, HACCP plans may need to include control of hazards that are outside the legal definitions of adulteration.

Regulations for meat and poultry processing are located in Title 9 Parts 318 and 381 of the *Code of Federal Regulations (9 CFR 318 and 381)*. Those for egg products are found in 7 *CFR* 59. Under these regulations, any substance that is used in the preparation of any product must meet specific guidelines. For instance, the substance must be previously approved by FDA for use in meat, poultry or egg products as a food additive or color additive, or as a substance "generally recognized as safe" (refer to 21 *CFR* for approved food and color additives and specifications for their use). USDA determines if use of a substance is functional and suitable for particular meat, poultry or egg products. For example, USDA regulations specify the amount of sodium nitrite that can be used for bacon. For a complete list of substances and their usage amount for various products, refer to 9 *CFR* 318.7 for meat products or 381.147 for poultry products; for eggs, refer to the Egg Products Inspectors Handbook.

In addition to regulations on approved additives, FDA has a list of substances that are specifically prohibited in foods (21 *CFR* 189; see Table 6-1). The substances that are prohibited from direct addition to foods either were used or had been proposed for use in foods. These substances were used for a variety of functions, such as flavoring compounds (calamus, cinnamyl anthranilate, coumarin, safrole), artificial sweeteners (cyclamates, dulcin, P-4000), preservatives (monochloroacetic acid, thiourea), a foam stabilizer

Table 6-1—Chemicals Prohibited in Foods (21 *CFR* 189)

DIRECT ADDITION	
Calamus and its derivatives	Dulcin
Chlorofluorocarbon propellants	Monochloracetic acid
Cinnamyl anthranilate	Nordihydroguaiaretic acid (NDGA)
Cobaltous salts and derivatives	P-4000
Coumarin	Safrole
Cyclamate and its derivatives Diethylpyrocarbonate (DEPC)	Thiourea

INDIRECT ADDITION
Flectol H
Lead solders
Mercaptoimidazoline and 2-mercaptoimidazoline
4,4′-Methylenebis (2-chloroanaline)
Hydrogenated 4,4′-isopropylidene-diphenolphosphite ester resins
Tin-coated lead foil capsules for wine bottles

(cobaltous salts), an antioxidant (NDGA), or a fermentation inhibitor (DEPC). Table 6-1 contains a list of substances prohibited from uses that could lead to their indirect incorporation into foods. These compounds were used previously for packaging or other food-contact materials, either as adhesives or as resin components. Every establishment must ensure that none of these chemicals is present in ingredients or in packaging or supplies that could come into contact with product.

CHEMICALS OF CONCERN TO THE FOOD INDUSTRY

Chemicals which pose a public health hazard can find their way into foods by any of three general routes: they could occur naturally in one or more of the product ingredients; they could be intentionally added during processing; or they could be added unintentionally. Consideration also must be given to allergens, which may pose significant health problems for a small percentage of the population that may be sensitive to them.

Naturally Occurring Substances

Some chemical hazards are naturally present in foods. Such chemicals occur in a variety of plants (e.g., mushrooms), animals (e.g., shellfish) or can be created by microorganisms (e.g., certain molds and bacteria). Although many naturally occurring toxic substances are biological in origin, they have been traditionally categorized as chemical hazards.

Naturally occurring toxic substances are generally prohibited in foods beyond a certain level. In some cases, the food itself is toxic and should be avoided; for example, certain types of mushrooms or shellfish containing toxins. In other cases, the hazardous substance is a natural defect of the food and in many cases, is unavoidable; for example, aflatoxin on some grains and nuts.

Unavoidable Poisonous or Deleterious Substances

By law, the presence of poisonous or deleterious substances in food renders the food adulterated. However, the presence of a poisonous or deleterious substance may be unavoidable—either because the substance is necessary in the production of a food product or the substance cannot be avoided by the use of current good manufacturing practices (cGMPs). In such cases, FDA is authorized to establish a tolerance or action level for the substance. Action levels for those unavoidable chemicals, which include aflatoxins, lead,

Table 6-2—Unavoidable Poisonous or Deleterious Substances

Aflatoxin	Ethylene dibromide (EDB)
Aldrin and Dieldrin	Heptachlor and Heptachlor epoxide
Benzene hexachloride (BHC)	Lead
Cadmium	Lindane
Chlordane	Mercury
Chlordecone (Kepone™)	Methyl alcohol
DDT, DDE, and TDE	Mirex
Dicofol (Kelthane™)	N—Nitrosamines
Dimethylnitrosamine (nitrosodimethylamine)	Paralytic shellfish toxin
	Polychlorinated biphenyls (PCBs)

and paralytic shellfish toxins (see Table 6-2), have been established for specific commodities and are published in a booklet titled ''Action Levels for Poisonous or Deleterious Substances in Human Food and Animal Feed.'' The booklet is available from FDA by contacting Industry Programs Branch (HFF-326), Center for Food Safety and Applied Nutrition, FDA, 200 C Street S.W., Washington, D.C. 20204, or FDA's website (www.fda.gov). In the absence of a tolerance or action level for a specific hazardous chemical in a specific food product, none is allowed.

In all cases, foods containing levels of unavoidable substances that are higher than established tolerances or action levels are considered adulterated and are subject to legal action. Each establishment must ensure that if any unavoidable poisonous substances are present in ingredients or food-contact materials, they meet established tolerances or action levels and are not present due to a lack of adherence to cGMPs.

Toxins of Microbial Origin

Histamine, also called scombrotoxin, is a problem only when certain species of fish are temperature abused. It can produce an allergic-type response in consumers of contaminated fish. Histamine is formed when bacteria (primarily species such as *Morganella morganii*, *Klebsiella pneumoniae*, and *Hafnia alvei*) produce the enzyme histidine decarboxylase during growth in fish containing large amounts of free histidine. The enzyme reacts with free histidine to form histamine. Histamine formation resulting from the growth of these microorganisms is generally due to inadequate postharvest time/temperature control.

There are other toxins associated with seafood products that can cause neurological symptoms. Most of these toxins originate in marine animals called dinoflagellates that are used as food by fish or are filtered from water by molluscan shellfish. The toxins these dinoflagellates produce include paralytic shellfish poisons (or saxitoxin), diarrhetic shellfish poisons, neurologic shellfish poisons, and domoic acid, which is responsible for amnesic shellfish poisoning. In finfish the primary natural toxin of concern is ciguatoxin. Histamine and ciguatoxin accounted for about half of the cases of chemical foodborne disease of known etiology between 1983 and 1987 (Bean and Griffin, 1990) and for 74% of the cases between 1988 and 1992 (CDC, 1996). Controls for this category of toxins are currently limited to harvesting fish or shellfish only from waters that have been approved by health authorities or harvested from waters where problems are unlikely to occur.

Mycotoxins represent another category of chemical compounds that present a potential risk to consumers. These chemicals are produced in foods or feeds as byproducts from the growth of specific types of mold, including *Penicillium*, *Fusarium*, *Aspergillus* and *Claviceps*. Contamination with mycotoxins may occur in grains, nuts, cottonseed, and other plant material prior to harvesting, or the mycotoxins can be produced during storage if moisture conditions permit growth of certain types of molds. While adverse health effects due to mycotoxins in foods are rare, certain mycotoxins have both an acute toxicity as well as a chronic toxicity in humans and animals. There is much to be learned about toxigenic molds and their role in human health. An establishment's ability to control mycotoxins in ingredients or feeds depends on an understanding of sources of supply, growing conditions in the production area, and the establishment of specifications along with testing when appropriate.

Allergens

Allergens are proteins that trigger a specific type of immune response by the human body. Responses range from relatively mild symptoms, such as the development of a rash, to severe reactions, such as anaphylaxis, involving respiratory and circulatory problems that can, in the extreme, lead to death. Foods known to cause allergic reactions include peanuts, tree nuts (walnuts, pecans, etc.), eggs, dairy (milk), soy, wheat, fish, and shellfish. Although theoretically almost any protein in a food could be allergenic, these commodities have been reported to account for more than 90 percent of the allergic reactions in adults. It has been estimated that 1-2 percent of the adult population and a somewhat larger percentage of children have an allergy to some type of food. An allergen is principally of concern in products where its presence may not be expected. Peanuts would not be considered a hazard in peanut butter or in candy that has peanuts identified as an ingredient, such as peanut brittle. Peanuts would be considered a hazard in a chili containing peanut butter in which peanuts were not declared on the label. Sensitive consumers must be informed of the intentional incorporation of potential allergens into a food product by appropriate ingredient labeling.

Since even minute amounts of an allergen are capable of triggering reactions in some extremely sensitive individuals, the control of allergenic ingredients in product formulation and prevention of cross contamination are essential for food safety. Thus, establishments producing formulated products must consider all routes of cross contamination with even small amounts of an allergen, including inclusion of an allergen from airborne contaminants, reworked product, inappropriately labeled ingredients, etc.

The most effective measure to prevent cross contamination is the use of separate facilities or totally segregated and dedicated production lines whereby one style of product containing an allergen can be produced exclusively. For practical purposes, however, cross contamination is usually prevented by other measures, including:

- Separately storing ingredients and work-in-process that contain allergens.
- Scheduling production to ensure that non-allergen-containing products are produced before products containing allergens.
- Carefully and thoroughly cleaning all equipment and establishment areas after the production of allergen-containing products.
- Establishing traffic patterns to ensure that allergen-containing materials are not moved through areas where non-allergen containing materials and products are being handled.

Other important control measures to minimize allergen-related problems include:

- Equipment and systems that are designed to facilitate cleaning and to enable verification that the systems are residue free.
- The ability to lock out equipment that contains residues of allergenic material, thereby physically preventing cross-contamination of allergen-free product.
- Careful control of product labels to ensure they accurately represent the product inside the container.
- Training of employees.

Intentionally Added Chemicals

Some chemicals are intentionally added to foods during growing, harvesting, storing, processing, packaging, or distribution. Intentionally added chemicals are safe when used at established safe levels but can be hazardous if improperly used. Examples of potentially hazardous additives include pesticides, fungicides, insecticides, herbicides, fertilizers, growth hormones, antibiotics, preservatives, coloring agents, and even some vitamins. Properly used, these chemicals are beneficial and sometimes necessary to maintain our food supply. Federal regulations control the level of use and maximum allowable residues of these and other chemicals in our foods.

Chemical Sensitivities

Sulfites present in sulfiting agents also are known to trigger allergic type reactions in a small percentage of the population. As in the case of an allergen, the reaction may be mild, such as a feeling of light-headedness or dizziness. Although rare, the reaction of individuals with severe asthma may be immediate and extremely severe, including respiratory problems that can lead to death. The use of sulfites in foods, including ingredients, must be declared on the product label if the level is greater than 10 ppm in the finished product. Processors should also be aware that some consumers may be sensitive to certain food-coloring agents (e.g., FD&C Yellow #5). Therefore, FDA requires that all food-coloring agents used in a product be included in the list of ingredients on the product label. As with allergenic ingredients, control of substances that consumers may be sensitive to will involve appropriate labeling, ingredient specifications, knowledge of the composition of formulated components used in or on products, and in-house control programs for tracking chemical use.

Antibiotics and Hormones in Meat and Poultry

The use of antibiotics and growth-regulating hormones are closely controlled by regulatory agencies. There have been no reported human health problems associated with appropriate uses of approved antibiotics and hormones. However, there is some concern that the widespread use of antibiotics in animal husbandry could give rise to pathogenic microorganisms that possess multiple resistance to antibiotics, a situation that has public health implications. Approvals of veterinary drugs used in the animal production industry are made by the FDA's Center for Veterinary Medicine (CVM). CVM regulates the manufacture and distribution of drugs and feed additives intended for animals. These include animals from which human foods are derived, as well as drugs and feed additives for pet (or companion) animals. Assurance that the drugs are used correctly is currently a shared responsibility between USDA's Animal and Plant Health Inspection Service (APHIS) and the Animal Production Food Safety Program of USDA's Food Safety and Inspection Service (FSIS). The Animal Production Food Safety Program concentrates on the link between animal production and slaughter and processing operations. Responsibility for verifying that meat and poultry products are free from illegal residues of these compounds belongs to FSIS. Controlling residues of these compounds in meat and poultry products will include assurances that they have been used in accordance with label directions and appropriate withdrawal times.

Pesticide Chemicals

The manufacturing, distribution, sale, and uses of all pesticide chemicals including chemicals used to sanitize food contact surfaces (insecticides, rodenticides, fungicides, herbicides, plant regulators, defoliants, desiccants, etc.) are closely regulated by the Environmental Protection Agency (EPA) under the authority of the Federal Insecticide, Fungicide, and Rodenticide Act (FIFRA) and the FD&C Act as amended by the Food Quality and Protection Act (FQPA). In addition, pest control substances must be approved by FSIS prior to use. (This requirement is expected to be eliminated by new sanitation performance standards that have been proposed but not yet finalized.) EPA approval of each pesticide formulation includes specific limitations regarding the means by which the chemical may be applied, conditions of application, permitted concentrations, the target organisms against which the chemical may be employed, use restrictions, and requirements for the disposal of the pesticide and its containers. Legislation passed in 1998 gives FDA jurisdiction over products that are used to control microbial populations in process water. Additionally, each agricultural pesticide is approved only for specific crops. The use of any pesticide, including those used in an establishment's pest control program, must comply strictly with the instructions and information on the label. In addition to determining which pesticides may be used on agricultural crops, EPA also has the responsibility to determine tolerances or exemptions from tolerances for pesticide residues on raw agricultural commodities and processed foods (40 *CFR* 180). FDA enforces the pesticide tolerances in or on raw agricultural commodities and processed foods, while USDA enforces the tolerances for residues in meat and poultry products.

The potential occurrence of illegal residues of pesticides, veterinary drugs, growth hormones, etc. must be considered by each food establishment. Control of these chemicals involves close working relationships with ingredient suppliers, animal production operations, and growers of raw agricultural commodities. The use of pesticide chemicals in establishment programs, including the use of sanitizing agents, also must be checked closely through an effective sanitation prerequisite program.

DESIGNING THE CHEMICAL CONTROL PROGRAM

Potential hazards may be created by the use of various chemicals at several points in the food production chain or by chemicals that may be produced naturally within foods and feeds. The categories of chemicals discussed above provide guidelines for identifying potential chemical hazards. If potential hazards are present, they may be addressed at one or more of the following points:

- Prior to receipt of food ingredients and packaging materials.
- Upon receipt of these materials.
- During establishment operations.
- During the use of toxic chemicals.
- Prior to the shipment of finished goods.

(Note: See Table 6-3 at the end of this chapter for examples of chemicals used in food production, points of control and types of control.)

Prior to Receipt

Suppliers should be involved in reducing the occurrence of potential chemical hazards associated with animals presented for slaughter, ingredients used in formulated items and supplies of all types. Examples of such potential hazards include pesticide residues on raw agricultural commodities; illegal residues of hormones or antibiotics; naturally occurring poisonous chemicals such as mycotoxins in grains and paralytic shellfish toxins in mollusks; additives in packaging materials; and residues of maintenance supplies.

All food establishments should develop specifications for ingredients and packaging materials as well as maintenance, sanitation, and other chemicals used in the establishment. References to regulations or regulatory approval should be cited when pertinent. For example: "only approved pesticides may be applied to agricultural commodities" and "pesticide residues must comply with established tolerances;" food-coloring agents must be FDA-certified and each container must clearly show the FDA batch certification number; "sanitizing agents must be approved by FDA" for specific uses.

A letter of guarantee should be obtained from all suppliers and vendors. The letter should state that the supplier or vendor guarantees that every item shipped to the establishment meets the specifications that have been provided, and that they comply with all applicable government requirements.

Many establishments certify or qualify suppliers and vendors before purchasing ingredients and supplies. The primary purpose of certification is to insure that the supplier or vendor is complying with pertinent regulatory requirements, such as the FDA cGMP regulations, and is capable of providing items that meet specifications. Where appropriate, some establishments are also requiring that their suppliers develop and implement HACCP programs.

Upon Receipt

Although specifications, letters of guarantee, and vendor certifications will help insure the chemical safety of animal products, ingredients, and supplies, additional measures should be taken when materials are received at the establishment. Each vehicle should be inspected before any items are unloaded. If a chemical odor or spilled substance of unknown origin is noted inside of a trailer or railcar or on a pallet or container, the shipment should either be rejected or placed on hold for further evaluation. Materials also should be inspected during the unloading process to insure that there are no indications of extraneous chemicals among the individual containers in the shipment.

The controls instituted prior to receipt of ingredients and supplies eliminate the need to routinely test received materials. However, a periodic sampling and testing protocol is prudent for checking supplier performance.

Establishment Operations

An important step for control of chemicals used in a food establishment is to ensure that only approved chemicals are used at the facility. Specifications and letters of guarantee may be used for this purpose. Additionally, a knowledgeable individual should be assigned the responsibility for assuring that all chemicals received, stored, and used in the establishment are approved. The processing steps where individual ingredients, processing aids, and food additives are used must be evaluated during the development of the HACCP plan.

The points of use for each chemical should include some means for controlling the in-house use of the chemicals. Batching sheets must be posted whenever formulated products are being manufactured. Logs should be developed for recording the usage of chemicals, especially such substances as nitrites, sulfiting agents, and allergenic products or ingredients. Since employee practices, including proper storage, handling, and use of chemicals in exposed food areas, are important, all food handlers must be thoroughly trained. Unlabeled chemical containers can be a serious problem in any food manufacturing facility and can be avoided only by thorough employee training and a strong establishment policy regarding the use, storage, and labeling of chemicals in food production areas.

Regularly scheduled in-house audits should be performed to insure that hazardous chemicals are being adequately controlled in processing areas. Each audit should include: observations of production practices; review of product formulations; verification of batching sheets and usage logs, where applicable; and confirmation that only approved chemicals are being used, and that they are being stored and handled appropriately.

Storage

Cross contamination is always a concern in a warehouse if hazardous chemicals are stored in close proximity to raw ingredients, packaging materials, or finished products. Additionally, storage of allergens in close proximity to other ingredients can enhance the possibility of cross contamination. All chemicals must be stored in tightly sealed containers. Hazardous or toxic chemicals must be stored in physically separated, secured enclosures accessible only to authorized personnel. Food additives and other chemicals, especially ingredients such as nitrites and sulfiting agents, as well as allergenic ingredients, must be stored in a manner that will minimize the possibility of cross contamination. Packaging materials in storage must be covered to protect against contamination. Common sense and strict adherence to cGMPs should provide adequate control.

Sanitation and Maintenance

All chemicals used during sanitation and maintenance programs should meet appropriate regulatory requirements. Proposed new rules would replace prescriptive requirements with a performance standard that specifies that cleaning compounds and sanitizing agents be safe and effective under the conditions of use and that their use must not result in adulterated product. The compounds would still have to meet use requirements promulgated by EPA and FDA. FDA publishes lists of specific approved chemical compounds, but not brand names, of sanitizers, water treatment and other chemicals (see 21 *CFR* 178). The individual responsible for purchasing such chemicals used in the establishment should refer to these lists. If a question arises regarding the acceptability of a chemical, the supplier of the chemical should be asked for a copy of a letter from a regulatory agency stating that the chemical has been approved for use in food facilities.

Chemical Residues

Misuse or negligent use of cleaning and sanitizing chemicals may create potential chemical hazards in foods. These potential hazards should be addressed by means of appropriate prerequisite programs, such as through Sanitation Standard Operating Procedures (SSOPs). To augment written SSOPs, establishments should also develop detailed, written cleaning and sanitizing procedures covering each piece of equipment and every line in the facility. The cleanup crew should be thoroughly trained to insure that the procedures are understood and explicitly followed. In addition to assuring proper cleaning and sanitizing, the procedures also should ensure that no harmful chemical residues are left on food contact surfaces or in equipment. The written procedures should cite any regulatory restrictions and limitations that may be associated with use of each chemical.

Pesticide Usage

Even a well designed integrated pest management system will require the occasional use of pesticide chemicals, such as fogging inside the establishment with a non-residual insecticide or applying residual sprays outdoors. Whether an outside pest control operator is contracted or the total pest management program is handled in-house, detailed written procedures should be developed. Copies of labels of all pesticide chemicals being used at the facility should be kept on file. Pesticide usage records should be maintained to show when each pesticide is used, the quantity used, and where and how the application was made.

Pesticide labels clearly state the concentration, method of application, and the target organism for each chemical. Using a pesticide in any other manner, including against a pest not identified on the label, constitutes a violation of FIFRA and could result in all foods stored in a mistreated area being deemed adulterated.

When poison baits are being considered for controlling rodents at a facility, ensure compliance with all regulations. Bait stations containing poisons, when properly used outdoors, will not create food safety problems. However, the chance for food contamination from interior bait stations is of great concern. Therefore, it is strongly recommended that no bait be placed inside a food-processing establishment. Although regulations vary from state to state, the use of poison baits should be limited strictly to the outside of the establishment.

The storage of pesticides, as with all hazardous chemicals, must be strictly controlled. Good hygienic practices as well as cGMPs require that such chemicals be stored securely in an enclosed area accessible only to authorized employees. Appropriate warning signs must also be posted at these storage locations.

Prior to Shipment

All vehicles should be inspected prior to loading finished goods. Each vehicle must be free of chemical or other objectionable odors and residues of unknown materials. Although there are regulations and regulatory guidelines that address chemical contamination of foods in commercial vehicles, nothing substitutes for in-house awareness through routine, careful inspection and documentation of the vehicle inspection.

SUMMARY

Table 6-3 provides examples of chemicals used in food production, points of control and types of control. The following steps are recommended for developing and implementing a system to control potential chemical hazards in a food processing facility:

- Use only approved chemicals. Develop specifications and obtain letters of guarantee from all suppliers of chemicals, ingredients, and packaging materials.
- Keep an inventory of all potentially hazardous chemicals, including food additives and coloring agents, which are used in the establishment.
- Review product formulations and current procedures for receiving, storing, and using all potentially hazardous chemicals, as well as procedures for inspecting vehicles for shipping finished products.
- Audit the use of all potentially hazardous chemicals, including the monitoring of employee practices.
- Institute appropriate in-house testing.
- Assure adequate employee training.
- Keep abreast of new regulations and information on allergens and the toxicity of chemicals.

Table 6-3—Examples of Chemicals Used in Food Production, Points of Control, and Types of Control

Chemical	Point of Control	Types of Control
	RAW MATERIALS	
Pesticides, toxins, hormones, antibiotics, hazardous chemicals	Prior to receipt	Specifications, letters of guarantee, vendor certification, approved uses.
	Upon receipt	Vehicle inspection, tests, controlled storage conditions.
Color additives, prohibited substances in packaged ingredients and packaging material	Prior to receipt	Specifications, letters of guarantee, vendor certification, approved uses.
	Upon receipt	Vehicle inspection, proper storage.
Allergens	Upon receipt	Shipped separately, not with non-allergens; handled to prevent cross contamination.
	PROCESSING	
Allergens	Point of use	Handling/storage practices; thorough cleaning of equipment/areas after use.
Color additives	Prior to receipt	Review purpose, labeling, exempted/certified requirements.
	Point of use	Handling practices, quantities used.
Water additives	Boiler/water treatment systems	Approved chemicals, handling practices, quantities used.
	BUILDING AND EQUIPMENT MAINTENANCE	
Indirect food additives, paints, coatings, lubricants	Prior to use	Specifications, letters of guarantee, approved chemicals.
	Point of use	Handling practices, quantities used, proper storage.
	SANITATION	
Pesticides	Prior to use	Approved chemicals, procedures, uses.
	Point of use	Handling practices, label instructions, surfaces protected, cleaned after application.
Cleaners, sanitizers	Prior to use	Approved chemicals, procedures.
	Point of use	Procedures, adequate rinsing.
	STORAGE AND SHIPPING	
Cross contamination	Storage area	Organized by type of materials; toxic chemicals secured/limited access; inventory all chemicals.
All types of chemicals	Shipping vehicles	Inspect and clean vehicles before loading; ship food and chemicals separately.

REFERENCES

Bean, N.H. and P.M. Griffin. 1990. Foodborne disease outbreaks in the United States, 1973–1987: pathogens, vehicles and trends. *J. Food Protect.* 53:804.

CDC. 1996. Surveillance for foodborne-disease outbreaks—United States, 1988–1992. *Morbid. Mortal. Weekly Rep.* 45 (No. SS-5), October 25.

Corlett, D.A., Jr. and R.F. Stier. 1991. Risk assessment within the HACCP system. *Food Control* 2:71.

Deibel, K. E., T. Trautman, T. DeBoom, W. H. Sveum, G. Dunaif, V. N. Scott and D. T. Bernard. 1997. A comprehensive approach to reducing the risk of allergens in foods. *J. Food Protect.* 60: 436.

EPA. 1998. Tolerances and exemptions from tolerances for pesticide chemicals in or on raw agricultural commodities. Title 40, *Code of Federal Regulations*, Part 180. U.S. Government Printing Office, Washington, DC. (Issued annually.)

EPA. 1998. Tolerances for pesticides in food. Title 40, *Code of Federal Regulations*, Part 185. U.S. Government Printing Office, Washington, D.C. (Issued annually.)

FDA. 1999. Color additive regulations. Title 21, *Code of Federal Regulations*, Parts 70-82. U.S. Government Printing Office, Washington, DC. (Issued annually.)

FDA. 1999. Food additive regulations. Title 21, *Code of Federal Regulations*, Parts 170–189. U.S. Government Printing Office, Washington, DC. (Issued annually.)

FDA. 1999. Unavoidable contaminants in food for human consumption and food-packaging material. Title 21, *Code of Federal Regulations*, Part 109. U.S. Government Printing Office, Washington, DC. (Issued annually.)

O'Neill, C.E. and S. B. Lehrer. 1995. Scientific status summary—Seafood allergy and allergens: A review. *Food Technol.* 49 (10): 103.

Samson, H.A. 1993. Adverse reactions to foods. In: *Allergy Principles and Practice*, 4th ed., E. Middleton, Jr., C.E. Reed, E.F. Ellis, N.F. Adkinson, Jr., J.W. Yunginger, and W.W. Busse (eds). Mosby Yearbook, St. Louis, MO.

Sperber, W. H., K. E. Stevenson, D. T. Bernard, K. E. Deibel, L. J. Moberg, L. R. Hontz and V. N. Scott. 1998. The role of prerequisite programs in managing a HACCP system. *Dairy, Food, Env. Sanit.* 18: 418.

Winter, C. K. and F. J. Francis. 1997. Scientific status summary—Assessing, managing and communicating chemical food risks. *Food Technol.* 51(5): 85.

Chapter 7

PHYSICAL HAZARDS AND CONTROLS

Allen M. Katsuyama and Michael Jantschke

INTRODUCTION

Biological hazards represent potential public health risks that may affect large numbers of people, while chemical hazards represent health risks that may affect a smaller, but still significant, number of people. Physical hazards, however, usually create problems only for an individual consumer or relatively few consumers. Physical hazards typically result in personal injuries such as a broken tooth, cut mouth, a case of choking, or other usually non-life-threatening problem. Therefore, consideration must be given to potential physical hazards and their controls when developing a HACCP plan.

FOOD SAFETY VS. AESTHETICS

Potential physical hazards consist of foreign objects or extraneous matter not normally found in food, including such items as metal fragments, glass particles, wood splinters, rock fragments, or stones. Extrane-

ous matter by regulatory definition also includes such materials as bone fragments in meat and poultry, mold, insects and insect fragments, rodent and other mammalian hairs, sand, and other usually non-hazardous objects. Whether or not these potential physical hazards are controlled in the HACCP plan will depend upon an evaluation of the actual likelihood of occurrence and severity of the hazard as determined during the hazard analysis.

For HACCP purposes, differentiation is made between foreign objects that are capable of physically injuring a consumer and those that are aesthetically unpleasing. Since HACCP deals solely with food safety, only those physical contaminants capable of causing injuries, such as glass, metal, or objects which could cause a consumer to choke, must be considered when conducting a hazard analysis.

Until recently there had been no regulatory or "official" established tolerances or acceptable limits for contaminants that have the potential to be a safety hazard. Each incident was reviewed and evaluated on a case-by-case basis to determine the risk to public health. Recently the U.S. Food and Drug Administration (FDA) updated their Compliance Policy Guide (CPG) to include Section 555.425, "Foods—Adulteration Involving Hard or Sharp Foreign Objects'' (FDA, 1999). This new guidance classifies a product that is ready-to-eat as being adulterated if it contains a hard or sharp foreign object that measures 7 mm to 25 mm in length. The CPG is based on information recently published by the Agency on the size of hard, sharp foreign objects associated with recall situations (Olsen, 1998). The conclusion of this study was that any sharp, pointed object equal to or greater than 7 mm would be considered a hazard. In addition, the Public Health Hazard Analysis Board to the Food Safety and Inspection Service (FSIS) of the U.S. Department of Agriculture (USDA) has made a recommendation on the size of bone particles in meat and poultry products. The Board concluded that bone particles less than 2 cm (0.8 inch) in size do not pose a significant safety hazard to consumers.

The decision to include or to exclude a specific potential physical hazard in the HACCP plan will ultimately depend on the result of the hazard analysis, including an assessment of the effectiveness of control by current Good Manufacturing Practices (cGMP) or other prerequisite programs (see Chapter 3 for further discussion of this topic).

Foreign objects are responsible for the vast majority of consumer complaints, as will undoubtedly be confirmed by a review of consumer complaint files. Filth in foods is often the basis for alleged ''mental anguish'' and similar litigious claims. Note that although extraneous matter normally categorized as filth may not actually injure a consumer, the regulatory agencies can initiate action when it is deemed that foods are adulterated by filth, whether or not a public health threat actually exists. Thus, even though control of filth is not normally addressed in a HACCP plan, firms must still ensure compliance with pertinent legal requirements, such as the ''defect action levels'' established by the FDA for natural, unavoidable contaminants in certain foods.

SOURCES AND CONTROL OF POTENTIAL PHYSICAL HAZARDS

As with biological and chemical hazards, there are numerous sources of physical hazards. Potential physical hazards in finished products may arise from sources such as:

- Contaminated raw materials.
- Poorly designed or poorly maintained facilities and equipment.
- Faulty procedures during production.
- Improper employee practices.

Raw Materials

Controlling foreign objects in incoming raw materials and ingredients begins prior to receipt. Material specifications, letters of guarantee, and vendor inspection and certification will eliminate or minimize foreign objects associated with received goods. All raw materials and ingredients also should be inspected upon receipt.

Equipment capable of detecting and/or removing potential foreign materials can be placed in-line for added protection. Some appropriate pieces of equipment are listed in Table 7-1. Proper installation, regularly scheduled maintenance, and regular calibration and inspection are essential for all equipment, for preventing potential physical hazards in finished products. This is particularly true for equipment that is designed to detect and remove physical objects from product.

Table 7-1—Equipment for Detecting or Removing Physical Hazards

Equipment	Function
Magnet	Removes metals with magnetic properties
Metal detector	Detects ferrous and nonferrous objects
X-ray equipment	Detects glass, metal, and other foreign objects
Screen or sifter	Removes foreign objects larger than size of openings (mesh)
Aspirator	Removes materials lighter than product
"Riffle board"	Removes stones from dry beans and field peas
Bone separator	Removes bone chips from meat and poultry products

Facility

Strict compliance with the cGMPs will insure that the facility does not become a source of potential physical hazards in foods. Properly protected light fixtures, appropriately designed facilities and equipment, and adequate establishment and equipment maintenance should prevent contaminants from the facility from becoming incorporated into product. Keeping the facility free of pests will also protect products from foreign materials of pest origin. (See Chapter 4 for more information.)

Processes/Procedures

Since processes and procedures are unique to each facility, a comprehensive, thorough evaluation must be made to identify inappropriate practices and operational areas that may contribute foreign materials to foods. If a process or procedure can create a potential hazard, such as a bucket elevator or meat grinder in which the generation of metal fragments due to contact between equipment components is a common problem, a change in the process, procedure, or equipment may be warranted. As another example, a written glass breakage policy is highly recommended for all glass filling operations; the policy should include procedures for stopping the line and removing potentially affected containers whenever a breakage occurs. Additionally, special precautions, such as the installation of magnets, metal detectors, or x-ray equipment may be necessary to provide adequate control of potential physical hazards. If warranted by the hazard analysis, control measures such as these will be included in the HACCP plan.

For meat or poultry products that have been identified as having foreign particle contamination, salvage procedures must be conducted in accordance with USDA/FSIS Directive 7310.4. This directive requires that all product be inspected using equipment capable of detection of particles of 1/32 inch (0.8mm) in the greatest dimension. This directive covers only product in which a known incident has occurred and does not address requirements for routine monitoring of product.

Employee Practices

Unfortunately, poor employee practices are responsible for the majority of physical contaminants entering product during production. Jewelry, hairpins, pens, pencils, and paper clips are examples of contaminants from employees. Adhering to regulatory guidelines regarding proper outer attire, hair restraints, and the absence of jewelry will help prevent many problems. Employee education and supervision are the primary means for controlling these foreign materials.

While maintenance personnel play a vital role in keeping establishments operating, it is important that they conduct work in a sanitary manner. Maintenance procedures should delineate specific steps to be followed whenever there are equipment malfunctions and after routine maintenance work. The steps should include a careful inspection of the equipment and surrounding areas for loose hardware and tools, and a complete cleaning and sanitizing of the line prior to restarting the operations. Working with the maintenance department to establish an effective protocol will help the company avoid problems with potential physical hazards attributable to maintenance and repair activities. In addition, a strict policy against using food containers as storage bins for repair parts, ashtrays, or chemical containers should be in place and enforced. Food containers should be used only for food.

POTENTIAL PHYSICAL HAZARDS AND CONTROLS

Many common physical contaminants, their sources, and controls are summarized in Table 7-2. This sum-

mary may be used as a guide to potential physical hazards that should be considered during the hazard identification stage of the hazard analysis.

As previously discussed, some of these potential physical hazards, such as glass from light fixtures and metal fragments from processing equipment, may be adequately addressed in prerequisite programs and may, therefore, be excluded from the HACCP plan. However, some physical hazards may need to be controlled at specific CCPs, thereby requiring the development of detailed procedures through the application of the HACCP principles.

An example of a control procedure that may or may not be designated a CCP, is the glass breakage program for products packed in glass. If identified as a CCP, detailed procedures should be developed for addressing the breakage of jars just prior to or at the filler where glass fragments may enter open containers. If an operator is stationed at the filler, that employee is usually responsible for immediately stopping the line whenever a breakage occurs and for removing and discarding all containers in the vicinity of the broken jar. An alternate procedure is to establish an inspection regimen whereby the area around the filler is inspected at specified intervals. Any evidence of broken glass since the previous inspection results in the placement of a "hold" on all product produced during the intervening time period. All broken glass is then removed from the area. The suspect containers may be subjected to 100% examination by appropriate testing methods such as x-ray examination. Documentation of inspections and follow-up actions is essential. Additionally, a time-related code on individual containers is a benefit to effective control when using this type of procedure.

SUMMARY

Prevention and control of potential physical hazards at each facility includes the following:

- Complying with good manufacturing practice regulations.
- Using appropriate specifications for ingredients and supplies.
- Obtaining letters of guarantee from all suppliers.
- Utilizing vendor certification.
- Identifying types and sources of physical hazards.
- Installing equipment that can detect and/or remove physical hazards.
- Monitoring the controls and documenting performance.
- Training employees.

Table 7-2—Examples of Physical Contaminants, Sources and Types of Control

Contaminant	Sources	Types of Control
Glass	Light fixtures	Shatter-proof bulbs, shields
	Clock faces, mirrors	Replace with plastic
	Thermometers, glass containers	Glass breakage procedure
Metal fragments, nuts, bolts, screws, etc.	Ingredients	Specifications, letters of guarantee
	Machinery	Inspection, preventive maintenance
	People/process related	Education, supervision of production and maintenance personnel
		Magnets, metal detector, x-ray equipment
Wood	Building	Inspection, maintenance
	Equipment/utensils	Eliminate
	Palletized goods	Inspection
Twist-ties, wires, clips	Packaged ingredients	Inspection, remove before use, sieves/screens, magnets
Stones in dry beans	Incoming dry beans	Stone traps ("riffle boards"), floatation washers, etc.
Hypodermic needles, bullets, shot, BBs	Incoming meat/poultry	Metal detector, x-ray equipment, specifications and letters of guarantee

REFERENCES

Corlett, D.A., Jr. and R.F. Stier. 1991. Risk assessment within the HACCP system. *Food Control* 2:71.

FDA. 1998. *The Food Defect Action Levels*. FDA/CFSAN. Washington, D.C. (Revised periodically)

FDA. 1999. Section 555.425: Foods—adulteration involving hard or sharp foreign objects. *Compliance Policy Guides Manual*. Food and Drug Administration, Washington, DC. (Revised periodically). (The document is available on the following FDA website: http://www.fda.gov/ora/compliance_ref/cpg/cpgfod/cpg555-425.htm)

Imholte, T. J. 1984. *Engineering for Food Safety and Sanitation*. Technical Institute for Food Safety. Crystal, MN.

Olsen, A. R. 1998. Regulatory action criteria for filth and other extraneous materials. I. Review of hard or sharp foreign objects as physical hazards in food. *Reg. Tox. Pharm. 28:181*.

Public Health Hazard Analysis Board. 1995. *Bone Particles and Foreign Material in Meat and Poultry Products* (a report to the Food Safety and Inspection Service). USDA/FSIS, Washington, D.C.

Rhodehamel, E. J. 1992. Overview of biological, chemical, and physical hazards. In, Pierson, M. D. and D. A. Corlett, Jr. (eds.), *HACCP Principles and Applications*. Van Nostrand Reinhold, New York, NY.

Chapter 8

INITIAL TASKS IN DEVELOPING HACCP PLANS

K. E. Stevenson

INTRODUCTION

The preceding chapters in this manual have described the development of the HACCP system, and provided examples of how HACCP was first implemented. In addition, the document containing the recent revision of the HACCP principles (NACMCF, 1998) was presented, along with detailed information on various types of hazards and controls, and prerequisite programs, with special emphasis on sanitation standard operating procedures (SSOPs). This chapter, and several chapters that follow, describe the procedures to use in applying the HACCP principles to develop a HACCP plan for specific products and processes.

As described in Chapter 3, prerequisite programs are the foundation for a successful HACCP program. Reports from the Food and Drug Administration's (FDA) HACCP pilot program (FDA, 1996 and 1997) stressed the importance of conducting an in-depth evaluation of prerequisite programs prior to application of the HACCP principles. Only establishment programs that support the HACCP plan need to be considered as prerequisite programs. Those programs should be evaluated carefully, since the hazard analysis is based, in part, upon an evaluation of the level of control provided by these programs. As a result, reliance on well developed and consistently maintained prerequisite programs can simplify a HACCP plan.

The latest NACMCF document describing use of HACCP concepts and the HACCP principles (see Chapter 2) states that HACCP plans may be specific for the product and process (NACMCF, 1998). Generic HACCP plans developed for a common product or group of products may be very helpful in providing a substantial amount of material for a HACCP plan, but each plan must be developed based upon the unique ingredients and conditions that define and produce each food product. These include, but are not limited, to the following:

Suppliers	Processing parameters
Ingredient specifications	Employee practices
Batches of ingredients	Packaging materials
Formulation	Storage and warehousing
Product specifications	Distribution
Facility and layout	Retail handling and display
Types of equipment	Product shelf-life
Equipment design	Label instructions to consumers
Preparation procedures	Operating conditions

Upper management must make a commitment to support the use of HACCP—both financially and in spirit. Once this key element has been established, the NACMCF (1998) identified five "preliminary tasks"

Table 8-1—Preliminary Tasks

    1. Assemble the HACCP team.

    2. Describe the food and its distribution.

    3. Describe the intended use and consumers of the food.

    4. Develop a flow diagram, which describes the process.

    5. Verify the flow diagram.

(Table 8-1) which need to be completed before the seven HACCP principles are applied to a specific product and process. Note: In a similar approach with a different terminology, the Codex (1997) HACCP guidelines specify 12 "tasks" in the development of the HACCP Plan; these tasks include similar versions of the five preliminary tasks and the seven HACCP principles which are listed in the NACMCF document.

ASSEMBLE THE HACCP TEAM

HACCP Coordinator

The first procedure in assembling a HACCP team is to appoint a HACCP coordinator. This individual will have overall responsibility for the development, organization and management of the HACCP program. The HACCP system is normally associated with the Quality Assurance (QA) function in a company. In large companies, the HACCP component may be given high visibility by placing the HACCP unit under the auspices of a Vice President in charge of food safety.

Whether in a large company or a small one, the HACCP coordinator must have the management skills and must be provided the resources necessary to implement the company's HACCP policy and objectives. A more extensive discussion of this topic is presented in Chapter 16.

The HACCP Team

The HACCP team is a multidisciplinary unit that has the responsibility of developing HACCP plans in accordance with the HACCP concepts and the company HACCP policy and objectives. This team should not be just another group of QA personnel; it should consist of personnel with skills and expertise in supervision and a wide variety of technical areas. This includes representatives from Engineering, Maintenance, Microbiology, Production, QA, Regulatory, Product Development, etc.

While one or more members of the team may have extensive knowledge of, and/or experience with HACCP systems, this is not a prerequisite for membership on the HACCP team. In many instances, particularly with small companies, it may be necessary to obtain assistance from consultants and other outside experts in order to ensure the proper development and application of HACCP.

The HACCP team does not need to have knowledge concerning every facet and detail of the products and processes in a facility or within a company. Ad hoc groups and project-specific teams can be utilized to provide local knowledge and expertise associated with various products and operations as they need to be addressed.

After the HACCP team is appointed, they will begin to plan, develop and implement a HACCP plan. Once the planning is done, they will need to gather a considerable amount of information before they can apply the HACCP principles to the operations. This will include information on the facilities, equipment, processes, products, packaging materials, and other items and operations which may affect food safety. This background material is crucial to the development of HACCP plans because it provides detailed information to which the HACCP principles are applied. The remainder of this chapter provides further descriptions of the types and nature of the materials which are useful. (See Chapter 16 for additional information concerning the responsibilities and duties of the HACCP team.)

DESCRIBE THE FOOD AND ITS DISTRIBUTION

Although the importance of descriptive information about the product and its distribution is often underrated, the purpose of this step is to obtain as many details concerning the product and its distribution as are practicable. Describing the product may be accomplished by answering questions, such as:

- What is the product? (e.g., frozen fried chicken thighs, buttermilk pancake mix, chocolate ice cream)
- What is the nature of the product? (e.g., fresh, canned, dried, vacuum packaged)
- What type of storage and distribution is required? (e.g., frozen, refrigerated, ambient)
- What is the shelf life of the product?
- Are there any other special considerations that need to be addressed?
- How is the product produced/processed?

Note that this list seeks mainly to describe the product in consumer terms, and it is not exhaustive. Also, the questions will vary since the product description for HACCP must be tailored to the individual product. A short description of how the product is produced/processed is also essential to prepare for the hazard analysis.

The next element involves preparing a detailed formula for the product. Also, it is important to develop a list of every ingredient or chemical, which may find its way into the product, whether or not the items are listed on the label. This should include items such as pesticides used during growth of crops, processing aids, chemical sanitizers, etc.

The importance of such a list can be illustrated by the following example. Historically, sulfites have been used as processing aids for a variety of products and processes. In many instances, sulfites were not listed specifically on product labels since they were only used as processing aids and the levels of sulfites in the final products were quite low. When it became apparent that sulfites represented a health hazard to some individuals who were extremely sensitive, manufacturers were required to label products that contained relatively low amounts of sulfites. For manufacturers who had developed detailed knowledge of their products and ingredients, this amounted to a detailed computer search to determine what ingredients and products contained sulfites. However, for others who did not have this type of information, numerous recalls of products were initiated when low levels of sulfites were found to be present in some ingredients.

Detailed information of the formula and ingredients also alerts the HACCP team to potential problems. Certain types of ingredients are known to be sources of specific microbiological hazards. For example, some dairy products, meat, eggs and other products of animal origin are recognized as sources of salmonellae, while cured meats and pasta may support staphylococcal growth and enterotoxin formation under certain conditions.

Nitrite in cured meats and antibiotics in milk and products of animal origin are examples of potential chemical hazards associated with specific ingredients. In many instances, the use of certain types of ingredients and equipment lead to contamination by specific foreign objects, which represent physical hazards. The use of wire brushes, bucket elevators and sifters may lead to product contamination with wire, metal components and metal shavings. Ingredients and products packaged in glass, or manufactured in an establishment that packs products into jars, represent potential sources of contamination with broken glass.

The nature of the food, the shelf life and packaging are also important to food safety. Historically, packaging has been used to protect food from adulterants and contamination. However, today's microwave-active packaging, selective barrier films, vacuum packaging, and recycled packaging materials present new and more complex food safety issues. Key issues concerning microbiological hazards associated with packaging are the potential growth and toxin production by *Clostridium botulinum* in products packaged in selective barrier films, and vacuum or modified atmosphere packaging, and the potential growth of *Listeria monocytogenes* in extended shelf-life refrigerated products.

DESCRIBE THE INTENDED USE AND CONSUMERS OF THE FOOD

Information concerning the intended use and consumers may also impact on the safety of a particular food. Preparation procedures (particularly cooking), potential product abuse after reconstitution, and other factors related to intended use might drastically affect food safety. For example, after botulism outbreaks associated with refrigerated garlic-in-oil products which had been improperly stored, FDA issued a notice indicating that such products were not safe if refrigeration was the only barrier to potential growth and toxin formation by *C. botulinum.*

Similarly, there are obvious safety issues if the product specifically is intended for use by a segment of the population consisting primarily of immunocompromised individuals. (Note: The intended use of a food should be based upon the normal use of the food by end users or the consumers.) Answering questions such as the following will assist in describing the consumer and intended use of the product:

- What is the intended use? (e.g., retail, food service, further manufacturing)
- What is the potential for mishandling?
- What preparation procedures are required? (e.g., ready-to eat, heat-and-serve, prepare and bake, reconstitution)
- Is the product intended for use by immunocompromised individuals? (e.g., infant foods, dietary supplements)

DEVELOP A FLOW DIAGRAM WHICH DESCRIBES THE PROCESS

Development of the flow diagram should be considered a detailed compilation of material associated with the ingredients, storage, preparation, processing, packaging, storage and distribution of the product. The basic document is a simple (block) flow diagram showing the locations where specific ingredients are added in the system, the individual preparation and processing steps which occur, as well as, the associated machinery used in these operations.

The information in the flow diagram is used to evaluate whether or not potential hazards may be associated with the various stages. Experience has shown that this document should not be comprised of engineering drawings because their level of complexity detracts from the food safety analyses. However, the type of equipment used in an operation is important and additional information concerning the equipment, and possibly tolerances or specifications, should be available to the HACCP team.

Mixing, cutting, conveying, chopping, grinding, sifting and screening are examples of events that may have consequences with respect to physical hazards. Likewise, storing ingredients, cooking, pasteurizing, cooling, refrigerating, freezing and thawing are examples of events that may affect the safety of the product with respect to microbiological hazards. Addition of a schematic or establishment layout is also useful. Information from the establishment layout can reveal areas of potential cross contamination from raw product to cooked product, or other areas of potential concern.

Note that the flow diagram is used during the hazard analysis associated with Principle 1. And, critical control points (CCPs) will be added to the flow diagram when they are identified using Principle 2.

VERIFY THE FLOW DIAGRAM

Once a flow diagram of the process has been prepared, it is imperative that the flow diagram be verified for accuracy and completeness by an on-site inspection of the facility, equipment and operations. In many instances, the simple task of verifying the flow diagram will identify deficiencies in the document, which need to be corrected. (Note: This flow diagram, by necessity, is a dynamic document; it must be updated and modified so that it accurately reflects the current processes and operations.) In addition, the relationship and location of various operations will be important factors to consider during the hazard analysis.

SUMMARY

Several tasks must be taken prior to applying the seven HACCP principles to a specific product and process. The initial task includes appointing a HACCP coordinator and assembling the HACCP team. Once in place, this group accomplishes the remaining preliminary tasks by gathering necessary information to (a) describe the food and its distribution, (b) describe the intended use and consumers, (c) develop a flow diagram and comprehensive information concerning preparation and processing operations, and (d) verify, on-site, that the flow diagram is accurate and complete.

REFERENCES

Codex. 1997. *Hazard Analysis and Critical Control Point (HACCP) System and Guidelines for its Application.* Alinorm97/13A. Codex Alimentarius Committee on Food Hygiene, Rome.

FDA. 1996. *Hazard analysis critical control point (HACCP) pilot program for selected food manufacturers—interim report of observations and comments.* CFSAN, Division of HACCP Programs. Washington, D.C.

FDA. 1997. *Hazard analysis and critical control point (HACCP) pilot program for selected food manufacturers—second interim report of observations and comments.* CFSAN, Division of HACCP Programs. Washington, D.C.

NACMCF. 1998. Hazard analysis and critical control point principles and application guidelines. *J. Food Protect.* 61: 762.

Chapter 9

HAZARD ANALYSIS

Dane T. Bernard, K. E. Stevenson, and Allen M. Katsuyama

PRINCIPLE 1: Conduct a Hazard Analysis

INTRODUCTION

After addressing the preliminary tasks discussed in previous chapters (developing a flow diagram, etc.), the HACCP team conducts a hazard analysis and identifies appropriate control measures. While most authorities agree that the hazard analysis is the heart of the HACCP system, everyone is not in agreement that the HACCP system should be reserved for addressing only food safety hazards. In the U.S., however, both FDA and USDA/FSIS have acknowledged that HACCP should focus only on food safety hazards. Thus, quality and economic issues (not involving safety) should be excluded.

Hazard analysis is the process used by the HACCP team to determine which potential hazards present a significant health risk to consumers. Only those hazards that pose significant risk to the health of consumers need to be included in a HACCP plan. Chapters 5–7 on potential biological, chemical and physical hazards and possible control measures cover much of the background information needed to initiate a hazard analysis.

According to the National Advisory Committee on Microbiological Criteria for Foods (NACMCF, 1998),

"The purpose of the hazard analysis is to develop a list of hazards which are of such significance that they are reasonably likely to cause injury or illness if not effectively controlled." Conducting a hazard analysis with this specific purpose distinguishes HACCP from other systems for managing food safety. It is essential that this process is conducted appropriately, since successful application of HACCP principles 2–7 depends on the output from the hazard analysis.

The NACMCF HACCP guidelines define a hazard as "a biological, chemical, or physical agent that is reasonably likely to cause illness or injury in the absence of its control." They describe the hazard analysis process as consisting of the following stages:

- Hazard identification, and
- Hazard evaluation.

A list of potential hazards that may be associated with the food is assembled during the hazard identification stage. After assembling the list, each potential hazard is evaluated based on its likelihood of occurrence and the severity of its effects (illness, injury, mortality, etc.) to consumers in order to determine which of the potential hazards presents a significant risk. The potential hazards that present a significant risk to consumer health are the hazards that should be addressed in the HACCP plan.

Once hazards that present significant risks have been identified, a control measure(s) must be described for each hazard that will prevent, eliminate or reduce the hazard to an acceptable level. If a hazard presenting a significant consumer safety risk has been identified and no control measure is available within the establishment's current processes, product formulation or operating procedures, then modifications to the system must be considered.

Hazards identified as significant for product produced in one operation or facility may not be significant for the same product produced in another establishment. This is attributable to differences in sources of supply, product formulation, production methods, effectiveness of prerequisite programs, etc. For example, due to differences in equipment and/or an effective maintenance program, metal contamination may be reasonably likely to occur in one facility but unlikely to occur in another.

IMPORTANCE OF CONDUCTING A HAZARD ANALYSIS

If the hazard analysis is not conducted correctly and the hazards warranting control within the HACCP system are not identified, the plan may not be effective in protecting consumers regardless of how well it is followed. In addition, the exercise of reviewing establishment operations during the hazard analysis often results in identifying elements of a process or product that should be modified. When an establishment's operations are thoroughly analyzed, the team may find that changing "traditional" procedures or upgrading equipment will eliminate a potential hazard or will provide more effective control over it. Thus, there is more benefit to conducting a thorough hazard analysis than just the identification of significant hazards.

The hazard analysis is necessary for providing a basis for determining CCPs (Principle 2). As you will learn in the next chapter, many establishments have made the incorrect assumption that identifying CCPs can be done merely by applying the decision tree without conducting a rigorous hazard analysis. If this is the practice at an establishment, the result may be the identification of far more CCPs than are actually needed.

CONDUCTING A HAZARD ANALYSIS

The proper analysis of biological, chemical and physical hazards associated with food ingredients and finished products is a subjective process that requires good judgement, detailed knowledge of the properties of the materials and manufacturing processes, and access to appropriate scientific expertise. To assist in this process, many tools have been proposed. Some of them are outlined below. As noted above, the NACMCF describes the process of conducting a hazard analysis as involving two stages: hazard identification and hazard evaluation.

HAZARD IDENTIFICATION

Hazard identification is sometimes described as a brainstorming session designed to facilitate the HACCP team's development of a list of potential hazards for consideration during the hazard evaluation stage. During the hazard identification stage, the HACCP team assembles or reviews information about:

- The raw materials and/or ingredients used in the product.
- The activities conducted at each step in the process.
- The equipment used to make the product.
- The method of storage and distribution.
- The intended use and consumers of the product.

Using this and other relevant information, the team develops a list of potential biological, chemical and physical hazards that may be introduced, increased (e.g., pathogen growth), or controlled at each step described on the flow diagram. Knowledge of any adverse health-related events historically associated with the product is important. The background information on hazards and controls contained in Chapters 5–7 should be useful at this stage.

To assist in the process of identifying potential hazards, the NACMCF HACCP document contains "Examples of Questions to be Considered when Conducting a Hazard Analysis" (Chapter 2, Appendix 2-C). Answering these questions will help the HACCP team to develop the list of potential hazards by assisting them in assembling the type of information they will need to consider. Some of the questions suggested by the NACMCF, along with others we find useful in certain situations are listed in Appendix 9-A.

HAZARD EVALUATION

Hazard evaluation, the second stage of the hazard analysis, is conducted after the list of potential biological, chemical or physical hazards is assembled. In the hazard evaluation, the HACCP team decides which of the potential hazards listed during the hazard identification stage present a significant risk to consumers. According to the NACMCF, each potential hazard should be evaluated based on two factors: severity (seriousness of the potential illness or injury resulting from exposure to the hazard), and likelihood of occurrence. Evaluating severity to establish public health impact of a potential hazard will require consideration of certain factors including susceptibility of intended consumers to foodborne illness, possible impact of secondary problems (e.g. haemolytic uremic syndrome from an *E. coli* O157:H7 infection), and magnitude and duration of the illness or injury.

Estimation of the likely occurrence of the hazard in the food as consumed is usually based upon a combination of experience, data from past outbreaks of foodborne illness, information in the scientific literature and historical information gathered by the establishment. Factors that may influence likelihood of occurrence of the potential hazard in the final product include:

- Effectiveness of prerequisite programs.
- Frequency of association of the potential hazard with the food or an ingredient.
- Method of preparation in the establishment.
- Conditions during transportation.
- Expected storage conditions.
- The likely preparation steps before consumption.

Based on the hazard evaluation, the HACCP team will determine which hazards need to be addressed in the HACCP plan. The HACCP team has the ultimate responsibility to make this decision. During this process, the HACCP team may rely upon the opinion of experts called upon to assist in the development of the HACCP plan. But, as the NACMCF notes, there may be differences of opinion, even among experts, as to the likely occurrence and severity of a potential hazard.

One tool developed to help explain the concept of evaluating potential hazards according to a qualitative estimate of risk is contained in Table 9-1. This table is an adaptation of a table developed by the NACMCF (1998) (Chapter 2, Appendix D) to help explain the two stages of conducting a hazard analysis. Table 9-1 gives three examples using the logic sequence described above for conducting a hazard analysis.

Another tool developed to assist in teaching the use of likelihood of occurrence and severity of a potential hazard during the hazard evaluation is the risk-ranking grid presented in Appendix 9-B to this chapter. Using the grid may clarify use of likelihood of occurrence and severity to develop a qualitative categorization of risk for any potential hazard being evaluated.

The Influence of Prerequisite Programs in the Hazard Analysis

As noted earlier in this chapter and in Chapter 3, each operation must have a firm foundation of prerequisite programs before developing a HACCP plan. The question often arises as to how prerequisite programs, such as adherence to good manufacturing practices (GMPs), influence the hazard evaluation stage of the hazard analysis. Remember that the primary factor to be considered in the hazard analysis is the team's evaluation of actual risk to consumers posed by the potential hazard. Considering likely occurrence and severity is how this evaluation is made. But during this evaluation, the team should consider how the likely occurrence of the hazard is affected by normal adherence to GMPs. In addition, the HACCP team needs to consider the degree of control necessary to feel comfortable that the potential hazard is adequately controlled. It is assumed that occasional nonconformance with a prerequisite program will not result in a health threat to consumers. The same cannot typically be said for critical control points.

Prerequisite programs normally include objectives other than food safety. Thus, it may not be easy to associate performance of a prerequisite program, e.g., pest control or chemical storage programs, with specific production lots or batches. Consequently, it is usually more effective to manage non-food safety objectives and hazards that present a low risk within a quality system rather than including their performance and control as part of the HACCP plan. This is appropriate provided that uninterrupted adherence to the prerequisite program is not essential for food safety.

Occasional nonconformance from a prerequisite program requirement alone is not expected to result in a significant risk to consumers. Nevertheless, prerequisite programs play an important role in consumer protection. Deviations from compliance with a prerequisite program usually do not result in action against the product, whereas deviations from compliance in a HACCP system normally result in action against the product, e.g. evaluation of product to determine appropriate action (rework, destroy, etc.). This is a key consideration that can aid in distinguishing between control points within prerequisite programs and CCPs that should be included in HACCP plan.

Some authorities consider the potential for recontamination of cooked products by organisms like *Listeria monocytogenes* as an example of a potential hazard that normally is unlikely to occur, and is therefore controlled adequately by prerequisite programs. Controlling establishment environments for *L. monocytogenes* involves a diverse set of activities such that management solely within a HACCP program will be extremely difficult. More importantly, failure to conduct a single activity at the prescribed time is not likely to result in contamination of product by *L. monocytogenes*. Although some distinct CCPs can be identified for control of *L. monocytogenes*, complete control of this potential hazard may not be compatible with HACCP because no distinct CCPs or critical limits (CLs) can be developed that would provide for adequate control.

Similarly, management of the establishment environment and operations is used to prevent or minimize cross contamination of product by allergens. In most instances, this is accomplished using a diverse set of control strategies (e.g., supplier guarantees, storage and handling procedures, air-handling systems, production schedules, cleaning and sanitizing procedures, etc.) that

Table 9-1—Example of How the Stages of Hazard Analysis are Used to Identify and Evaluate Hazards

Hazard Analysis Stage		Frozen cooked beef patties produced in a manufacturing establishment	Product containing eggs prepared for foodservice	Commercial frozen pre-cooked, boned chicken for further processing
Stage 1 Hazard Identification	Determine potential hazards associated with product.	Enteric pathogens (i.e., *E. coli* O157:H7 and *Salmonella*)	*Salmonella*	*Staphylococcus aureus* enterotoxin
Stage 2 Hazard Evaluation	Assess severity of health consequences if potential hazard is not properly controlled.	Epidemiological evidence indicates that these pathogens cause severe health effects, including death among children and elderly. Undercooked beef patties have been linked to disease from these pathogens.	Salmonellosis is a food borne infection causing a moderate to severe illness that can be caused by ingestion of only a few cells of *Salmonella*.	Certain strains of *S. aureus* produce an enterotoxin, which can cause a moderate foodborne illness.
	Determine likelihood of occurrence of potential hazard if not properly controlled.	Likely occurrence of *E. coli* O157:H7 is low to remote while the likelihood of salmonellae is moderate in raw beef trimmings.	Product is made with liquid eggs, which have been associated with past outbreaks of salmonellosis. Recent problems with *Salmonella* serotype Enteritidis in eggs cause increased concern. Probability of *Salmonella* in raw eggs cannot be ruled out. If not effectively controlled, some consumers are likely to be exposed to *Salmonella* from this food.	Product may be contaminated with *S. aureus* due to human handling during boning of cooked chicken. Enterotoxin capable of causing illness will only occur if *S. aureus* multiplies to about 1×10^6/g. Operating procedures during boning and subsequent freezing are unlikely to permit growth of *S. aureus*, thus the potential for enterotoxin formation is very low.
	Using information above, determine if this potential hazard is to be addressed in the HACCP plan.	The HACCP team decides that enteric pathogens are hazards for this product.	HACCP team determines that uninterrupted control is needed to prevent an unacceptable health risk.	The HACCP team determines that the potential for enterotoxin formation is very low due to normal good operating practices. While it is still desirable to keep the initial number of *S. aureus* organisms low, this does not require control in the HACCP plan.
		Hazards must be addressed in the plan.	**Hazard must be addressed in the plan.**	**Potential hazard does not need to be addressed in plan.**

are included in the establishment's prerequisite programs. The objective of executing these strategies is to minimize the potential for products to become contaminated by allergens. While this program is important to minimize contamination by allergens, occasional nonconformance with any one of these elements would not be expected to result in contamination of product with an allergen.

CONTROL MEASURES

When the hazard analysis has been completed and all significant biological, chemical, and physical hazards have been listed with their points of occurrence, the HACCP team must identify measures to control these specific hazards. The term control measure was substituted for preventive measure in the 1998 NAC-MCF HACCP document because not all hazards can be prevented, but virtually all can be controlled to some degree. More than one control measure may be required for a specific hazard. On the other hand, more than one hazard may be addressed by a specific control measure. This information will be used in Principle 2, to assist in identifying CCPs.

When reviewing the identified hazards, processors usually will be able to identify control measures that can be used to reduce or eliminate the risk posed by these hazards. For example, heating the food to a specific minimum temperature for a specified period of time can control biological hazards such as pathogenic microorganisms. Chemical and physical hazards can often be controlled through the use of appropriate procedures and detection/removal equipment. Table 9-2 provides some examples of "points of occurrence," identified hazards, and control measures.

SUMMARIZING THE HAZARD ANALYSIS

Upon completion of the hazard analysis, the hazards associated with each step in the production of the food should be listed along with any measure(s) that are used to control the hazard(s). USDA/FSIS requires that a hazard analysis be conducted and that a written hazard analysis be available for inspectors to review. The FDA seafood rule, however, only requires that the hazard analysis be conducted, not that it be recorded. The FDA proposal on HACCP for juice products, on the other hand, would require a written hazard analysis. Regardless, it is recommended that the HACCP team keep some record of its deliberations for future reference by the establishment.

Table 9-2.—Examples of Hazards and Possible Control Measures

Point of Occurrence	Identified Hazard	Control Measures
Raw milk	Vegetative pathogens	Pasteurization
Lake water intake	Giardia lamblia	Disinfection
Vegetables for canning	C. botulinum	Adequate thermal process, container integrity
Batching of acidified foods	C. botulinum	Proper acidification
Finished product from raw materials or processing step	Metal fragments	Metal detectors
Product packed in glass	Glass	Glass breakage procedure
Fermenting sausages	S. aureus enterotoxin	Proper fermentation

The hazard analysis summary could be presented in several different ways. One format is a table similar to that shown in Table 9-3. Another possible approach is a text summarizing the hazard analysis, along with a summary table listing only the hazards that will be addressed in the plan and associated control measures. For official purposes, the final hazard analysis record need only note those hazards being addressed in the plan. Thus, the complete list of potential hazards evaluated by the HACCP team need not appear on the official record.

STRUCTURE FOR CONDUCTING A HAZARD ANALYSIS AND DETERMINING CCPs

The following brief example of a hazard analysis work sheet is patterned after an example used in the 1998 NACMCF guidelines for a fully cooked beef patty. The format below provides a useful template for conducting a hazard analysis. This format is useful not only for instructional purposes, but also for setting up a HACCP plan.

When using this form, begin by listing each step in the production process in the first column, according to product flow as depicted on the flow chart. In the example above, we have included only the cooking step from the flow chart for producing fully cooked beef patties.

In the second column, the HACCP team should list all potential hazards (chemical, physical, and biological) introduced, controlled or enhanced at each process step. For convenience, only some of the pathogenic bacteria that may be associated with raw beef are included in the table.

After the list of potential hazards at each step is complete, the HACCP team then evaluates each to determine which ones are reasonably likely to cause adverse health consequences if they are not properly controlled. As described earlier, the hazard evaluation should focus on the likelihood of occurrence and severity of each potential hazard. The question at the top of the third column asks if the hazard will be addressed in the HACCP plan. The answer to this question will be based on the results of the hazard evaluation. After evaluating the potential hazards, enter a yes in the third column beside each potential hazard that needs to be addressed in the HACCP plan. In the example above, the team determined that enteric pathogens are reasonably likely to be associated with this product and that the potential health consequences can be severe. Thus, they decided that enteric pathogens will be addressed in the HACCP plan and they entered a ''yes'' into column three.

In the fourth column, provide the rationale or justification for decisions regarding hazards to be addressed in the HACCP plan. The rationale should focus on the likely occurrence and severity of the hazard. Documenting the rationale for decision making will be important during any reevaluation of the HACCP plan.

Table 9-3—Example of a Hazard Analysis Worksheet

Ingredient or Processing Step	Potential hazards introduced, controlled or enhanced at this step.	Does this potential hazard need to be addressed in HACCP plan? (Yes/No)	WHY? (Justification for decision made in previous column)	What measures can be applied to prevent, eliminate or reduce the hazards being addressed in your HACCP plan?	Is this step a critical control point (CCP)?
Cooking	BIOLOGICAL Enteric pathogens: e.g., Salmonella, verotoxigenic E. coli	Yes	Enteric pathogens are associated with foodborne illness from undercooked ground beef. Hazard from pathogenic microorganisms is reasonably likely to occur.	Proper cooking	Yes CCP(B)

For each significant hazard that will be addressed in the HACCP plan, determine if an effective control measure exists at that step or at a later step. If so, document the control measures in the fifth column. In the example outlined above, cooking is noted as the control measure.

Next, determine whether the step or steps where effective control measures are identified is a CCP. A decision tree can be used to assist in determining CCPs (see Chapter 10). Enter the decision regarding CCPs in column six. In the example above, proper cooking at the establishment is used to reduce the occurrence of the hazard to an acceptable level, so cooking is a CCP.

REGULATORY REQUIREMENTS REGARDING HAZARD ANALYSIS

Current federal requirements for HACCP are contained in 21 *CFR* 123 for FDA's rule on HACCP for seafood and 9 *CFR* 417 for the USDA/FSIS rule on HACCP for meat and poultry products. While there are a few differences between these rules, they are very consistent regarding definitions and concept. These regulations are discussed in depth in Chapter 17.

Regarding hazard analysis, neither the FDA nor the USDA/FSIS HACCP rules specifically mention consideration of severity. In addition, there are some apparent differences in the definition of a hazard and in the description of the hazard analysis process. Because of these perceived differences, there is currently some uncertainty as to how the agencies will view hazards identified through use of the NACMCF hazard analysis protocol. However, a properly conducted and well documented hazard analysis will result in scientific documentation concerning the hazards that a processor includes in the HACCP plan and those potential hazards determined to be of low risk and not included in the HACCP plan. This scientifically developed rationale will be invaluable in assisting establishments when dealing with inspectors who are evaluating the HACCP plan.

One point of perceived difference between the NACMCF recommendations and the current regulatory requirements is that both USDA/FSIS and FDA define a "food safety hazard" as, "Any biological, chemical or physical property that may cause a food to be unsafe for consumption," rather than the definition given at the beginning of this chapter. Both HACCP rules state that HACCP plans should address those food safety hazards that are "reasonably likely to occur." Both agencies explain that, in their opinion, a food safety hazard that is reasonably likely to occur is one for which a prudent processor would establish controls because it has occurred or because there is a reasonable possibility that it will occur in the particular type of product being processed in the absence of controls [9 *CFR* 417.2(a)(1); 21 *CFR* 123.6(a)].

In addition, the Agencies require that every official establishment or processor conduct, or have conducted for it, a hazard analysis to determine the food safety hazards reasonably likely to occur in the production process and to identify the preventive measures the establishment can apply to control those hazards. The hazard analysis shall include food safety hazards that can occur before, during and after entry into the establishment. Further, both FDA [21 *CFR* 123.6(c)(1)(a)] and USDA/FSIS [9 *CFR* 417.2(a)(3)] provide a list of potential sources of food safety hazards, although the list seems to be of limited utility. This broad list notes that food safety hazards may be expected to arise from the following: natural toxins, microbiological contamination, chemical contaminants, pesticides, drug residues, decomposition, parasites, unapproved use of direct or indirect food or color additives, and physical hazards. To this list, FSIS adds zoonotic diseases. Although the intent of the agencies with regard to this list is not clear, processors should consider addressing each category during the hazard analysis and at least noting that no hazards were found in a specific category if this is the case.

The FDA Office of Seafood has assembled and published a "Fish & Fisheries Products Hazards & Controls Guide," which serves as guidance in preparing a HACCP plan for seafood (FDA, 1998). The guide suggests hazards that may be of concern for the various species of fish and fishery products and various processes that they may used for such products. While this guide is not a mandatory part of the seafood HACCP rule, a processor of seafood products would be wise to understand the potential hazards listed by FDA. If a processor disagrees about the potential risk posed by a hazard in a product, a solid, science-based rationale should be developed to support this position.

Both agencies require that the individual responsible for developing the HACCP plan (presumably including the hazard analysis) be trained in accordance with the training requirements contained in each rule. In addition, a HACCP-trained individual must reassess the HACCP plan, including the hazard analysis, at least annually or more often if changes in products, equipment, formulations, etc., necessitate such a review.

SUMMARY

A thorough hazard analysis is vital to an effective HACCP plan and is required by U.S. government agencies that administer mandated HACCP programs. Identification of hazards to be addressed in a HACCP plan will be facilitated by the utilization of the two-stage process (hazard identification and hazard evaluation) proposed by the NACMCF. By using the concepts of likelihood of occurrence and severity to evaluate potential hazards, the establishment will focus on those hazards that pose significant risk to consumers. These are the hazards that deserve the attention and focus of a HACCP food safety management system.

REFERENCES

Bernard, Dane T. 1997. Hazard Analysis and Critical Control Point system: use in controlling microbiological hazards. Chapter 41 In: *Food Microbiology Fundamentals and Frontiers*. M.P. Doyle, L.R. Beuchat, and T.J. Montville, eds. ASM Press, Washington, D.C.

Bryan, F.I. 1990. Application of HACCP to ready-to-eat chilled foods. *Food Technol.* 45(7):70.

FDA. 1995. Procedures for the safe and sanitary processing and importing of fish and fishery products; final rule. *Federal Register* 60 (242): 63096. (December 18).

FDA. 1998. *Fish & fisheries products hazards & controls guide*, 2nd. ed. Food and Drug Administration, Washington, D.C.

NAS. 1985. *An Evaluation of the Role of Microbiological Criteria for Foods and Food Ingredients*. National Academy Press, Washington, D.C.

NACMCF. 1998. Hazard analysis and critical control point principles and application guidelines. *J. Food Protect.* 61:762.

Pierson, M.D. and D.A. Corlett, Jr. (eds.). 1992. *HACCP: Principles and Applications*. Van Nostrand Reinhold, New York, NY.

Sperber, W.H. 1991. The modern HACCP system. *Food Technol.* 45(6):116.

USDA/FSIS. 1996. Pathogen reduction; Hazard Analysis and Critical Control Point (HACCP) systems; final rule. *Federal Register* 61 (144): 38806. (July 25)

APPENDIX 9-A
List of questions that may be useful in assembling a list of potential hazards for consideration during the hazard evaluation stage of hazard analysis

Identifying Potential Biological Hazards

A biological hazard is a pathogenic bacterium (or its toxin), virus or parasite that is reasonably likely to result in foodborne illness if not properly controlled. While the organisms of primary concern are pathogenic bacteria, such as *Clostridium botulinum, Listeria monocytogenes, Salmonella* species, and *Staphylococcus aureus* (see Chapter 5), the other categories of biological pathogens also need to be considered during the hazard analysis.

1. Review the list of ingredients used in the manufacture of the food item.
   a. Are there pathogenic microorganisms known to be associated with any of the ingredients? (e.g., *Salmonella* in raw chicken; various pathogens in raw milk; *C. botulinum* in vegetables; pathogenic *E. coli* in ground beef.)
   b. Are any of the ingredients capable of supporting pathogen growth or are they susceptible to biological hazards due to contamination or mishandling?
2. Review the flow diagram for the selected product, placing emphasis on the handling procedures and manufacturing operations, as well as the storage methods and practices for the ingredients and the finished product.
   a. Are there any situations that may allow pathogens to multiply such that consumer risk is significantly increased? (e.g., *Salmonella enterica* serotype Enteritidis in pooled eggs held for extended periods at room temperature.)
   b. Are there any situations where ingredients, work in process, or the finished product may become contaminated with pathogens? (e.g., *S. aureus* in batter due to poor employee hygiene; pathogens from handlers of foods after a heat treatment step that is designed to destroy harmful microorganisms.)
   c. Are there any risks from biological hazards that may be created or made worse by mishandling of the finished product? (e.g., improper hot holding of a cooked item.)
3. List the potential biological hazards that have been identified during the hazard identification stage and the point at which each potential hazard enters the process (e.g., raw material, incoming ingredient, handling procedure, manufacturing operation, storage, and distribution). An individual or group with expertise in food microbiology and familiarity with past microbiological problems can provide valuable assistance in this process.

Identifying Potential Chemical Hazards

Potential chemical hazards (see Chapter 6) include toxic substances and any other compounds that may render a food unsafe for consumption, not only to the general public, but also to the small percentage of the population that may be particularly sensitive to a specific chemical. For example, sulfiting agents used to preserve fresh leafy vegetables, dried fruits, and wines have caused allergic-type reactions in sensitive individuals. Examples of other chemical hazards that should be considered include aflatoxin and other mycotoxins, fish and shellfish toxins, scombrotoxin (histamine) from the decomposition of certain types of fish, and ingredients, such as tree nuts or shellfish, known to contain proteins that trigger allergic reactions.

As in the case of biological hazards, the HACCP team must identify all potential chemical hazards associated with the production of the food commodity before evaluating the significance of each. The following outline will assist in identifying potential chemical hazards.

1. Review the list of raw materials, ingredients, and packaging materials that are used to manufacture the finished product.
   a. Are there any hazardous chemicals associated with the growing, harvesting, processing, or packaging of any item? (e.g., pesticide chemicals on raw agricultural commodities; aflatoxin in nuts and grains; sulfites used on shrimp, dehydrated fruits and vegetables.)
   b. Are all of the food additive ingredients approved for their intended uses? Would any chemical pose a significant safety risk if used inappropriately?
   c. Are food-contact packaging materials made from approved chemicals? If the finished product is intended to be prepared in its package, such as in a microwave or conventional oven, are the packaging materials approved for such use?
   d. Are there labeling requirements associated with any food additive, such as for sulfites and some coloring agents? If so, do the product labels comply?

2. Review the flow diagram for the product and the manufacturing facility, placing emphasis on all of the equipment with food-contact surfaces. Consider the chemicals that are used in the establishment for water treatment, equipment and building maintenance, cleaning and sanitizing, and pest control.
   a. Are food contact surfaces free of toxic substances?
   b. Are all water treatment chemicals, such as boiler water additives, approved for use and used appropriately?
   c. Are only food-grade lubricants used in the establishment? If non-approved lubricants are used, are they restricted to uses where there is no chance of product contamination?
   d. Are paints and other coatings on food-contact surfaces approved for such use?
   e. Are cleaning and sanitizing chemicals approved for use in food establishments? Are they used appropriately?
   f. Are pesticides (insecticides, rodenticides) used for pest control in the establishment? If so, are they approved for such use and are they being used appropriately?
   g. Are all hazardous chemicals handled and stored in a manner that precludes contamination of food-contact surfaces, raw materials, ingredients, packaging materials, and finished product?
   h. Are any ingredients used that contain an allergenic component? What possibilities exist for cross contamination of allergenic compounds during storage, preparation, processing, or the handling of rework? Are allergen-containing products appropriately labeled?
   i. Would any of the chemicals used pose a significant risk to consumers if used inappropriately.
3. List all of the potential chemical hazards that have been identified during the hazard identification stage and the point at which each enters the system.

Identifying Potential Physical Hazards

Foreign objects that are capable of injuring the consumer represent potential physical hazards (see Chapter 7). The HACCP team must identify the potential physical hazards associated with the finished product. The following outline will assist in identifying potential physical hazards.
1. Review the list of raw materials, ingredients, and packaging materials that are used to manufacture the finished product.
   a. Are there foreign objects capable of causing injury associated with any of the raw materials or ingredients? (e.g., stones in dry beans and field peas, wood splinters in palletized materials.)
   b. Are there physical hazards associated with any packaging material? (e.g., metal clips on sausage casings or other types of packaging; glass fragments in empty jars and metal slivers in empty cans.)
2. While referring to the flow diagram for the finished product at the selected establishment, inspect the physical facilities.
   a. Are there environmental sources of physical hazards in and around food storage and processing areas? (e.g., unprotected light fixtures; loose nuts, bolts, screws, or other fasteners on overhead structures; exposed or deteriorating insulation on pipes; corroded metal fixtures, such as support structures and louvers on ventilation ducts; wire, tape, twine and other impermanent materials used for "temporary" repairs.)
   b. Is any equipment capable of generating physical hazards? (e.g., splinters from wooden materials, including pallets; nuts, bolts, screws, or rivets; metal fragments from metal-to-metal contact, such as in choppers, grinders, emulsifiers, screw conveyors and bucket elevators; glass fragments from unprotected thermometers and gauges.)
   c. Are there tools, utensils, and other implements used on or near the lines where there is a likelihood that they may fall into equipment or exposed foods? (e.g., meat hooks, shovels, cleaning supplies, small wrenches, sampling or measuring devices, writing implements, thermometers, gauges.)
3. List all of the potential physical hazards that have been identified during the hazard identification stage and the point at which each hazard enters the system. Past history of problems with foreign objects is valuable for this exercise.

APPENDIX 9-B
Grid for the Qualitative Ranking of
Risk Resulting from a Hazard in Food

Versions of this table have been incorporated in training materials used by the Food and Agriculture Organization of the United Nations, Agriculture and Agri-Food Canada, and the United States National Marine Fisheries Service. In using the table, likelihood of occurrence is categorized as Remote, Low, Medium, or High; severity is categorized as Low, Medium or High. When these categories are established, the appropriate grid coordinate is located.

Severity				
High	H-*R*	H-*L*	H-*M*	H-*H*
Medium	M-*R*	M-*L*	M-*M*	M-*H*
Low	L-*R*	L-*L*	L-*M*	L-*H*
	Remote	*Low*	*Medium*	*High*

Likelihood of Occurrence

Once potential hazards are categorized in terms of likelihood of occurrence and severity, a decision still must be made as to whether the potential hazard needs to be addressed in the HACCP plan. This risk ranking method is primarily a tool to facilitate teaching. There are no guidelines for which grid blocks would qualify a potential hazard to be included or excluded from a HACCP plan based on a specific grid location. However, most would probably agree that hazards that are remote and of low severity do not demand the time and resources needed to manage them in a HACCP plan. Likewise, a potential hazard that is estimated to be highly likely to occur and results in a highly severe health effect would probably be included in a HACCP plan. Using this logic, the closer a hazard is ranked to the "**H-*H***" grid block, the more likely it is to be addressed in a HACCP plan, and the closer to the "**L-*R***" grid block, the less likely the potential hazard would be included within a HACCP plan. The decision, however, will still depend on the subjective judgment of decision-makers.

Chapter 10

CRITICAL CONTROL POINTS

Lisa M. Weddig

PRINCIPLE 2: Determine Critical Control Points (CCPs)

INTRODUCTION

The HACCP team determines critical control points (CCPs) based upon the results of the hazard analysis. The potential hazards that need to be addressed in the HACCP plan are those that were identified during the hazard analysis procedure as being reasonably likely to cause injury or illness if not effectively controlled. Using the list of control measures developed in Principle 1 for each hazard, the HACCP team must identify the steps at which the control measures can be applied. Each of these steps is then assessed, and the appropriate CCP(s) is (are) selected for each hazard. Each hazard must be controlled at one or more CCPs.

CONTROL POINTS AND CRITICAL CONTROL POINTS

Control points (CPs) and CCPs can be differentiated based upon the following definitions developed by the National Advisory Committee on Microbiological Criteria for Foods (NACMCF, 1998):

Control Point: Any step at which biological, physical, or chemical factors can be controlled.

Critical Control Point: A step at which control can be applied and is essential to prevent or eliminate a food safety hazard or reduce it to an acceptable level.

There can be several steps in a food processing system where biological, chemical or physical hazards can be controlled to some extent. (A step has been defined by the NACMCF as a point, procedure, operation or stage in the food system from primary production to final consumption.) However, there are likely to be only a few steps where a loss of control will result in the production of a potentially unsafe food. These steps are the CCPs in the HACCP plan.

For example, levels of pathogens in a product intended to be pasteurized may be prevented from increasing in the product by controlling temperature during storage and processing and by maintaining a sanitary environment. While good temperature control and sanitation are important CPs, they alone cannot ensure that the finished product is free of the pathogens. Only the pasteurization process is capable of doing so. Therefore, if the presence of pathogens is identified as a food safety hazard, the pasteurization

Table 10-1—Examples of Control Measures & Possible CCPs/CPs

PRODUCT	IDENTIFIED HAZARD	CONTROL MEASURE	POINT OF CONTROL	CCP or CP
Milk	Enteric pathogens	Pasteurization	Pasteurizer	CCP
		Prevention of recontamination	Post-process handling	CP
Canned beets (low-acid food)	C. botulinum	Thermal Process	Retort	CCP
Pickled beets (acidified food)	C. botulinum	Proper acidification	Brine kettle (proper acidification of brine)	CCP
Ground beef	Metal fragments	Magnets	After each grinder	CP
		Equipment inspection	Each grinder	CP
		Metal detection	After packaging	CCP
Cheddar cheese	S. aureus enterotoxin	Proper rate & level of acid development during ripening	Ripening	CCP

process is the CCP in this example. Other examples of CCPs and CPs are outlined in Table 10-1.

DETERMINING CCPs

CCP decision trees have been developed to assist establishments in determining CCPs in the process; both the NACMCF (1998) and Codex (1997) HACCP documents include various versions of this tool. Figures 10-1 and 10-2 contain the CCP decision trees presented in the NACMCF document. The HACCP team may utilize a CCP decision tree to evaluate each of the steps where food safety hazards can be prevented, eliminated, or reduced to acceptable levels. Each of these steps should then be categorized as either a CP or a

---

Figure 10-1—NACMCF CCP Decision Tree #1

Important considerations when using the decision tree:

>   The decision tree is used after the hazard analysis.

>   The decision tree then is used at the steps where a hazard that must be addressed in the HACCP plan has been identified.

>   A subsequent step in the process may be more effective for controlling a hazard and may be the preferred CCP.

>   More than one step in a process may be involved in controlling a hazard.

>   More than one hazard may be controlled by a specific control measure.

Q1. Does this step involve a hazard of sufficient likelihood of occurrence and severity to warrant its control?

```
         ↓                        ↓
       YES                  NO → Not a CCP
         ↓
```

Q2. Does a control measure for the hazard exist at this step?

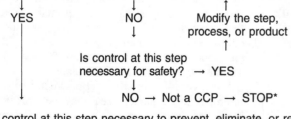

```
         ↓              ↓              ↑
       YES             NO        Modify the step,
         |              ↓       process, or product
         |                            ↑
         |       Is control at this step
         |       necessary for safety?  →  YES
         |                   ↓
         ↓           NO  →  Not a CCP  →  STOP*
```

Q3. Is control at this step necessary to prevent, eliminate, or reduce the risk of the hazard to consumers?

```
         ↓                        ↓
       YES                  NO  →  Not a CCP  →  STOP*
         ↓
  CRITICAL CONTROL POINT
```

   *Proceed to next step in the process.

Figure 10-2—NACMCF CCP Decision Tree #2

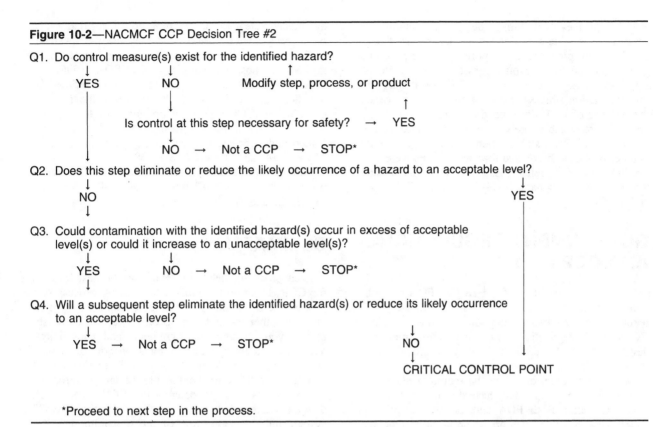

Q1. Do control measure(s) exist for the identified hazard?

    ↓   ↓   ↑

  YES   NO   Modify step, process, or product

               ↓   ↑

      Is control at this step necessary for safety? →   YES

                  ↓

               NO → Not a CCP → STOP*

Q2. Does this step eliminate or reduce the likely occurrence of a hazard to an acceptable level?

   ↓   ↓

  NO   YES

  ↓

Q3. Could contamination with the identified hazard(s) occur in excess of acceptable level(s) or could it increase to an unacceptable level(s)?

   ↓   ↓

 YES   NO → Not a CCP → STOP*

  ↓

Q4. Will a subsequent step eliminate the identified hazard(s) or reduce its likely occurrence to an acceptable level?

    ↓   ↓

 YES → Not a CCP → STOP*   NO

                                      ↓

                                   CRITICAL CONTROL POINT

*Proceed to next step in the process.

CCP. The results of this evaluation should be summarized and added to the supporting documentation for the HACCP plan.

The most common problem with using a CCP decision tree is trying to apply the questions prior to the completion of the hazard analysis. By applying the questions to potential hazards that are not reasonably likely to cause illness or injury, the HACCP team may unintentionally identify CCPs that are not directly related to controlling product safety. Experience also has shown that strictly following a decision tree sometimes results in a decision that common sense says is incorrect. Thus, a decision tree should be used with appropriate caution.

Remember the CCP decision trees are only tools that can be used to assist establishments in determining appropriate CCPs; establishments are not required to use them. Many HACCP teams are comfortable determining CCPs based on their experience and knowledge of the process and existing control measures.

Designating CCPs

CCPs may be designated in the HACCP plan in different manners. CCPs can be sequentially numbered for convenience (e.g., CCP #1, CCP #2, etc.). In some instances, companies prefer to number CCPs sequentially within each hazard category (e.g., CCP P1, CCP C1, for the first CCP addressing a physical hazard and

a chemical hazard, respectively). While these numbering systems are primarily beneficial, in some cases they may cause confusion when CCPs are added or deleted due to changes in the specifications, ingredients or operations. Some establishments avoid the problems with numbering systems by designating CCPs by process step name (e.g., oven, packaging, etc.). An establishment should select a CCP designation system that is best suited to the operation.

Number of CCPs

HACCP teams often ask, "How many CCPs should we have?" There is not a simple answer to that question because the number of CCPs is dependent on the product produced, the ingredients used, the processing methods employed and the prerequisite programs implemented. It is more common, though, for establishments to select too many CCPs than it is to select too few. Proper attention should be given to the CCP determination process in order to select the appropriate CCPs for the operation. Too few CCPs may not allow for adequate control of food safety hazards. On the other hand, too many CCPs may over burden the HACCP plan by attempting to control non-safety issues with the same intensity as food safety hazards.

It is important for the HACCP team to remember that HACCP plans can be modified. The number or location of CCPs may be changed at any time as the

HACCP plan evolves during the implementation process. This was demonstrated quite clearly in FDA's HACCP pilot program. The reports from the pilot program indicated that the majority of the establishments involved changed the number of CCPs during the implementation process. Establishments that increased the number of CCPs realized that some potential hazards were reasonably likely to occur, thus necessitating additional CCPs. Establishments that decreased the number of CCPs discovered that some CCPs were controlling non-safety related issues or potential hazards that were not reasonably likely to occur (FDA, 1996 and 1997).

GOVERNMENT REGULATIONS AND CCPs

The current regulations for HACCP (FDA's regulation for fish and fishery products and USDA/FSIS's regulation for all meat and poultry products) address CCPs. Both regulations require establishments to develop CCP(s) for each food safety hazard identified during the hazard analysis.

One may assume, based on the requirements, that a product with no food safety hazard would not require a HACCP plan. Both FDA and USDA recognize in their regulations that there are some products that may not have any food safety hazards. USDA/FSIS however has made it clear in the preamble to the regulation and on several other occasions that they are not aware of any meat or poultry process that can be deemed categorically to pose no likely hazard (USDA, 1996).

At this time, establishments producing acidified or low acid canned foods which fall under the purview of either HACCP regulation do not have to establish CCPs to address the biological hazards which are controlled under the existing canning regulations (21 *CFR* 113 or 114, and 9 *CFR* 318 or 381).

Further information on the current HACCP regulations can be found in Chapter 17, as well as Appendices B, C, and D.

SUMMARY

Each processor needs to determine the best location for CCPs to control identified hazards. A process step that is a CCP at one processing location may not be one at another location due to differences in establishment layout, equipment, ingredients and control systems. Each identified hazard must be controlled with at least one CCP. When using a CCP decision tree, it is important to complete the hazard analysis for the entire process prior to determining CCPs. The CCPs that are identified serve as the basis for the HACCP system and the application of the remaining HACCP principles.

REFERENCES

Bernard, Dane T. 1997. Hazard analysis and critical control point system: Use in controlling microbiological hazards. Chapter 41 In: *Food Microbiology Fundamentals and Frontiers*. M.P. Doyle, L.R. Beuchat, and T.J. Montville, eds. ASM Press, Washington, D.C.

Codex. 1997. *Hazard analysis and critical control point (HACCP) system and guidelines for its application*. Alinorm 97/13A. Codex Alimentarius Committee on Food Hygiene, Rome.

FDA. 1995. Procedures for the safe and sanitary processing and importing of fish and fishery products; final rule. *Federal Register* 60 (242): 63096. (December 18).

FDA. 1996. *Hazard analysis critical control point (HACCP) pilot program for selected food manufacturers—interim report of observations and comments*. CFSAN, Division of HACCP Programs. Washington, D.C.

FDA. 1997. *Hazard analysis and critical control point (HACCP) pilot program for selected food manufacturers—second interim report of observations and comments*. CFSAN, Division of HACCP Programs. Washington, D.C.

NACMCF. 1998. Hazard analysis and critical control point principles and application guidelines. *J. Food Protect.* 61:762.

USDA/FSIS. 1996. Pathogen reduction; hazard analysis and critical control point (HACCP) systems; final rule. *Federal Register* 61 (144): 38806. (July 25)

Chapter 11

CRITICAL LIMITS

Lisa M. Weddig

PRINCIPLE 3: Establish Critical Limits

INTRODUCTION

Up to this point, considerable time has been spent on the hazard analysis and identification of critical control points (CCPs). Potential hazards, biological, chemical and physical, have been identified and evaluated to determine which ones are likely to cause illness or injury if not controlled. Measures have been identified which can control these hazards. In addition, points in the process have been identified where these control measures can be used to prevent, eliminate, or reduce the hazards to an acceptable level. While these CCPs are the heart of the HACCP system, there is considerably more work to be done in developing the HACCP plan.

WHAT ARE CRITICAL LIMITS?

When a CCP is identified, parameters need to be established to signify whether the control measure at a CCP is "in" or "out" of control. These parameters are referred to as "critical limits" (CLs). A CL, as defined by the National Advisory Committee on Micro-

biological Criteria for Foods (NACMCF, 1998), is a maximum and/or minimum value to which a biological, chemical, or physical parameter must be controlled at a CCP to prevent, eliminate, or reduce to an acceptable level the occurrence of a food safety hazard. The Codex (1997) definition of a CL is more simply stated—a criterion which separates acceptability from unacceptability. Some typical biological, chemical, and physical parameters that may be CLs are found in Table 11-1.

Table 11-1—Examples of Parameters that May Be Critical Limits

temperature	time	physical dimensions
pH	flow rate	weight
moisture level	water activity	viscosity
line speed	salt concentration	

Not meeting a CL should indicate that the CCP is out of control, and therefore a potential for the development of a health hazard exists. For HACCP purposes, not meeting the CL may indicate any one of the following:

- Evidence of the existence of a direct health hazard (e.g., detection of *Salmonella* in a ready-to-eat product).
- Evidence that a direct health hazard could develop (e.g., underprocessing of a retorted, low-acid food).
- Indications that a product was not produced under conditions assuring safety (e.g., metal detector at a CCP adjusted incorrectly).

SETTING CRITICAL LIMITS

The application of scientific principles for identifying and controlling food safety hazards is the basis of the HACCP system. The hazard analysis provides for a science-based identification of hazards, whereas CLs provide for a science-based control of food safety hazards. During its deliberations, the HACCP team will determine the food safety criterion that must be met at each CCP. The HACCP team will determine what standard or benchmark must be met in order to prevent, eliminate, or reduce to acceptable levels the occurrence of a food safety hazard. This will include selecting appropriate CLs.

Food safety criteria may be established by regulatory standards and guidelines. These are often referred to as performance standards. Examples of performance standards include the mandatory pasteurization times and temperatures for milk (e.g., 161°F for 15 seconds), and requiring a 7-$\log_{10}$ reduction of *Salmonella* in fully cooked poultry products. Processing authorities and others with food safety expertise also may be good sources for establishing performance standards if government standards do not exist. Based on the appropriate performance standard, CLs are then established to assure that the performance standard will be achieved. The HACCP Team may consult additional technical and scientific sources for information on establishing CLs. Some examples of sources are found in Table 11-2.

Table 11-2—Sources to Assist in the Establishment of Critical Limits

---

- articles in scientific journals/literature surveys
- government documents (regulations, guidelines, directives, performance standards, tolerances and action levels)
- trade association guidelines
- university extension publications
- in-plant studies or research
- processing authorities
- university extension agents
- industry experts and consultants
- equipment manufacturers

In many instances, when CCPs are identified the appropriate CL will not be readily apparent. Experts may be able to provide a conservative recommendation on a CL that will protect the product; however,

research may be necessary to further refine this CL. For example, the chill step may be identified as a CCP for a cooked, beef product. The HACCP team determined that an appropriate performance standard for the chill step is to limit the growth of the pathogen *Clostridium perfringens* to no more than a 1-$\log_{10}$ increase. This was selected because it is the performance standard for certain meat and poultry products mandated by the Food Safety and Inspection Service (FSIS) of the U.S. Department of Agriculture (USDA/FSIS, 1999a). CLs for the rate of cooling necessary to prevent the 1-$\log_{10}$ increase would need to be determined. Without any in-plant research, a microbiologist may recommend cooling the product to an internal temperature between 130°F and 80°F within 1.5 hours after heat processing and additional cooling between 80°F and 40°F within 5 hours to ensure meeting the performance standard. This recommendation is one of the options provided by USDA/FSIS in their compliance guidelines as being acceptable for meeting the performance standard regulations (USDA/FSIS, 1999b). In reality, there is not just one cooling rate limit that would ensure that the performance standard is met, but many different combinations. Research would be able to identify the appropriate cooling temperature/time relationships for the product, thereby providing the establishment with more flexibility while still producing a safe product.

The HACCP team will need to develop CLs that are best suited to the capabilities of the establishment. For example, research may have indicated that to achieve a 5-$\log_{10}$ reduction of *Salmonella* within a beef patty, the patty must be heated to an internal temperature of 151°F and held at that temperature for ≥ 41 seconds as required in the USDA/FSIS performance standard regulation (USDA/FSIS, 1999a). An establishment may decide to set CLs to correspond to these two parameters (internal temperature of patty and time duration). Another establishment may elect to ensure the safety of the product by controlling and monitoring the cook process. Through heat penetration tests, the establishment may have determined that by running an oven at a specific temperature, circulating the hot air at a certain speed and holding the patty in the oven for a specific period of time, the necessary internal temperature of the patties will be met provided that the patties do not exceed a specified thickness. In this example, the CLs would be a minimum oven temperature, minimum air-flow rate, minimum time, minimum initial temperature of patties, and maximum thickness of patties. Periodically checking the internal temperature of the patty and time duration could be a verification procedure.

While it may seem more complicated to control and monitor the process rather than the product temperature, some establishments feel this approach provides more consistent control of the process. Focusing on controlling a properly designed process will provide greater assurance of product safety than periodically monitoring product temperatures where assurance of control is limited by the frequency and accuracy of the temperature checks.

Establishments may find they need to conduct tests or experiments to establish CLs or to ensure that the control measure will deliver the desired results for ensuring food safety. Table 11-3 lists several tests that may be used to establish CLs.

Table 11-3—Examples of Experiments Used to Establish Critical Limits

Test Type	Purpose
Heat Penetration	To measure the heating or cooling rate of a product.
Temperature Distribution	To map the temperatures within equipment which either heats or cools product (e.g., oven, pasteurizer, water bath, steam tunnel, retort, smoke house, chill bath, cooler, spiral freezer).
Thermal Death Time Studies	To determine the heat resistance of pathogens or other organisms in a specific product.
Inoculated Pack or Microbial Challenge Studies	To challenge a pre-designed process (either cook or cool) to determine whether or not the process will achieve the desired performance standard.

Operating Limits

An establishment may establish operating limits to help prevent the routine violation of CLs. In such instances, operating limits are parameters that exceed those necessary for safety and are established for reasons other than food safety. Operating limits provide the opportunity for an operator to adjust a process to bring it back into control before the CLs are exceeded. Establishing operating limits is a practical means of preventing deviations and avoiding the need to take corrective actions.

Some operating limits may be established for quality reasons. Some cooking temperatures are necessary to gelatinize starch, inactivate enzymes, or destroy spoilage organisms. These temperatures may exceed that necessary to destroy the pathogens of concern. Similarly, a storage temperature criterion may be established to extend shelf life or to provide a specific product quality attribute (e.g., texture of ice cream), and that temperature may be well below the minimum temperature criterion that prevents the growth of pathogens.

Operating limits also may be set to compensate for expected variation in operation of processing and monitoring equipment so that CLs are not violated. Remember that a CL is a maximum and/or minimum value, not an average value. For example, if the oven used to cook beef patties in the example cited earlier can only control temperature with a variability of $\pm 5°F$, the operating limits/settings for the oven temperature would need to take this into account and the temperature must be set so that the CL will be met consistently.

REGULATORY CONSIDERATION FOR CRITICAL LIMITS

The current Food and Drug Administration's (FDA) HACCP regulations for fish and fishery products (FDA, 1999) and USDA/FSIS's HACCP regulation for all meat and poultry products (USDA/FSIS, 1999c) address CLs. Both regulations require establishments to list CLs that must be met at each CCP. The USDA/FSIS regulation also stipulates that the CLs be designed to ensure that applicable targets, performance standards, or other requirements established by the agency are met. A CL which is less stringent than an Agency requirement must be supported with sound scientific data.

Further information on the current HACCP regulations can be found in Chapter 17, as well as Appendices B, C, and D.

SUMMARY

CLs are used to set criteria at the CCPs in the process. These are locations where lack of control will likely result in the development of a potential safety hazard. The CLs are the parameters that define whether the CCP is in or out of control. Other limits that are set to control situations that are of quality, non-safety regulatory, consumer, or economic consequence should not be designated CLs.

REFERENCES

Bernard, Dane T. 1997. Hazard Analysis and Critical Control Point System: Use in controlling microbiological hazards. Chapter 41 In: *Food Microbiology Fundamentals and Frontiers*. M.P. Doyle, L.R. Beuchat, and T.J. Montville, eds. ASM Press, Washington, D.C.

Codex. 1997. *Hazard Analysis and Critical Control Point (HACCP) System and Guidelines for its Application*. Alinorm 97/13A. Codex Alimentarius Committee on Food Hygiene, Rome.

FDA. 1999. Fish and fishery products. Title 21, *Code of Federal Regulations*, Part 123. U.S. Government Printing Office, Washington, D.C. (issued annually).

Moberg, L. J. 1992. Chapter 6. Establishing critical limits for critical control points. In, Pierson, M. D. and D. A. Corlett, Jr. (eds.), *HACCP Principles and Applications*. Van Nostrand Reinhold, New York.

NACMCF. 1998. Hazard Analysis and Critical Control Point Principles and Application Guidelines. *J. Food Protect.* 61:762.

NAS. 1985. *An Evaluation of the Role of Microbiological Criteria for Foods and Food Ingredients*. National Academy Press, Washington, D.C.

National Seafood HACCP Alliance for Training and Education. 1997. Chapter 7. Principle 3: Establish Critical Limits. In: *HACCP: Hazard Analysis and Critical Control Point Training Curriculum*, 2nd ed. North Carolina Sea Grant, Raleigh, N.C.

USDA/FSIS. 1999a. Performance standards for the production of certain meat and poultry products; final rule. *Federal Register* 64 (3): 732. (January 6)

USDA/FSIS. 1999b. *Appendix B: Compliance Guidelines for Cooling Heat Treated Meat or Poultry Products (Stabilization)*. Food Safety and Inspection Service, Washington, D.C. (Issued January 1999, updated May 1999). (The document is available on the following USDA website: http://www.fsis.usda.gov/OA/fr/95033F-b.htm)

USDA/FSIS. 1999c. Hazard Analysis and Critical Control Point (HACCP) systems: Part 417. Title 9, *Code of Federal Regulations*, U.S. Government Printing Office, Washington, D.C. (issued annually).

Chapter 12

MONITORING CRITICAL CONTROL POINTS

D. E. Gombas, K. E. Stevenson and Dane T. Bernard

PRINCIPLE 4: Establish Monitoring Procedures

INTRODUCTION

Once critical limits (CLs) are established for the critical control points (CCPs), procedures must be established to monitor the CCPs to determine and document whether these CLs are being met. Thus, monitoring is a key element in determining if specific product/process operations are conducted in a manner that is sufficient to control the identified hazards. The National Advisory Committee on Microbiological Criteria for Foods (NACMCF) describes monitoring as a planned sequence of observations or measurements to assess whether a CCP is under control and to produce an accurate record for future use in verification (NACMCF, 1998).

Examples of monitoring activities include visual observations and measurements of temperature, time, pH and moisture level. Application of Principle #4 involves describing the type of monitoring procedures (what will be monitored), specifying the procedures used for monitoring (how it will be monitored), establishing the frequency or maximum time lapse between application of monitoring procedures (when it will be monitored), and identifying the person(s) responsible for conducting the monitoring procedures (who will perform the monitoring procedures).

WHAT WILL BE MONITORED

At every CCP, a control measure is used to control an identified hazard. To assure product safety, the control measure must operate within one or more established CLs. Monitoring is conducted at the CCP to determine if the process is operating within those CLs. It is important that the CL and monitoring activity are suited to each other, such that the monitoring activity will provide reliable and definitive information on whether the CL is being met. For example, if cooking was a CCP in the processing of ready-to-eat chicken pieces and the CL was "every chicken piece is cooked to at least 165°F internal temperature," an appropriate monitoring activity would be to measure the internal temperature of the chicken pieces at the end of cooking. However, if the CLs at the same CCP were "oven temperature greater than or equal to (≥) 350°F and belt speed through the oven no greater than 5.0 feet per minute," in order to achieve a minimum internal temperature of 165°F, then the appropriate monitoring activities would be to measure the oven temperature and the belt speed.

HOW WILL IT BE MONITORED

Monitoring activities will involve measurement and/ or observation. If the CL is a numerical value (e.g., ≥350°F), then monitoring will usually involve a measurement (e.g., with a thermometer or other temperature-measuring device). If the CL is defined as the presence or absence of an attribute (e.g., screen is in place and intact), then monitoring may involve observation (e.g., observe the screen to determine if it is in place and intact).

When a deviation from a CL occurs, an appropriate corrective action must be taken. Monitoring activities should be designed to determine when deviations occur and to alert the person conducting the monitoring so that appropriate corrective actions can be initiated.

No matter what monitoring procedures are used, it is important that the results of monitoring are accurate and precise. First, it is important to select an appropriate monitoring "device." If the monitoring activity is an observation, then the person performing the monitoring procedure must be adequately trained to provide objective, accurate observations. This will be discussed further below. If the monitoring activity involves making a measurement, then the device selected to make the measurement must have sufficient accuracy and precision relative to the parameter being monitored and the CL. Accuracy of measuring instruments also must be adequate for the needs of the particular monitoring activity at the CCP.

Remember that a CL is a specific value that must be met for each control measure. They are not "average values." If the HACCP plan specifies that a product must be cooked to a minimum internal temperature of 160°F, this means that 159°F is not acceptable. Thus, monitoring equipment should be selected or designed to assure enough accuracy for the purpose intended. For example, if a cooling temperature CL is easily achieved and cooling is expected always to be several degrees on the safe side of the CL, then a dial thermometer (which typically has an inherent variability of plus or minus a few degrees) may suffice as a monitoring tool. However, if the monitored temperature is likely to be within a few degrees of the CL, then a more precise temperature-sensing device is probably necessary. As another example, if a company determines that a fermented product must achieve a pH level of <4.7 for safety reasons but the pH after fermentation is always 4.0 or less, then pH test paper may be appropriate as a measurement device. But, if the pH is close to 4.6 after fermentation, then a calibrated pH meter may be more appropriate as a monitoring device. To assure accuracy of the measurements taken, monitoring devices must be in calibration when they are used for monitoring, and they should be recalibrated frequently enough that the accuracy of the device is assured. Calibration typically is considered part of verification, and is discussed further in Chapter 14.

The monitoring activity must provide a real-time assessment of the status of the CCP. Analytical testing of a raw material that can remain in storage until the results are available can take several hours or even days without compromising the HACCP plan. However, if the test results are needed immediately, then such testing may not be an appropriate monitoring technique.

Most food processors conduct various sampling and testing procedures to detect or measure one or more attributes in raw materials and/or finished products. These attributes may be related to product quality, economics or safety. However, a sampling and testing procedure is rarely an appropriate monitoring activity for microbiological hazards. First, even rapid microbiological test methods do not yet provide "real-time" results. Turnaround times of several hours to several days for microbiological tests are impractical for on-line monitoring. As a result, these tests may only be useful for ingredient or finished product testing when the sampled materials can be held until results are available. Secondly, sampling and testing suffers from poor precision in detecting sporadic contamination. In most instances, large numbers of samples are not analyzed on a routine basis. Thus, when a statistical sampling of a lot is analyzed for a defect such as a microbiological hazard, the probability of detecting such a defect is directly related to the level of that defect in a sampled lot. Since most microbiological hazards are absent or, if present, are found at relatively low levels, the probability of detecting such hazards is quite low. Conversely, the probability of accepting a lot with hazardous microorganisms is quite high. For example, if *Salmonella* was present in a batch of product at a rate of 1 out of every 1000 units of product and 60 samples were examined for the pathogen, there would be greater than a 94% chance of accepting the contaminated batch of product. Therefore, note with caution that sampling and testing of ingredients or products provides only limited assurance that hazards have been detected (unless very large-scale sampling is employed).

Some monitoring activities involve placing devices in direct contact with the product (e.g., measuring a product's internal temperature with a thermometer probe). It is important that the monitoring activity does not introduce another potential hazard. Dipsticks, thermometers, and pH probes are examples of devices that usually must contact the product during monitoring. Each instrument or device should be considered for the potential of introducing anything that may represent a potential hazard. For example, will the dipstick transfer any unsafe chemicals, or could the dipstick itself create a physical hazard if lost in the product? Mercury-in-glass thermometers are the standard for temperature measurement in many systems, but direct product contact could create a potential for physical (e.g., glass) and/or chemical (e.g., mercury) hazard. In addition, using the same thermometer to monitor many samples of product may create an opportunity to transfer a pathogen from one sample to the others. Where feasible, it is preferable to use a non-invasive monitoring procedure. Where product contact must occur, procedures should be developed to ensure that no new hazards would be created by the monitoring activity. For example, the sample of product could be discarded after the monitoring activity is completed. To avoid cross contamination with microorganisms, measuring devices should be cleaned and sanitized with appropriate frequency.

An important aspect of monitoring is that the monitoring activity is expected to produce an accurate record for future use in verification. Therefore, when monitoring involves an instrument or device that makes a measurement, the monitoring activity must provide a value that can be recorded, and, where feasible, should provide a record of the measurement. Devices that do not provide measurements or values, such as alarms and divert valves, are not appropriate for monitoring, unless there is a record of their action (e.g., their action is documented or automatically recorded). However, such devices may be useful when operated together with instruments that provide a readable measurement, e.g., a thermometer or temperature readout. Some monitoring devices, such as temperature chart recorders, automatically provide a record. With such devices, the chart can be used as the official monitoring record for a CL, provided that the person responsible for the monitoring activity adds appropriate comments and signs or initials and dates the chart. Where records are not automatically created, forms must be developed for documenting the actual values collected during monitoring. (Refer to Chapter 15 for additional information.)

WHEN WILL IT BE MONITORED

In order for HACCP to be a truly preventive system, monitoring activities must be conducted with sufficient frequency that they can detect when potentially hazardous foods may have been produced and prevent such products from reaching consumers. These monitoring activities may be continuous or discontinuous. If a monitoring activity is conducted on a discontinuous basis, it is important that it be performed frequently enough to detect any deviations from the specified CL, and to allow for corrective actions to be taken before products leave control of the establishment.

Continuous monitoring at a CCP is preferred, but may not always be practical or necessary. Continuous monitoring is necessary when variations, spikes or drift in the CL parameter may otherwise go unnoticed. For example, if an oven at a cooking CCP has historically had a tendency for the operating temperature to drift or cycle over time, then taking periodic temperature readings may not provide sufficient information on whether the oven has operated continuously within the CLs. In such a situation, monitoring should be automatic and continuous. Automatic and continuous monitoring is possible with many types of physical and chemical measurements. For example, the temperature and time of operation of the oven can be recorded continuously on a temperature recording chart. If the temperature falls below the CL temperature or the cooking time is insufficient to meet the CL, the extent of the deviation is recorded on the chart. Other examples of parameters that can be monitored continuously include making pH or pressure measurements in fluids by use of in-line probes.

Discontinuous monitoring is appropriate when it is not feasible or practical to measure parameters continuously. For example, if a CL is a minimum internal temperature for cooked turkey breasts or surimi at the end of cooking, it may not be practical to measure the internal temperature of every piece of turkey or every package of surimi after the cooking process. However, monitoring could be designed to sample temperatures at the "worst case," such as the largest turkey pieces or the largest packages of surimi and/or the units from the slowest heating position. When there is no known worst case, monitoring could be designed to collect random samples at a statistically determined frequency. Of course, sampling and testing must be used with caution when applied for monitoring purposes, and sampling and testing procedures are inappropriate for some types of monitoring activities. It is advisable to consult with a statistician when developing a sampling procedure, in order to select sampling and testing procedures that provide the sensitivity and statistical confidence desired.

Discontinuous monitoring may also be used when variability in the monitored parameter is low, and/or the operating parameters are well above the CL. For example, if the CL for oil in a roaster is "≥300°F" and the temperature of the oil is normally 350°F ± 10°F for quality purposes, it may be adequate to monitor the oil temperature on a discontinuous basis. On the other hand, if the CL is closer to the normal temperature of the oil, or if the variability in the oil temperature is larger, then continuous monitoring (e.g., using a temperature recording chart) may be preferable.

While continuous monitoring is preferred, there may be situations when monitoring activities may be too frequent to be practical. It is important to avoid setting monitoring frequencies which are burdensome. For example, some HACCP plans may describe monitoring activities such as "operator observes every container" in an attempt to ensure that a CL is met. If such monitoring were performed on a conveyor line, this could mean that the operators would not be able to take their eyes off of the conveyor, or even take a break without stopping production.

One consequence of overly burdensome monitoring is that some monitoring activities are more likely to be missed. It is important to realize that missing a monitoring activity can have the same consequences as not meeting a CL. Remember that if the plan specifies a monitoring activity will be conducted every two hours, conducting the task at three hours is a violation of the HACCP plan. When monitoring does not occur as specified in the HACCP plan, then it is unknown whether the process has deviated from the CL. Therefore, the safety of the process is in question, and corrective action must be taken. Corrective actions, and other consequences of deviations from CLs, will be described further in the next chapter.

WHO WILL PERFORM THE MONITORING

Assignment of the responsibility for monitoring activities is necessary for each CCP. Many establishments have found that operations staff (e.g., line supervisors, or selected line workers) should be assigned to monitor CCPs and to record the results when monitoring is performed on-line. The operator is often in the best position to detect deviations and may be in the best position to take corrective actions immediately. However, for those monitoring procedures that require sampling and testing, quality control personnel may be more appropriate. In any case, the person (usually described by job title rather than name) conducting the monitoring:

- Must be designated in the HACCP plan as being responsible for that monitoring activity.
- Must be adequately trained to perform the monitoring procedures and to prepare the monitoring records.
- Signs or initials the monitoring records.

The individual(s) responsible for conducting the monitoring activities should be trained in the specific monitoring techniques and procedures that are used. Each individual involved in monitoring should be educated so that they fully understand the purpose and importance of monitoring, and that the monitoring and reporting needs to be done accurately and in an unbiased way. Likewise, each individual should be instructed to report immediately unusual occurrences to the individual responsible for initiating corrective actions, especially if a process or product does not meet CLs. Alternatively, the person should be trained to make process adjustments or, if so designated in the HACCP plan, to take the appropriate corrective action.

While the responsible individual must be designated in the HACCP plan, in order to avoid confusion, it is also advisable to avoid too restrictive a designation. As noted above, generally, the responsible individual is described by job title (e.g., "oven operator" or "maintenance technician"). If monitoring is primarily the responsibility of a single individual (e.g., "Quality Control Supervisor"), some HACCP teams have included wording such as "or designated employee" to allow for times when the primary individual is on vacation or otherwise not available to conduct the monitoring activity. However, in such instances it is important that the "backup" individuals are aware that they are responsible for conducting the monitoring activity and are adequately trained for this task.

REGULATORY REQUIREMENTS

Both the meat and poultry HACCP regulation (9 *CFR* 417) and the seafood HACCP regulation (21 *CFR* 123) contain regulatory requirements related to monitoring. These regulations require that the written HACCP plans list the monitoring procedures, and the frequency of monitoring, that will be used to monitor each CCP to ensure compliance with the CLs [9 *CFR* 417.2(c)(4) for meat and poultry and 21 *CFR* 123.6(c)(4) for seafood]. At the time monitoring occurs, the monitoring information, date and time the activity took place must be entered in the monitoring records, and the person conducting the monitoring procedure must sign or initial each entry on the record sheet. In addition, the monitoring records are subject to other regulatory requirements as described in Chapter 14 for verification and Chapter 15 for record-keeping.

OTHER CONSIDERATIONS

Information gathered through monitoring can be used for purposes that are not formally a part of the HACCP plan. For instance, monitoring may reveal discrepancies from normal processing parameters or other abnormalities that are not actual deviations from CLs. The production personnel then have several options to pursue depending upon the nature of these discrepancies. In some instances, an adjustment can be made that will avoid a deviation.

Reviewing monitoring records over time may reveal trends that could adversely affect product safety in the future. Recalibrating instruments, repairing or replacing equipment, and altering processing procedures are some of the activities that may be useful in averting future problems. From a production standpoint, it is important and highly beneficial to adjust a process and avoid a future deviation.

REFERENCES

Corlett, D.A., Jr. 1998. *HACCP User's Manual*. Chapman & Hall, New York.

FDA. 1999. Fish and fishery products. Title 21, *Code of Federal Regulations*, Part 123. U.S. Government Printing Office, Washington, D.C. (issued annually).

Hudak-Roos, M. and E.S. Garrett. Chapter 7. Monitoring critical control point critical limits. In, Pierson, M.D. and D.A. Corlett, Jr. (eds.), *HACCP Principles and Applications*. Van Nostrand Reinhold, New York.

Mortimer, S. A. and C. E. Wallace. 1998. *HACCP: A Practical Approach,* 2nd ed. Chapman & Hall, London.

NACMCF. 1998. Hazard Analysis and Critical Control Point Principles and Application Guidelines. *J. Food Protect.* 61:762.

USDA/FSIS. 1999. Hazard Analysis and Critical Control Point (HACCP) systems: Part 417. Title 9, *Code of Federal Regulations*, U.S. Government Printing Office, Washington, D.C. (issued annually).

Chapter 13

CORRECTIVE ACTIONS

K. E. Stevenson and Allen M. Katsuyama

PRINCIPLE 5: Establish Corrective Actions

INTRODUCTION

Since a deviation from a critical limit (CL) for a critical control point (CCP) will result in an actual or potential hazard to the consumer, appropriate "corrective action" must be taken to address the problem. For HACCP purposes, a corrective action is defined as procedures followed when a deviation occurs (NAC-MCF, 1998). The specific corrective action to use depends on the process parameters in use and the type of food being manufactured. Due to the diversities in possible deviations, corrective actions must be developed for each CCP when they are identified and the CL(s) and monitoring parameters are set. In a well designed HACCP program, whenever a deviation occurs immediate corrective action is already assigned, the CCP will be brought back into control before production continues, and no potentially violative product will leave the facility.

In most cases the establishment will have to place the product in question on hold pending a thorough investigation of the problem. This investigation may require record review or analyses. All product deviations at CCPs must be recorded and should remain on file for the term mandated by applicable regulations or the HACCP plan. These deviation records become an integral part of the HACCP program and, where appropriate, must be made available to the authorities for review.

It is of paramount importance that food establishments covered by federal regulations read and understand the requirements regarding corrective actions contained in those regulations. When deviations occur, each establishment must comply with the requirements in 9 *CFR* 417.3 for meat and poultry products or 21 *CFR* 123.7 for fish and fishery products. These specific requirements will be discussed later in this chapter.

ADJUSTMENTS AND CORRECTIVE ACTIONS

Ideally, information gathered through monitoring at each assigned CCP should detect trends toward potential violation of the CL, thereby enabling the operator to make adjustments before there is a need to take corrective actions that are described in the establishment's HACCP plan. Remember that HACCP takes a "preventive approach." One goal of monitoring in HACCP is to alert the operator of a potential problem in time for the operator to take action in order to avoid rejection of the product. Unfortunately, due to the complexity of many systems, complete control is not possible, and some deviations will occur.

The following provides examples of different options that might be exercised when dealing with potential or actual deviations:

1. Immediately adjust the process and keep the product in compliance within the critical limits. In this case the action is immediate, and no product is placed on hold because there was no deviation.

2. Stop the line. Hold all product not in compliance. Correct the problem on the line, and then continue with production. These are "corrective actions," and while this is a less desirable solution, it is often the scenario in food manufacturing. If this action is taken, the product involved in the deviation must be clearly distinguished from product made before and after the deviation.

3. If the deviation is the result of a problem in line design or equipment malfunction, a "quick fix" may be applied in order to continue running, but a long-term solution must be sought. Non-compliant product must be placed on hold and clearly distinguished from non-compliant product. The re-evaluation process also is a part of the HACCP approach, and the system may be changed if warranted.

If the CCPs have been carefully identified and monitoring programs are designed appropriately, then actions such as number 3 above can be kept to a minimum.

Adjusting the Process

Some potential deviations can be prevented by automatically controlling and monitoring a process. For example, flow diversion valves may be installed to divert product when the temperature of the product, or another critical factor, drops below a minimum set criterion. Examples of where this type of control is employed are in a pasteurization system for milk and a filling operation in a hot-fill-hold system. The same concept can be applied to meat or poultry cookers where temperature is continually monitored and alarms or automatic temperature adjustments are made when data indicate a trend toward a deviation.

When automatic control is not feasible, an operator can intercede and take action through the decision process that management has outlined for this specific processing step. Whether or not the product in question can be "saved" by this method of intervention depends on the product and the process. For example, a batch system for cooking chicken breasts could be adjusted to increase the cook time and still reach the minimum internal temperature needed for microbial safety. If the

system is a straight flow oven where the time factor cannot be changed or the temperature cannot be increased, then product exiting the oven that may not have received the minimum thermal process must be placed on hold or immediately reprocessed. Whenever possible, "in-process adjustments" should be designed into the product line (and the HACCP system) so that almost all potential deviations are eliminated in-line, thereby avoiding the need to hold product.

Other examples of adjustments include:

1. Control all time/temperature dependent operations, by adjusting either of the two variables while the line is still running, to prevent deviations.

2. Reroute ingredients not meeting specific criteria to another process line where the criteria are not crucial to the final safety of the product. For example, if a load of beef trim is found to contain E. coli O157:H7, it could be diverted to fully cooked product.

3. If the pH of a brine is not low enough to provide an equilibrium pH of 4.6 or less when used for acidification of vegetables, do not use the brine until sufficient acid has been added so that a proper equilibrium pH will be achieved.

CORRECTIVE ACTIONS

The NACMCF (1998) stated that corrective actions should include the following elements: (a) determine and correct the cause of non-compliance; (b) determine the disposition of non-compliant product; and (c) record the corrective actions that have been taken. In addition, each corrective action should specify who is responsible for initiating the corrective action, the records which must be maintained, and who is responsible for oversight.

Since any deviation from a CL is a safety rather than quality concern, proper documentation is essential. The following questions should be asked regarding product held for deviations at CCPs.

1. What tests can be made to verify the safety of the product in question?

2. Does review of the data indicate the safety of the product is in serious question?

3. Can this product be diverted for use in another product where safety is assured?

4. Can the product be reprocessed or reworked in a manner resulting in adequate assurance of food safety? (Example: Sending product held for possible metal contamination, due to a malfunction in a metal detector, through a properly operating metal detector.)

5. If the product cannot be reused, what method should be used to discard or destroy the product safely?
   a. Send to animal feed (inedible/unfit for human consumption)?
   b. Bury in a landfill?
   c. Incinerate the product?

6. What forms must be filled out and what records should be maintained?

Corrective Action Records

The disposition of all product involved in deviations at CCPs must be adequately documented by listing the reasons for the action taken, the reasoning behind the disposition decision, the number of units and codes of all product in question, and the method of disposal (if product warrants destruction). It may be necessary to make these records available to regulatory agents during HACCP verification audits. In some cases an appropriate final disposition of a product may require the expertise of industry experts in toxicology, microbiology, thermal processing, or a related field. Recommendations from such authorities also should be part of the HACCP records dealing with the deviation. Records of corrective actions are required by both the FDA and USDA/FSIS HACCP regulations. Thus, records of corrective actions must be in compliance with 9 *CFR* 417.3 or 21 *CFR* 123.7 as appropriate.

The HACCP records for deviations should include the following:

1. The actual production records or a reference to the production records relating to any products involved in the deviation. (Note: When deviations are corrected immediately on the line and no violative product is produced, this should be noted on the production records in case a question ever arises regarding the safety of these products.)

2. A standard form listing the following: Hold number, deviation, reason for hold, number of containers held, date of hold, date and code of product held, disposition and/or release forms, name of individual responsible for decision on disposition.

3. Recommendations of authorities (either outside or in-house) regarding final disposition of product.

4. An accurate accounting of all units in question.

5. A statement of the standard operating procedure for handling the specific deviation(s).

REGULATORY REQUIREMENTS

The HACCP regulations for seafood (21 *CFR* 123) and meat and poultry products (9 *CFR* 417) include specific requirements concerning corrective actions, and there are slight variations in the requirements.

The HACCP regulation for meat and poultry products requires that the written HACCP plan describes the corrective action to be taken in response to a deviation and that the actions taken ensure that:

1. The cause of the deviation is identified and eliminated.

2. The CCP is brought back into control by the corrective action.

3. Measures are taken to prevent recurrence of the deviation.

4. No unsafe or otherwise adulterated product enters commerce.

It is important that the corrective action records address each of these points.

For unforeseen deviations, meat and poultry establishments must:

1. segregate and hold the affected product until steps 2 and 3 have been taken;

2. perform a review to determine if the product is acceptable to distribute;

3. prevent unsafe or otherwise adulterated product from entering commerce; and

4. determine if the newly identified deviation or unforeseen hazard should be incorporated into the HACCP plan.

Again, corrective action records must document each of these steps.

The HACCP regulation for seafood requires a seafood processor either to follow a corrective action plan appropriate for the deviation or to segregate and hold product for evaluation. Written corrective action plans may be included as part of the HACCP plan but they are not required. A corrective action plan appropriate for a deviation describes the steps to be taken to ensure that:

1. No unsafe or otherwise adulterated product enters commerce.

2. The cause of the deviation is corrected.

When a deviation for which no appropriate corrective action plan has been established occurs, the processor must:

1. Segregate and hold the affected product until requirements 2 and 3 have been met.

2. Perform a review to determine if the product is acceptable to distribute.

3. Prevent unsafe or otherwise adulterated product from entering commerce.

4. Take action to correct the cause of the deviation.

5. Have a trained individual determine the need to modify the HACCP plan and modify it as necessary.

As with the meat and poultry regulations, the corrective action records must fully document the actions taken. The required records will be subject to close scrutiny during regulatory investigations. Furthermore, these records are critical to the verification of the HACCP system (see Chapters 14 and 15).

RESPONSIBILITY FOR DECISION MAKING

To ensure the success of the HACCP system, it is crucial to delineate clearly the responsibility for making decisions about taking corrective actions. An individual thoroughly familiar with the CCP, control measure and the product should have the authority to make decisions on the production floor in order to maintain appropriate control of a line operation.

Whenever a deviation occurs and corrective action is taken, that individual also must be responsible for keeping appropriate records. This may include keeping records (on the CCP data sheet) of the corrective action(s) taken and who took them. In addition, records should be kept of other pertinent information regarding any product that was placed on hold due to the deviation.

SUMMARY

Corrective actions are a key element of the HACCP system. Although deviations may occur infrequently, an appropriate corrective action must be initiated when a deviation occurs. The overall objectives of the corrective action(s) are to protect the consumer, by ensuring that no unsafe or adulterated product is distributed into interstate commerce, and to correct the cause of the deviation.

If a HACCP plan is properly designed and implemented, all deviations will be discovered and appropriate corrective actions will be initiated before any product leaves the facility. Thus, record-keeping and record review associated with corrective actions are important elements to the success of the HACCP program.

REFERENCES

Corlett, D.A., Jr. 1998. *HACCP User's Manual.* Chapman & Hall, New York.

NACMCF. 1998. Hazard Analysis and Critical Control Point principles and application guidelines. *J. Food Protect.* 61:762.

NAS. 1985. *An Evaluation of the Role of Microbiological Criteria for Foods and Food Ingredients.* National Academy Press, Washington, D.C.

Tompkin, R. B. 1992. Chapter 8. Corrective action procedures for deviations from the critical control point critical limits. In, Pierson, M. D. and D. A. Corlett, Jr. (eds.). *HACCP Principles and Applications.* Van Nostrand Reinhold, New York.

Chapter 14

VERIFICATION PROCEDURES

K. E. Stevenson and D. E. Gombas

PRINCIPLE 6: Establish Verification Procedures

INTRODUCTION

Verification is defined as those activities, other than monitoring, that determine the validity of the HACCP plan and that the system is operating according to the plan (NACMCF, 1998). It is important to realize that application of this principle includes a wide array of activities in two major areas—validation, and verification of compliance.

VALIDATION

Validation is defined as that element of verification focused on collecting and evaluating scientific and technical information to determine if the HACCP plan, when properly implemented, will effectively control the hazards (NACMCF, 1998). Thus, the primary objective of validation is to make an overall review and evaluation of the HACCP plan to determine if the plan will work. This type of evaluation is conducted after the development of the HACCP plan—the initial validation—and subsequently on a periodic basis—revalidation or reassessment.

Initial Validation

After completion of the hazard analysis and development of the HACCP plan (both of which usually take longer than anticipated), it is important to conduct an "initial validation" of the HACCP plan. This is an attempt to assure that the plan is valid for controlling food safety hazards associated with the ingredients, process and product, and also to verify that the plan can be implemented as written.

The HACCP regulation for meat and poultry products requires that establishments conduct an initial validation designed to determine if the HACCP plan is functioning as intended [9 *CFR* 417.4(a)(1)]. Furthermore, the regulation specifies that the establishment "shall repeatedly test the adequacy of the CCP's, critical limits, monitoring and recordkeeping procedures, and corrective actions set forth in the HACCP plan," and review records generated by the HACCP system.

The initial validation is performed during implementation of the HACCP plan. During the first few weeks or months, the hazard analysis and the HACCP plan are reviewed to determine if they are valid. This includes a review of the hazard analysis by the HACCP team to confirm that all significant hazards were identified, and that the control measures specified are appropriate to control the specific hazards. The HACCP team also should conduct reviews to confirm that the critical control points (CCPs), critical limits (CLs), monitoring activities and other aspects of the HACCP plan are providing adequate control of the hazards. Information needed to validate control of hazards may include (1) expert advice and scientific studies to justify the control parameters selected, and (2) in-plant observations, measurements, and evaluations to verify delivery of the intended process. For example, validation of the cooking process for beef patties could include the scientific justification for the heating times and temperatures used to destroy enteric pathogens in the beef patties, and studies to confirm that the conditions of the cooking step will deliver the required time and temperature to each beef patty. Monitoring, corrective action and CCP verification records are reviewed to determine if the records are being prepared as expected, and to assess whether the records provide evidence that the identified hazards are being controlled. During this initial validation, the HACCP team must revise the HACCP plan accordingly and implement changes as quickly as possible.

Revalidation

It is important to validate HACCP systems again when any changes are made that could affect the hazard analysis or the HACCP plan. These subsequent validations or revalidations are termed "reassessments" in the HACCP regulations for seafood (21 *CFR* 123) and meat and poultry products (9 *CFR* 417). Both of those regulations require reassessment at least annually or whenever any changes occur that could affect the hazard analysis or alter the HACCP plan [21 *CFR* 123.8(c) and 9 *CFR* 417.4(a)(3)]. These may include changes in:

prerequisite programs	suppliers
raw materials	storage conditions
equipment	preparation procedures
employee practices	processing operations
product formulation	product specifications
shelf-life	product storage & distribution
packaging	labeling, etc.

Likewise, a revalidation of the hazard analysis and HACCP plan may be required if new information is available concerning potential deficiencies in the HACCP plan, or other factors that could affect its adequacy. Sources and types of information that may trigger a need for revalidation include:

- New information concerning the safety of the product or an ingredient.
- The product or product category is linked to a foodborne disease outbreak.
- Regulatory agency alerts related to the product or process.
- Process authority recommendations.
- Multiple deviations from a CL.

- Inadequate record-keeping.
- Recalls or product withdrawals.
- Scientific or technical literature articles.
- Test results obtained on products and/or ingredients.
- Consumer complaints.

An overall revalidation or reassessment is performed in a manner similar to that used for the initial validation. The HACCP team usually performs this procedure, but it could be performed in conjunction with an independent individual or team. The product description, flow chart and other information collected in the preliminary tasks are reviewed to determine if they accurately reflect the product, its manufacture and its uses. The team reviews quality audit reports to determine whether any potential hazards have become more or less likely to occur as a result of current performance of prerequisite programs. They also review any new information related to the likelihood or severity of hazards associated with the product/process, and potential control measures. With the aid of this information and the reviews of records and on-site observations, the team reassesses the hazard analysis and the adequacy of the HACCP plan to control the identified hazards.

Examples of questions that may be asked during reassessments include:

- Are there any additional hazards that should be addressed in the HACCP plan?
- Have any changes occurred or is there any new information for the hazard analysis that would indicate that a previously identified hazard does not need to be addressed in the HACCP plan?
- Are the CCPs and control measures being used to control the identified hazards still appropriate for the product/process?
- Are the current CLs still adequate based on the latest available information?
- Are the activities described for monitoring, corrective actions, verification and record-keeping still adequate and appropriate for controlling the identified hazards?

When the reassessment is complete, the HACCP team should issue a report detailing their findings, and this report must be maintained as a HACCP record. If changes in the HACCP plan are warranted, the HACCP plan must be revised and the changes implemented. The regulations for meat and poultry products [9 *CFR* 417.4(a)(3)] and seafood [21 *CFR* 123.8(a)(1)] require that the HACCP plan be modified immediately whenever a reassessment reveals that the plan is no longer adequate to fully meet the requirements of the respective regulation. In addition, it is important that out-of-date versions of the HACCP plan be replaced, and that sufficient training be performed to educate pertinent employees concerning the specific modifications in the HACCP plan and their responsibilities and duties.

While the HACCP regulations require reassessment, those revalidation procedures may be limited in scope if they are evaluating the effects of a single change. For example, if a change were made in the formulation, then only the portions of the hazard analysis and HACCP plan affected by the formulation change would need to be evaluated. In many instances this would be a rather simple, focused procedure. However, with respect to an overall reassessment of the HACCP plan, that type of activity would need to be conducted within one year of the last overall evaluation of the plan.

VERIFICATION

While validation is designed to check the validity or adequacy of the HACCP plan, the on-going verification activities are designed to ensure that the HACCP plan is being implemented properly. Thus, various types of reviews and audits are employed to check the practices used in the establishment (i.e. the HACCP system) to determine if they are consistent with the HACCP plan.

Since verification includes assessing overall compliance with the HACCP plan, it includes a wide range of activities. In broad terms, these compliance checks include:

- Verification of prerequisite programs.
- Verification of CCPs.
- Verification of the HACCP plan.

These verification procedures may be conducted by internal and external sources.

Verification of Prerequisite Programs

HACCP verification procedures for prerequisite programs are fairly simple. For example, from the standpoint of the HACCP plan, verification of premises-related prerequisite programs may simply entail a periodic (e.g., annual) review of written procedures and quality systems audit reports to ensure that the programs are operating in a manner that would not require a change in the current hazard analysis or HACCP plan.

However, in some instances elements of prerequisite programs may be incorporated into the HACCP plan. For example, many monitoring procedures for CCPs entail the use of instruments for detection or measurement, and the calibration of such instruments must be a part of the formal verification procedures for the HACCP plan. Many facilities have a prerequisite or quality assurance program that includes calibration of all detection and measurement instruments, including those used at CCPs. While it is not necessary to perform the calibration activity separately from the establishment-wide program, calibration procedures used in HACCP monitoring or verification should be included

under HACCP verification. Thus, if a temperature recorder is used to monitor the temperature of the product during processing (to determine if it meets the CL), calibration of the temperature recorder should be included as a HACCP verification procedure, even if the facility has a prerequisite program for calibration. Furthermore, the records generated during calibration of instruments used for HACCP monitoring or verification would be considered HACCP records.

Verification of CCPs

Verification of CCPs involves evaluating the day-to-day compliance of the activities at each CCP to determine if they comply with the intent and/or specifics of the HACCP plan. These verification activities are developed by the HACCP team and usually are performed by establishment management or other specially trained personnel. The three primary verification activities for CCPs include:

- Calibration of processing and monitoring instrumentation.
- Review of monitoring records and corrective action records.
- Where possible, an independent check on the adequacy of the CCP to control the identified hazard.

Calibration

Since HACCP plans frequently rely on accurate measurements of parameters (e.g., temperature, pressure, pH, flow rate, water activity, etc.), to ensure that CLs are met, it is important to use properly calibrated instruments or equipment to measure these criteria. These instruments or equipment and their calibration frequencies, along with the individual responsible for calibration, should be described in the HACCP plan.

The obvious goal of the calibration procedures is to ensure that all measurements are accurate. If the procedures show that a measuring device is not within tolerance, then it must be recalibrated or replaced, and all records that reflect measurements taken with that device must be reviewed back to the last acceptable calibration. This review must evaluate whether there were any deviations from CLs and assess the potential impact of any deviations to product safety. Since the frequency of calibration will determine the amount of product potentially affected, this is an important consideration when determining the frequency of calibration for various measuring devices.

Records Review

The review of monitoring records is a key function in implementing the HACCP plan. For mandatory HACCP plans, the regulations require an appropriate review, and the reviewer must sign and date the record [21 *CFR* 123.8(a)(3) and 9 *CFR* 417.4(a)(2)]. While the regulations provide varying requirements concerning the time frame for the review, in most instances monitoring records will be reviewed daily. The purpose of this review is to verify that:

- Records were prepared correctly.
- Monitoring activity and frequency were performed as required in the HACCP plan.
- No monitoring activities were missed.
- All monitoring results were within the CLs, or any Deviation was identified.

Whenever the monitoring record shows there is a deviation, there must be corresponding corrective action records. Again, the HACCP regulations enforced by FDA and USDA/FSIS require different time frames for completion of the record review. The seafood HACCP regulation requires that the CCP monitoring and corrective action records are reviewed within one week of the day the records were made [21 *CFR* 123.8(a)(3)]. The meat and poultry HACCP regulation requires that the CCP monitoring and corrective action records be reviewed prior to shipping product [9 *CFR* 417.5(a)(3)(c)]. The purpose of the review of corrective action records is to verify that:

- There is a corrective action record for every deviation.
- The nature and extent of the deviation was recorded appropriately.
- Affected product was identified and isolated, if necessary.
- Corrective actions were conducted according to the HACCP plan.
- The final disposition of the affected product was appropriate and recorded.
- The individuals (i.e., positions) responsible for the corrective actions are identified.
- All decisions are justified.
- The report was prepared correctly.

Independent Check

In many instances it is not sufficient to ensure that monitoring is performed accurately and reliably. It may be advisable or necessary to perform a periodic observation or measurement in addition to, and independent of the monitoring activities to verify that the identified hazard is being controlled adequately. The methodology and frequency of such testing should be specified in the HACCP plan, and the records associated with these tests will become a part of the HACCP records. For example, cooking might be used to control pathogens in hot dogs. CLs for cooking time and smokehouse temperature could be routinely monitored for each batch. Periodically, measurements (with a properly calibrated thermometer) of the internal temperature of one or more hot dogs could be performed as an independent check on the adequacy of the cooking operation.

Another type of independent check could be to have a second individual perform or observe the monitoring activity. Using another hot dog example, if the HACCP plan called for the smokehouse operator to monitor the cooking step by measuring the internal temperature of one or more hot dogs, then another individual (e.g., Quality Assurance) periodically would check the hot dog temperature with another calibrated thermometer, or just observe the operator performing the monitoring activity. In short, where practical, CCP verification should include an independent check designed to provide a second level of assurance that the CCP is providing adequate control of the hazard and/or that the hazard is being controlled as intended.

As described in Chapter 12, microbiological testing is rarely an appropriate activity for monitoring. However, in some cases, microbiological testing may be a useful tool for CCP verification. For example, if purchasing an ingredient that must be free of pathogens for product safety reasons, conducting an occasional sampling and analysis for the specific pathogen(s) of concern (while holding this lot of ingredients until the testing is concluded) may be appropriate as a verification activity. However, since microbiological sampling and testing for verification has the same limitations as microbiological sampling and testing for monitoring, a preferred method would be to gain confidence in the microbial safety of the ingredient through verification that the vendor is using validated processing methods to eliminate the pathogen.

Verification of the HACCP Plan

In addition to the ongoing verification associated with reviews of CCP records, there must be a periodic verification that the implementation of the HACCP plan complies with the written HACCP plan. These audits involve two major activities, review of the HACCP records as cited above, and an on-site audit, which is normally conducted by trained internal or external auditors.

The review of HACCP records is intended to check compliance with the HACCP plan, not the validity. As such, the record review should include:

- The current HACCP plan.
- Audit reports of prerequisite programs.
- The product/process description and flow diagrams.
- Selected monitoring records.
- Selected CCP verification records, including calibration records.
- Selected corrective action records.
- Previous HACCP audit reports.

The HACCP plan forms the basis for verification. It should list the prerequisite programs considered to be prerequisite for this HACCP plan, and information gathered from the preliminary tasks, (e.g., product/process description, distribution, intended use and consumers, and flow diagram.) There is no need to conduct a full inspection of prerequisite programs. In addition, it is not necessary to determine adequacy since verification of compliance is all that is needed. A review of portions of the quality system audit reports dealing with the pertinent programs may be all that is needed.

Selected CCP monitoring, corrective action and verification records must be reviewed to ensure that the record-keeping, record review and other verification procedures are being performed as stated in the HACCP plan. This type of review of monitoring and corrective action records includes the same activities as a routine record review, and verification of the appropriate reviewer's signature and date of review, the required frequency of review, and any special comments or notations. It is important to check to see if any information or data is missing, and to determine if all deviations were addressed, and if corresponding corrective action records are available. Review of these records should confirm that all deviations from the CL and the respective corrective actions are well documented and all actions were performed as specified. In addition, these reviews of monitoring, corrective action and verification records should check to determine if the records were in compliance with any regulatory requirements (see Chapters 12, 13 and 15).

Review of the previous HACCP audit report(s) may help identify chronic problem areas. Also, items that were deficient during the last audit are obvious areas for scrutiny during the current audit.

The on-site audit should be conducted according to normal (QA-like) audit procedures. The portion dealing with prerequisite programs should be brief, and need only determine if these programs are being conducted as described in the quality audit reports. A key aspect of the on-site audit is to verify the product/process description and the flow diagram.

At a minimum, the auditing procedures at CCPs should include:

- Confirming the nature of the operation at that CCP.
- Confirming the operator's knowledge of that CCP's operation, the CL(s), and the monitoring and record-keeping activities required by the HACCP plan.
- Confirming the operator's knowledge of actions to take if there is a deviation from the CLs.
- Observing the operator performing monitoring activities.
- Observing how a deviation is handled (if one occurs during the audit).
- Examining some of the in-process monitoring records.

At the conclusion of the audit, a HACCP audit report should be written which documents findings during the record reviews and the on-site audit. The primary purpose of the audit report is to determine and document whether or not the facility has been operating according to the HACCP plan.

Verification by Regulatory Agencies

According to the NACMCF (1993), the major role of regulatory agencies is to verify that HACCP plans are effective and being followed. Along those lines, the current HACCP regulations in the United States relegate the responsibility for development and implementation of HACCP plans to industry. The HACCP regulation for meat and poultry products indicates that the agency (USDA/FSIS) will verify the adequacy of the HACCP plans, and such verification may include:

a. Reviewing the HACCP plan.
b. Reviewing the CCP records.
c. Reviewing and determining the adequacy of corrective actions taken when a deviation occurs.
d. Reviewing the critical limits.
e. Reviewing other records pertaining to the HACCP plan or system.
f. Direct observation or measurement at a CCP.
g. Sample collection and analysis to determine the product meets all safety standards.
h. On-site observations and record review.

There are obvious similarities between the verification activities used by industry and those employed by the regulators. Additional information on verification is available in some recent publications (Corlett, 1998; Gombas and Stevenson, 1998; Wallace and Mortimer, 1998).

SUMMARY

Verification is comprised of two primary functions: determining the validity of the HACCP plan to assure that it is adequate, and verifying the HACCP system complies with the HACCP plan. Validation of the HACCP plan is conducted during implementation ("initial validation"), and subsequently on a periodic and/or as needed basis ("revalidations" or "reassessments"). Validation of the HACCP plan includes assessments of the accuracy of the hazard analysis and the adequacy of the HACCP plan to control the identified hazards. Verification activities at CCPs generally include three activities: calibration, record review, and an independent check on the performance of the CCP. Verification of the HACCP system is accomplished by conducting routine and/or periodic record reviews and/or on-site audits, and assessing whether the monitoring, corrective actions and verification activities being performed at CCPs are in compliance with the HACCP plan. Individuals within an establishment, third-party experts or regulatory personnel may conduct these HACCP system verification activities.

REFERENCES

Corlett, D.A., Jr. 1998. *HACCP User's Manual*. Chapman & Hall, New York.

Gombas, D.E. and K. E. Stevenson. 1998. *Verification of HACCP Systems: An Advanced HACCP Workshop Manual.* The Food Processors Institute, Washington, D.C.

Mortimer, S. E. and C. A. Wallace. 1998. *HACCP: A Practical Approach*, 2nd ed. Chapman & Hall, London.

National Advisory Committee on Microbiological Criteria for Foods. 1994. The role of regulatory agencies and industry in HACCP. *Int. J. Food Microbiol.* 21:187–195.

NACMCF. 1993. *The Role of Regulatory Agencies and Industry in HACCP*. USDA/FSIS, Washington, D.C.

NACMCF. 1998. Hazard Analysis and Critical Control Point Principles and Application Guidelines. *J. Food Protect.* 61:762.

Prince, G. 1992. Verification of the HACCP program. In, Pierson, M.D. and D.A. Corlett, Jr. (eds.), *HACCP—Practices and Applications*. Van Nostrand Reinhold, New York.

Chapter 15

RECORD-KEEPING

Lisa M. Weddig and K. E. Stevenson

PRINCIPLE 7: Establish Record-keeping and Documentation Procedures

INTRODUCTION

Records are written evidence through which an act is documented. Record-keeping assures that this written evidence is available for review and is maintained for the required length of time.

Since part of the HACCP plan includes documentation relating to all critical control points (CCPs) identified in a food establishment operation, records are an integral part of a working HACCP system. All measurements at a CCP, and any action on deviations and final disposition of product, are among the records that must be correctly documented and kept on file.

Records are the only references available to trace the production history of a finished product. If questions arise concerning the product, a review of the records may be the only way to determine whether or not the product was prepared and handled in a safe manner in accordance with the establishment's HACCP plan.

The benefits derived from record-keeping and review go beyond food safety. For example, records can be used as a tool or mechanism by which an operator learns of equipment problems or other malfunctions and corrects potential problems before they lead to the violation of a critical limit (CL). Records of this type provide a history of equipment performance, as well as documentation of actions taken to prevent a problem.

Records are reviewed in-house by qualified staff members and also may be reviewed by outside parties, such as HACCP consultants, customers and regulators. The reviews are conducted to verify strict compliance with the HACCP plan. Prompt and careful review of well documented and maintained records is an invaluable tool in indicating potential problems and allowing corrective action to be taken before a public health problem occurs.

REASONS FOR KEEPING RECORDS

The reasons for keeping HACCP records are numerous. A record-keeping program should be viewed as a benefit rather than a burden.

Well-maintained records provide irrefutable evidence that procedures and processes are being followed in accordance with HACCP requirements. Adherence to the specific CLs set for control measures applied at each CCP is the best assurance of product safety. Documenting the results of monitoring procedures provides information for HACCP records that document the safety of products being produced.

During regulatory compliance audits, establishment records will be the single most important source of information for data review. Accurate records provide management with documentation of compliance. These records also facilitate the work of the inspector in determining the establishment's compliance with the HACCP plan.

Since HACCP records focus only on safety-related issues, problem areas can be identified and corrected quickly because these records provide an uncluttered view of product safety issues. It is best to keep all HACCP records separate from quality control records so that only the product safety records are reviewed during HACCP audits. If a product safety problem occurs requiring a recall or market withdrawal, HACCP records assist in identifying the lots of ingredients, packaging materials, and finished product that may be involved.

TYPES OF HACCP RECORDS

Record-keeping includes records that go beyond those that are maintained during the day-to-day operation of the HACCP plan. A well maintained HACCP system also includes records supporting the development of the HACCP plan. The National Advisory Committee on Microbiological Criteria for Foods (NACMCF, 1998) endorses the maintenance of four types of records:

1. Summary of the hazard analysis.
2. The HACCP plan.
3. Support documentation.
4. Daily operational records.

Summary of the Hazard Analysis

As discussed in Chapter 9, the hazard analysis establishes the scientific basis and justification of an establishment's HACCP plan. Establishments are encouraged to document the deliberations of the HACCP team during the hazard analysis process. This documentation will prove to be valuable to the HACCP team during the periodic verification of the HACCP plan. Thorough records will eliminate the need to start anew when reviewing the hazards associated with each product.

A documented hazard analysis also will support an establishment's decision on the hazards that are being controlled in the HACCP plan. A complete hazard analysis will discuss the potential hazards identified by the HACCP team and the hazards subsequently evaluated as being significant enough to warrant control in the HACCP plan. When the hazard analysis is based on sound science, any question regarding the adequacy of the plan may be answered by referring to the written hazard analysis.

The complete hazard analysis also will include justification or discussion of the control measures selected to prevent, eliminate or reduce to an acceptable level the identified food safety hazards. This will prove to be valuable when determining the appropriate CCPs and CLs necessary to control the hazards.

The hazard analysis summary could be maintained in several formats. A record describing the HACCP team's deliberations provides the most complete means of documentation. This document should be supplemented with a brief listing of the identified hazards and control measures. In many instances, the hazard analysis is presented in a table. An example of the table format can be found in Appendix E. Hazard analysis tables that provide a column for recording the justification for the HACCP team's decisions will retain the information needed for the periodic validations of the HACCP plan.

The HACCP Plan

The HACCP plan is a written document that outlines the formal procedures to be followed in accordance with the seven HACCP principles. It outlines the procedures the establishment will follow to ensure the production of safe product. The HACCP plan may be incorporated into a HACCP manual or working document that also would include support documents such as appropriate HACCP test methods, standard operating procedures (SOPs) and sample HACCP records.

In their respective regulations, both the U.S. Food and Drug Administration (FDA) and the Food Safety and Inspection Service (FSIS) of the U.S. Department of Agriculture (USDA) require the development of a HACCP plan for products that contain food safety hazards. The components of the HACCP plan vary slightly, depending on the agency. Table 15-1 lists the required components of the HACCP plans for seafood or meat and poultry products.

While not required by USDA/FSIS or FDA regulations, the NACMCF recommends that HACCP plan records include (in addition to the above):

- A list of the HACCP team and assigned responsibilities.
- A description of the food, its distribution, intended use and consumer.
- A verified flow diagram for the entire manufacturing process with CCPs indicated.
- A HACCP Plan Summary Table [that contains the information listed in Table 15-1].

Table 15-1—Required Components of HACCP Plans

HACCP PLAN COMPONENTS FOR EACH PRODUCT/PROCESS	Meat and Poultry 9 *CFR* 417.2	Seafood 21 *CFR* 123.6
List the food safety hazards which must be controlled	x	x
List the CCPs for controlling food safety hazards	x	x
List the CLs for each CCP	x	x
List the monitoring procedures and frequencies	x	x
List the corrective actions	x	*
Record-keeping system that documents the monitoring of CCPs	x	x
List the verification procedures and frequencies	x	x
Signature of acceptance of HACCP plan	x	x

*Processors of seafood products are not required to list pre-determined corrective action plans; they may use the corrective actions outlined in 21 *CFR* 123.7.

Support Documentation

It is important to develop and document the rationale necessary to support the HACCP plan. The support documentation is an important component of the information necessary to prove that the implemented HACCP plan will ensure the production of safe food. These records are part of the "HACCP Master File." Many establishments find that this information already exists in one form or another. The HACCP team will only need to fill in the missing pieces and data gaps. The written hazard analysis is part of the support documentation. Other components include records associated with establishing CCPs and CLs, monitoring, corrective action and verification procedures, and any prerequisite programs that support the HACCP system. Discussion of these components are discussed below.

Establishment of Critical Control Points

Records associated with establishing CCPs document the identification of specific hazards and the related control measures associated with each CCP. These hazards, biological, chemical and/or physical, could be related to an ingredient, a packaging component or the process (USDA/FSIS, 1997).

A diagram or flow chart of the entire manufacturing process with each CCP identified would be a portion of these records. Since each hazard being controlled by the HACCP plan requires the development of at least one CCP, the HACCP team should properly document the deliberations in determining the appropriate CCP(s) for each hazard. This may include an explanation of why one process step was selected as the CCP versus another step.

Some establishments find it useful to document the use of a CCP decision tree when determining the appropriate location of a CCP. Forms and computer programs have been developed to facilitate this process.

Establishment of Critical Limits

In order to support the CLs established for each CCP, studies may have to be conducted and experimental data collected. The rationale used to support the conclusions of these studies is important and should be included in the supporting documents. If the CLs were established based upon information from the scientific literature, then the pertinent articles should be cited and discussed. CLs based on existing government regulations or guidelines should be supported by citing the appropriate government document. The precision and accuracy of all test methods used in the establishment of CLs must be well documented before making such tests part of the supporting documents for the HACCP program.

Establishment of Monitoring Procedures

Establishment personnel such as line workers or laboratory analysts should have copies of all SOPs or appropriate test methods for which they are responsible. This will enable them to properly execute their individual HACCP assignments. Copies of these documents also should be retained in the HACCP master file. In addition, SOPs will serve as helpful training tools.

There are normal and/or acceptable fluctuations in the data collected from most operations, and these fluctuations will be apparent in the records. It is crucial that the individual responsible for recording the CCP data knows the difference between normal fluctuations and an indication of loss of control at any CCP location. This type of information should be included in SOP documents related to the CCP.

CCPs monitored with continuous procedures will require automated equipment designed to perform the desired task. The HACCP team will need to determine the precision and accuracy of the monitoring device to determine if the device is suitable for monitoring the particular control function being performed.

Establishment of Corrective Action Procedures

The corrective action procedures for deviations must be documented in the HACCP plan. If the corrective action involves alternate procedures, such as extending a process to correct for a low cook temperature, the parameters of the alternate process need to be established and documented. Written SOPs should be developed to guide designated personnel through any necessary corrective action procedures.

Establishment of Verification Procedures

The HACCP plan must contain verification procedures used to validate the HACCP plan and verify that implementation in the establishment complies with the HACCP plan. Support documentation for verification would include the justification of the calibration procedures and any end-product testing used as a verification procedure. Decisions involving the frequencies employed for various validation and verification procedures, including audits, also would be part of the support documentation.

Daily Operational Records

The daily operation of the HACCP plan will require the completion and maintenance of three basic types of records: 1) monitoring, 2) corrective action, and 3) verification. The purpose of these records is to document the data and observations generated during implementation of the HACCP plan. These records provide the tools for managers to ensure that the HACCP plan is functioning as intended to control the safety of the product and also can provide valuable information regarding trends in operations and deviations. Analyzing for trends may lead to modifications or adjustments in the operations that minimize future deviations.

Simple, daily operational records specific only to the HACCP plan are the most effective. Records that document information not related to HACCP may result in a loss of focus on food safety.

Monitoring Records

Monitoring records provide the backbone of the HACCP plan and are designed to document compliance with the plan. The records maintained will vary depending on the method of monitoring–continuous versus discontinuous.

Continuous monitoring methods using automated recording equipment will generate records such as circular charts that document time and temperature or electronic records of the performance of metal detectors. These records may be supplemented with charts, logs, check lists and laboratory analysis sheets for operator notations.

Discontinuous monitoring will require accurate documentation for each lot sampled or each test performed. For ease of documentation, standardized forms or logs should be developed for recording of data. CLs should be printed on each CCP record or data sheet for easy reference by the operator or attendant.

Corrective Action Records

Corrective actions taken when a CL is violated will require documentation. This requires a written record identifying the deviant lots. The records of final disposition and handling of all process or product deviations should contain sufficient detail to determine that the corrective actions taken are appropriate and must include an accurate accounting of all units of food involved. This includes quantities and codes of product released, destroyed, or used as rework. A Hold Summary or Deviation Log could be the master form for these deviations, with supporting documentation kept in a separate file and retained for the same period of time as other HACCP records.

Verification Records

The verification activities designated in the HACCP plan also will need to be documented. Calibration records will assist in confirming that the monitoring equipment is accurate. Any sampling and subsequent testing of product at a CCP will generate a record of the test results. Periodic observations or independent measurements of the monitoring activities can be noted on the monitoring record or on a separate verification record. Verification of the HACCP system will result in a HACCP audit report which documents the on-site audit and record review findings.

RECORD-KEEPING PROCEDURES

Personnel responsible for documenting daily operational HACCP records should never pre-record data in anticipation of the actual data, or postpone making entries and rely on memory. These records may be the establishment's only proof that a CCP was controlled or that appropriate corrective action was taken to assure the safety of the product. Thus, these records must be kept in a timely and accurate fashion.

Any modifications to the existing data should never be erased. If warranted, existing data may be lined out, corrected with the responsible individual's initials alongside the change, and an explanatory note.

To be used effectively, HACCP records should be on standardized forms for the establishment and must be reviewed regularly by a responsible individual for completeness. Deficiencies from standard documentation procedures must be brought to the attention of the individuals responsible for filling out the reports, and these deficiencies must be corrected immediately.

In their respective regulations, both the FDA and USDA/FSIS stipulate specific record-keeping requirements. The seafood HACCP regulation (FDA, 1999) requires that all HACCP records contain the following information:

- Name and location of processor or importer.
- Date and time of the activity reflected on record.
- Signature or initials of person performing operation.
- Product identification (code, name or identity), where appropriate.
- Processing information entered at the time observed.
- Actual observations or data values obtained during monitoring.
- Reviewer's signature and date of review.

The HACCP regulation for meat and poultry products (USDA/FSIS, 1999) mandates that HACCP records contain:

- Date and time of the activity reflected on record.
- Each record entry is date and time recorded and signed/initialed by employee making entry.
- Processing information entered at the time observed.
- Actual observations or data values obtained during monitoring.
- Reviewer's signature and date of review.

In addition to the regulatory requirements, HACCP records should contain the following additional information to assist in effective record-keeping.

- Company name and location of plant/establishment.
- Title of the record.
- CCP criteria such as CLs (monitoring records only).
- Corrective action to be taken and by whom (monitoring records only).

RECORD-KEEPING SYSTEM

Any revisions of the HACCP plan must be reflected immediately in the HACCP manual, thus, document control is important. All charts and forms should have issue numbers so CLs, SOPs, and other instructions are kept current. Outdated sections and forms should be discarded immediately to avoid confusion. A periodic review of departmental HACCP forms and procedures may be necessary to assure continued compliance with the HACCP plan.

When revisions to HACCP documents are made and sent to their respective departments, it is advisable to have routing slips attached so that the individuals responsible for the implementation of those revisions are properly notified. It is bad practice to have outdated HACCP documents on file and in use at a facility purporting to be operating under a comprehensive HACCP system.

Staff personnel should conduct investigative reviews in order to identify weaknesses in the documentation or record-keeping system. Having a well organized system for documentation will show that an establishment is in control of the overall operation as well as the product safety issues. In-house record reviews should be well documented with all deficiencies noted and remedial action(s) clearly outlined. When problems continue to occur in a certain area, there must be a written record of the cause(s) and the solution(s).

HACCP records may be maintained in a computerized format provided that appropriate controls are implemented to ensure the integrity of the data and electronic signatures. Some establishments find that use of computers assists in record-keeping, trend tracking, and tracing the disposition of lots of ingredients and products.

RECORD REVIEW

A designated, responsible individual must review records dealing with establishment operations at CCPs. A thorough review is necessary to ensure that all requirements have been satisfied and are accurately documented. FDA requires that all seafood HACCP records documenting the monitoring of CCPs, corrective actions and verification procedures be reviewed by an individual trained or knowledgeable in the application of HACCP principles. Required meat and poultry HACCP records are to be reviewed preferably by a HACCP-trained individual or the responsible establishment official.

The record reviewer must sign and date all records as they are reviewed. The frequency of record review will vary depending on whether or not the establishment is required by the regulatory agencies to maintain a HACCP plan. USDA/FSIS requires that HACCP records must be reviewed prior to shipping the product, while FDA requires that seafood HACCP records must be reviewed within one week. For non-regulated HACCP plans, establishments may find reviewing records on a daily basis to be the most manageable and effective frequency.

Any anomalies in records or record-keeping must be investigated thoroughly for potential problems or trends. In this regard, record review becomes the last control measure for assuring product safety. When this review reveals or identifies any deficiencies in the record-keeping and normal monitoring procedures, existing procedures must be reviewed and updated. Because maintenance of the HACCP program results in a dynamic system, continual updating and improvements are necessary and warranted.

RETENTION OF RECORDS

The regulatory requirements for retention of records are similar for meat, poultry and seafood products. Both USDA/FSIS and FDA have mandated that HACCP records be held for at least one year for slaughter activities or refrigerated products and for at least 2 years for frozen, preserved or shelf-stable prod-

TABLE 15-2—HACCP Record Requirements Mandated in HACCP Regulations

REQUIRED RECORDS	USDA/FSIS Meat & Poultry	FDA Seafood
Written hazard analysis, including supporting documentation	x	
Flow chart of process and product flow	x	
Documentation of intended use or consumers of product	x	
Written HACCP plan including components listed in TABLE 15-1	x	x
Decision making documents related to development of CCPs, CLs, monitoring and verification procedures	x	
CCP monitoring records	x	x
Monitoring instrument calibration records	x	x
Corrective action records	x	x
Verification records	x	x
Product codes, product name, or identity, or slaughter production lot records	x	
Records relating to adequacy of equipment or processes being used		x

ucts. The shelf life of products and other government regulations need to be taken into account when establishing record retention guidelines for products not covered by a mandatory HACCP requirement.

REGULATORY ACCESS

The question of regulatory access to HACCP records has been answered in the two HACCP regulations promulgated by USDA/FSIS and FDA. HACCP records that are required to be maintained and which the agencies are entitled to review are listed in Table 15-2. These records must be made available to an inspector or investigator upon request. It is anticipated that any future FDA HACCP regulations will contain similar records access requirements.

Records that deal with proprietary non-HACCP information normally would not be made available to the regulatory agencies. Records that clearly relate to product safety are identified already in the HACCP program and may be subject to the scrutiny of regulatory authorities. Having these records well organized makes data retrieval an easy task for both internal and external audits.

Many industry representatives are concerned about public access to HACCP records. Any HACCP record that is copied by a government inspector or investigator has the potential to be released to the public through the Freedom of Information Act (FOIA). To limit public access to establishment HACCP records, some legal counsels have recommended that establishments mark or stamp each page of the HACCP plan and accompanying support documentation as "Trade Secret" and each daily operational record as "Confidential Commercial Information." Establishments also are advised to develop SOPs outlining record access protocols. Sharing copies of HACCP plans and records with customers and entities other than the regulatory agencies may void the confidential nature of the records.

SUMMARY

Record-keeping and documentation provide an establishment with the evidence necessary to verify that product was produced in accordance with the HACCP plan. Management, supervisors and inspectors have a primary role in assuring that all HACCP records are accurate and complete, and that these records reflect the actual operating conditions. Assuring compliance with the written HACCP plan through records and record reviews will assist in ensuring product safety.

REFERENCES

Corlett, D.A., Jr. 1998. *HACCP User's Manual*. Chapman & Hall, New York.

FDA. 1999. Procedures for the safe and sanitary processing and importing of fish and fisheries products. Title 21, *Code of Federal Regulations*, Part 123. U.S. Government Printing Office, Washington, DC (Published annually)

Mortimore, S. A. and C. E. Wallace. 1998. *HACCP: A Practical Approach*, 2nd ed. Chapman & Hall, London, UK.

NACMCF. 1998. Hazard Analysis and Critical Control Point Principles and Application Guidelines. *J. Food Protect.* 61:762.

Stevenson, K. E. and B. J. Humm. 1992. Effective record-keeping system for documenting the HACCP plan. In, Pierson, M. D. and D. A. Corlett, Jr. (eds.), *HACCP—Principles and Applications*. Van Nostrand Reinhold, New York.

USDA/FSIS. 1997. *Guidebook for the Preparation of HACCP Plans*. Washington, DC.

USDA/FSIS. 1999. Hazard analysis and critical control point (HACCP) systems. Title 9, *Code of Federal Regulations*, Parts 416 & 417. U.S. Government Printing Office, Washington, DC (Published annually).

Chapter 16

ORGANIZING AND MANAGING HACCP PROGRAMS

K. E. Stevenson and Dane T. Bernard

INTRODUCTION

The preceding sections of this manual have reviewed and explained the principles and concepts of HACCP and provided detailed information on the development of a HACCP plan. Once an establishment decides to use HACCP as the system for assuring the safety of its products, then the establishment should commit to making the HACCP program an integral part of their operations. Since HACCP represents a structured approach to controlling the safety of food products, the HACCP system must be organized and managed in a manner that will assure that it will be operating correctly and maintained appropriately. This chapter contains information gleaned from industry successes and failures. The suggestions assembled here are offered to help in deciding how to manage the HACCP program. These suggestions can help assure that the foods produced are safe to consume and promote a systematic approach to operational control.

ORGANIZING AND MANAGING A HACCP PROGRAM

The structure for organizing a HACCP program varies considerably from establishment to establishment due to the variety of internal organizations and the differing responsibilities of groups already in existence. HACCP programs are often associated with the Quality Assurance (QA) group, or a similar group that has traditionally been responsible for technical activities including food safety. In recent years, however, an increasing number of food operations have established an office of food safety led by an individual who is solely responsible for food safety. We endorse this approach for a number of reasons. Forming an office of food safety sends a message to employees that the establishment is serious about food safety. In addition, it provides a visible demonstration of management's commitment to the process. Often, the individual leading this office is identified as the HACCP coordinator for the establishment.

Establishing an office or individual primarily responsible for food safety also may help alleviate problems that sometimes exist in an establishment. Relations between QA and Operations are sometimes strained. In such instances, appointing the QA function to be in charge of HACCP may result in unnecessary difficulties in starting a program. Allowing Operations and QA personnel to be involved in decisions can make HACCP successful. Thus, it is important that establishment managers and their representatives are involved in planning HACCP programs with the shared objective of producing safe food. Since Operations personnel are needed to make HACCP work, organizing a HACCP program to be managed through an office of food safety may help avoid potential problems during HACCP implementation.

After developing a HACCP plan, most establishments will find that their current operating practices already control many of the critical control points (CCPs) associated with a product and process. However, it is a mistake to assume that because an establishment is currently taking steps consistent with a HACCP plan, that it is already employing HACCP. When adopting HACCP, establishments should address all seven HACCP principles. Deficiencies in many HACCP programs often occur in two areas: (a) documentation of the HACCP plan and (b) management of the HACCP program. Deficiencies in plan documentation include inadequate "background" information for conducting a hazard analysis, no documented rationale for the CCPs identified, no scientific justification for critical limits (CLs) and no justification for monitoring frequency. Management problems often are related to inadequate verification that the HACCP plan is being applied correctly and followed as written.

Management Commitment

In order for HACCP to succeed within an establishment, there must be a clear commitment to food safety and the HACCP concept. The success of a HACCP program often hinges on management's commitment to installing a HACCP program to assure product safety. In addition, success will depend on detailed planning, providing appropriate resources and empowering employees to assist in producing safe food. Thus, two key steps in initiating work on a HACCP program are a corporate commitment to producing safe foods through use of HACCP, and communication of this goal throughout the establishment. A simple statement presenting the corporate policy with respect to HACCP is one way to communicate management's commitment. Making a public commitment to food safety is an important step in communicating the importance of HACCP to every employee in the organization. To further demonstrate commitment and to help facilitate the HACCP process, management should establish specific objectives and realistic implementation schedules in cooperation with the HACCP team.

Management also must recognize its responsibility to the HACCP system by providing for on-going review and assessment of the HACCP system. A systematic program for auditing the HACCP system is needed to provide for a long-term view of the objectives and functioning of this food safety program. Also, management should provide for regularly scheduled assessments of those programs discussed earlier for prerequisite programs (See Chapter 3) and for verification (See Chapter 14). These assessments may include audits of the following programs:

- Materials control (hold and release, chemical control, etc.).
- Equipment and instrument calibration.
- Hygiene and sanitation, (both facility and personnel).
- Record retention, control and review.
- Training.
- Vendor selection/approval/audits.

HACCP Coordinator and HACCP Team

In facilities where personnel are available to assist in the HACCP process, a HACCP coordinator should be appointed to work with a multidisciplinary team to develop and implement HACCP plans. The responsibility, authority and importance given to the HACCP coordinator and the HACCP team represent another key communications tool that can be used to emphasize the establishment's commitment to HACCP. The HACCP coordinator must be chosen carefully, since this individual will be the "champion" of HACCP within the establishment. The coordinator should possess the technical skills necessary to assist in the development of a science-based plan for managing food safety. The coordinator also will need interpersonal skills to facilitate the work of the HACCP team and to obtain buy-in and adoption of elements of the HACCP plan by various operational units. When identifying the HACCP coordinator, management should consider the duties that this individual may be expected to carry out and the skills necessary to successfully complete them. Other duties of the HACCP coordinator may include the following:

- Identifying key operators to serve as trainers.
- Writing instructions and check lists.
- Reviewing HACCP records.
- Reviewing operating instructions.
- Assuring follow-up on corrective actions.
- Performing internal audits.
- Initiating root-cause-analysis of problems.
- Assuring compliance with prerequisite programs.

The coordinator, in conjunction with management, should select the personnel who will become members of the HACCP team. The HACCP coordinator will also provide the leadership and guidance for development of the establishment's HACCP plan. Management should assure that resources are available for training the HACCP coordinator, the team and other personnel as appropriate.

The make-up of the HACCP team will vary according to the establishment, but, as stated earlier, experience has shown that a representative from facility management (Operations) must play a key role. Since HACCP is a system that depends to a great extent on the involvement of line personnel, it is vital that establishment Operations be represented on the HACCP team. If appropriate, a representative of Operations may be selected to be the HACCP coordinator. The HACCP team should include individuals that understand engineering and equipment performance, establishment sanitation, quality assurance, and food safety. A representative of management is often appointed to the HACCP team to assure that decisions are consistent with established policies and to assure that the team receives proper support.

When developing a HACCP plan, the HACCP team will often find technical areas where information is unclear. In these cases, additional study or assistance from outside consultants/experts may be needed to determine an appropriate course of action. This situation should be brought to the attention of management so that resources are available to obtain appropriate advice when needed.

In many smaller facilities, it is not unusual for an establishment owner to be the manager of Operations and perform other functions as well. In this environment, developing a multidisciplinary HACCP team composed of establishment employees is usually not practical. In this situation, other sources may be required to develop and implement a HACCP program. Developing a HACCP program that will be effective in producing a safe food product requires a certain amount of food safety knowledge and experience. There is no substitute for this essential knowledge base. Thus, smaller establishments may need to use trade associations, consultants, educators, extension agents, or other sources to assist in plan development. In addition, the number of good "generic" HACCP plans for specific products or product groups that can be adapted for specific operations is increasing. However, when using a generic HACCP plan, it must be thoroughly reviewed and adapted to the specific operation. Food safety expertise will be needed to complete this task.

A word of caution. HACCP is a relatively new field and there are many individuals that claim expertise in this discipline. While HACCP sounds simple, experience and food safety expertise are needed to write and implement effective plans. In other words, some of those who proclaim to be HACCP experts may not have the necessary background to perform this task well.

A Strategy for Developing a HACCP Plan

Once assignments to the HACCP team have been made, there is a tendency to become overwhelmed by the complexity of the operations and the amount of information and documentation that is needed to develop a HACCP plan. Like other complex jobs, careful planning, forming ad hoc groups to address specific jobs, and assigning small tasks will keep the job from becoming overwhelming.

In practice, the format of HACCP plans varies according to the needs of the particular process/product or of the industry segment being addressed. In the processing sector, plans are often product and process specific, although it is common to find a group of products covered by the same HACCP plan. Grouping products is only possible however when the hazards identified are the same for all products and the controls applied are also identical. For example, an establishment may make a particular sausage in five flavors, and the formulations and preparation procedures may be identical except for the flavoring ingredients. If the flavorings present no unique hazards, then the same HACCP plan may be used for all five products.

Some HACCP plans, however, may be based on a unit operations approach. While this is not the usual approach in the manufacturing sector, the trend for HACCP plans in the retail and foodservice sectors appears to focus on an operations approach. The operations approach focuses on unit operations that are common to a number of products (e.g., cooking) and establishes controls, CLs, monitoring practices, etc. that are applicable to a number of menu items.

Generic HACCP plans can serve as useful guides in the development of HACCP plans; however, it is essential that the unique conditions within each facility be considered during the development of all components of the HACCP plan. In the development of a HACCP plan, the five preliminary tasks need to be accomplished before the application of the HACCP principles. (See Chapter 8.)

Possibly the best approach to developing a HACCP program is to begin by working on a HACCP plan for one specific product and process or for a specific unit operation. The HACCP team should gather appropriate information and gain knowledge of the specified product(s), and then apply the HACCP principles in a stepwise manner. This approach also involves all of the preliminary tasks associated with describing the food, its intended use and distribution, and developing and verifying a flow diagram that describes the process.

Once developed, this HACCP plan can serve as the model for the development of additional HACCP plans for other products. The experience gained and the procedures used to develop this first HACCP plan will facilitate the development of additional plans for other products and/or product groups. As noted above, a single HACCP plan may be used for a group of very similar products, provided that the HACCP team assures that this plan is appropriate for each of the products and their processes. (Note: The process of developing HACCP plans for additional products and processes can be expedited by the formation of specific product/process teams to assist in their preparation. These ad hoc teams would have the responsibility of working with the HACCP team to develop plans involving specific products or processes.)

Implementing A HACCP Plan

Before implementation begins, appropriate training should be provided to all levels within the establishment. Training should focus on the knowledge and skills needed to carry out individual duties under the HACCP plan. Everyone in a facility does not need to become a HACCP expert, but they should know their duties within a facility operating under HACCP. It is especially important that they know why those duties are important for food safety purposes. Education and training should include a general overview of HACCP so that all employees understand the general concept and objectives, as well as specific training associated with individual jobs and tasks.

HACCP programs are no different than other management programs; unforeseen problems will be encountered during implementation. Thus, a trial period should be used to allow employees to become familiar with the HACCP plan and to attempt to discover any deficiencies, weaknesses or significant problems. During the trial period, the HACCP plan may undergo relatively constant review, evaluation, and revision. However, a formal review should be scheduled to specifically evaluate the current system and to recommend revisions, if appropriate. Food establishments that are facing mandatory requirements to develop and implement HACCP plans to fulfill government requirements should allow sufficient time for a proper implementation period.

During the initial phase of HACCP implementation, one of the more common errors is not conducting appropriate analysis and review of progress. In some cases, it may take months to develop a good HACCP plan. Implementation also should be expected to take a few months before operating according to the HACCP plan becomes routine. Management must realize that HACCP systems are complicated, and they should budget time accordingly. During the implementation period, the HACCP team should meet on a regular basis to check on progress. The team must be ready to assist in solving the problems that will arise during this period. As the frequency of problems diminishes, the team may meet less frequently, but regular meetings on a permanent basis are essential to long-term success.

MANAGING A HACCP PROGRAM

HACCP programs do not operate automatically. In order to succeed, HACCP programs need appropriate support and management systems. Some suggestions related to management of HACCP systems are included in the remainder of this chapter.

Coordination of Food Safety Operations

One person should have overall responsibility for the food safety system (HACCP and supporting programs) within an establishment. This responsibility extends to input, review, and approval of the documentation of the HACCP system. This individual also should be able to assure that the HACCP team has access to the variety of information that they will require when conducting their assignments.

Regardless of whether the establishment is large or small, every individual assigned to a HACCP-related task should receive appropriate written standard operating procedures (SOPs) and descriptions of their responsibilities and tasks. It is important to clarify the reporting structures and the relationships of the various groups involved. Since food safety issues are preeminent, HACCP issues must take precedence over quality and production issues.

Systems for Evaluating New Products

Once HACCP plans have been developed for all of the products being produced in an organization, there must be a structure established for evaluating new products and processes. In most instances, individuals working in product/process development areas do not have extensive training in food safety. Thus, it is imperative that a system be established to facilitate the evaluation of new products and processes with respect to food safety. It is beneficial to use a system for evaluating the safety of all new products and processes prior to scale-up and commercialization. First, this system can provide an early indication of any food safety-related problems, thereby saving time and money. Second, once such a system is in place; product development employees will be more cognizant of food safety considerations when they are designing new products and processes.

Other safeguards can be implemented as part of the overall management of the HACCP system. When an establishment is currently operating with HACCP plans in place, production of a new product should not begin until a HACCP plan has been developed for the new product/process. When operating within a government-mandated HACCP program, it may be a violation of regulations to produce product without having a formal HACCP plan that is specific for that process and product.

Systems for Evaluating Product/ Process Changes

An essential element of a HACCP system is that any proposed change related to a product or process is evaluated by the HACCP team for impact on safety of the food being produced. The decision concerning whether or not a change in the product/process is significant with respect to food safety should be made by the HACCP team or another group specifically appointed for that task. A mandatory evaluation process guarantees that a systematic evaluation will be made of any changes in the process or product. This will assure that any changes or revisions that might affect food safety will be thoroughly investigated prior to their implementation. A policy should also be in effect that prohibits changes from being made without such an evaluation.

Day-to-Day Management

Routine management of the HACCP plan is facilitated by the requirements associated with monitoring, corrective actions, verification, and the daily review of records associated with CCPs. Designing relevant assignments and records streamlines this task. Furthermore, documentation of reporting responsibilities also clarifies actions to be taken and helps assure that the correct individuals are notified immediately when a problem has been discovered.

One of the more visible benefits of a HACCP system is the fact that management can now receive daily reports related to food safety. In addition, this type of activity can frequently spot trends that may trigger adjustments to a process or operation before a food safety problem occurs.

Periodic Evaluation and Revision

Verification procedures assure that the HACCP system will be evaluated and revised on a periodic basis.

In some cases, a problem may occur that is not recognized on a day-to-day basis, due to carelessness, inadequate oversight/review and/or because of a failure to comprehend a potential problem. Therefore, regularly scheduled evaluations are invaluable in evaluating the HACCP system. In addition to evaluating long-term trends, these evaluations also are used to determine if any changes need to be made in the HACCP plan, SOPs, corrective action procedures or documentation forms or practices. An internal audit team should conduct this activity. In addition, many establishments have found it valuable to have an audit conducted by external experts who serve as an independent authority. A written report of the findings and recommendations of this verification procedure should be analyzed by the HACCP team. Then, the HACCP team should send the report, their specific responses to each observation, and their recommendations to management. These reports should become a part of the documentation in the HACCP master file.

SUMMARY

The HACCP concept is intended to provide a systematic, structured approach to assuring the safety of food products. The strength of a HACCP program is in providing a system that an establishment can use effectively to organize and manage the safety of the products produced. Successful implementation of the system depends on management commitment to the process, management commitment to provide the resources needed to provide appropriate education and training, and an ongoing commitment to evaluation and improvement of the HACCP plan and HACCP system.

REFERENCES

Corlett, D.A., Jr. 1998. *HACCP User's Manual.* Chapman & Hall, New York.
Mortimore, S. and C. Wallace. 1994. *HACCP: A Practical Approach.* Chapman & Hall, London, UK.
NACMCF. 1998. Hazard Analysis and Critical Control Point Principles and Application Guidelines. *J. Food Protect.* 61:762.

Chapter 17

HACCP AND THE REGULATORY AGENCIES

Lloyd R. Hontz and Virginia N. Scott

FEDERAL FOOD INSPECTION OVERVIEW

Until the end of 1997, the use of HACCP within the food industry was entirely voluntary. Since then, however, the U.S. food regulatory agencies have begun to mandate the application of HACCP for individual segments of the food industry. Seafood and meat and poultry were the first two food industry segments required to implement HACCP. Additional industry segments, such as juice and certain egg products, have been identified as candidates for mandatory HACCP. HACCP continues to grow in global importance as the basis for assuring the safety of food products in international trade.

Currently, there are two primary U.S. Federal agencies with food safety missions. They are the U.S. Department of Agriculture's Food Safety and Inspection Service (FSIS) and the Food and Drug Administration (FDA) of the U.S. Department of Health and Human Services.

USDA/FSIS Inspection of Meat and Poultry and Egg Products

As mandated by the Federal Meat Inspection Act, the Poultry Products Inspection Act and the Egg Products Inspection Act, USDA has jurisdiction over the production of the country's meat- or poultry-containing food products, as well as certain egg products. This jurisdiction encompasses continuous in-plant inspection of animal slaughter, as well as at least daily inspection of "further processing" operations. In general, USDA/FSIS has oversight authority for virtually all food products containing more than 2–3 percent meat or poultry. Since its reorganization in 1996, USDA/FSIS also conducts continuous inspection of egg processing establishments that manufacture liquid, frozen and dried egg products.

FDA Regulatory Jurisdiction Over Food Products

FDA has responsibility for all foods other than meat, poultry, and those egg products described above. This includes fruits, vegetables, seafood and shell eggs. FDA conducts periodic inspections at food processing establishments. Under the Federal Food, Drug and Cosmetic Act, FDA's mandate includes virtually all food products moving in interstate commerce, other than those inspected by USDA/FSIS.

Both USDA/FSIS and FDA conduct examinations of warehouses and points of entry of imported foods under

117

their respective jurisdictions. Responsibility for foods at retail and in restaurants and institutions is generally left to state and local governments. This is a simplistic view of the system, as there are several federal agencies that have some sort of responsibility for the regulation of food.

Pasteurized Milk Ordinance

Producers of milk and milk products also must comply with state regulations which are typically based on a model ordinance known as the Grade A Pasteurized Milk Ordinance (PMO). While this document is based on a HACCP-like approach to controlling certain hazards, it is very prescriptive in nature. Future revisions to the PMO are likely to contain additional HACCP-based provisions.

APPLICATION OF HACCP PRINCIPLES BY REGULATORY AGENCIES

Recent initiatives by both FDA and USDA/FSIS have shifted the focus of regulatory oversight to HACCP-based inspection systems. Both agencies nominally have based their initiatives on application of the National Advisory Committee on Microbiological Criteria for Food's publication "Hazard Analysis and Critical Control Point Principles and Application Guidelines" (NACMCF, 1998; see chapter 2). Table 17-1 briefly outlines the differences between the HACCP regulations for meat and poultry in comparison to those for seafood. Appendix D presents a more detailed side-by-side comparison of the requirements of the FDA seafood HACCP rule and USDA/FSIS meat and poultry HACCP rule.

USDA/FSIS MEGA-REG for Meat and Poultry

The Pathogen Reduction: Hazard Analysis and Critical Control Point Systems final rule (USDA/FSIS, 1996) covers not only slaughter establishments, but also "further processing" establishments—any establishment that has a USDA establishment number is covered. (Pertinent requirements of this rule are contained in Appendix B.) The meat and poultry HACCP rule was expected to create a new regulatory paradigm in which industry would be held accountable for food safety and USDA/FSIS would concentrate its oversight on the greatest food safety risks. This would replace the old USDA/FSIS inspection model in which establishments often looked to inspectors to dictate day-to-day food safety and sanitation requirements and the agency imposed "command and control" regulations on industry.

This massive rule, commonly referred to as the "Mega-Reg", included a variety of near term requirements for pathogen reduction in addition to the HACCP mandate for all meat and poultry operations. On January 27, 1997, all meat and poultry establishments were required to implement Sanitation Standard Operating Procedures (SSOPs) as required in 9 *CFR* 416, and slaughter establishments had to begin testing for generic *E. coli*.

The rule called for a 3-step phase-in of HACCP depending on the size of the establishment. In the early weeks of the implementation process many problems were encountered. These problems included the role of prerequisite programs in HACCP, concerns over a perceived lack of science in the agency's approach to HACCP, and major concerns about the lack of "due process" prior to Agency suspension of inspection based upon violations of the HACCP regulation. Several months of weekly meetings between industry representatives and key Agency officials were instrumental in resolving issues as they arose. Among other things, a letter from the USDA/FSIS Administrator clearly instructed inspection personnel that it was not their prerogative to dictate the content of establishment HACCP plans. A USDA/FSIS Notice was issued that requires notification of establishments of intended enforcement action related to HACCP system inadequacy determinations. Establishment of a HACCP Hotline at the USDA/FSIS Technical Service Center has provided the industry and Agency field staff with a single source for answers to implementation questions.

USDA/FSIS conducted an audit of the large establishment HACCP implementation process and made significant mid-course corrections in preparation for the second phase of implementation. Among other adjustments, inspector training began and concluded earlier in the process, allowing a period of time during which establishments and their inspectors worked out problems prior to the actual implementation date.

FDA Seafood HACCP Regulation

FDA published a final rule, "Procedures for the Safe and Sanitary Processing and Importing of Fish and Fishery Products," (FDA, 1995) mandating that each processor or importer of seafood products develop and implement HACCP plans to help assure the safety of its products (See Appendix C). The regulation also includes provisions for importers of seafood products to implement written verification procedures to ensure imported products meet the HACCP regulation as well. The regulation applies to any food product in which fish is a characterizing ingredient—a crab dip would be covered, but Worcestershire sauce, which contains anchovies, would not.

FDA Plans for HACCP for other Industry Segments

In 1994, FDA published an Advance Notice of Proposed Rulemaking (ANPR) on "Development of Haz-

Table 17-1—Differences between USDA/FSIS and FDA HACCP Regulations
(HACCP Portion Only)

USDA/FSIS Mega-Reg	FDA Seafood HACCP
Requires development of flow chart.	Flow chart not required.
Requires description of intended use of product.	No requirement for intended use of product.
HACCP plans for thermally processed/commercially sterile products do not have to address food safety hazards associated with microbiological contamination if produced in accordance with 9 *CFR* part 318, subpart G or part 381, subpart X (Canning Regs).	HACCP plans for thermally processed, commercially sterile products do not have to address food safety hazards associated with *Clostridium botulinum* toxin if produced in accordance with 21 *CFR* part 113 or 114 (Canning Regs).
Critical limits must meet targets or performance standards set up by USDA/FSIS.	No such requirement.
Plan signed and dated by responsible establishment individual who is person with overall authority on-site or a higher level official.	Plan signed and dated by most responsible individual on-site or by higher level official.
Requires written pre-planned corrective actions and assigned responsibilities.	Not required to have pre-planned corrective actions, but do have the option to develop pre-planned corrective actions.
Initial validation of plan required.	Review of consumer complaints as part of verification procedure.
Review monitoring records prior to shipping product.	Review monitoring and corrective action records within one week of processing.
	Shall take corrective actions when verification reveals need.
Written hazard analysis required along with decision-making documents for critical control point development and critical limits.	
Records may be retained off-site after 6 months if they can be returned within 24 hours.	Records may be retained off-site only if processing on a vessel or a seasonal or remote facility.
Record review can be performed by someone other than HACCP trained individual.	HACCP trained individual to perform the record review.
	HACCP training may be established through work experience.
	Defines requirements for imported products.
Defines an inadequate HACCP System.	
Defines Agency's verification steps.	
Implementation dates: 1/26/98—large establishments; 1/25/99—smaller establishments; 1/25/00—very small establishments	Implementation date: 12/18/97—all establishments

ard Analysis Critical Control Points for the Food Industry: Request for Comments'' (FDA, 1994a). This notice posed over one hundred rhetorical questions and requested comments on whether and how the agency should develop regulations to establish requirements for a new and comprehensive food safety assurance program to include products other than seafood.

FDA described the rationale for a HACCP approach in lieu of end-product testing and comprehensive GMPs for industry segments, and indicated that establishing HACCP throughout the industry could enable both the industry and FDA to carry out their responsibilities more efficiently and effectively. They requested comments on the scope of a HACCP regulation (all segments of the industry or only certain ones); the focus of HACCP (safety only or should quality issues be addressed as well); implementation of HACCP (time for implementation and costs); evaluation of the system (how to measure effectiveness; alternative approaches); roles for FDA, the States, and the food industry; international harmonization; potential costs and benefits; and potential environmental effects.

Pilot HACCP Program

FDA also published a notice inviting industry to participate in a voluntary HACCP pilot program (FDA,

1994b). The pilot program was intended to provide information that FDA could use in deciding whether to mandate HACCP for manufacturers, and, if so, information on developing and implementing such a system.

Establishments manufacturing products as diverse as hard cheese, salad dressing, pan breads, flour, frozen dough, quiche, breakfast cereal, and shelf stable juices have participated in this program, with several establishments having completed their efforts. The project is ongoing and FDA welcomes additional establishments to participate.

Two reports were issued by FDA regarding interim findings of the pilot program (FDA, 1996 and 1997). Both FDA and industry participants have found the HACCP pilot to be a positive experience. FDA had confidence that participants were taking appropriate corrective actions when deviations occurred, thus preventing release of potentially hazardous product and that HACCP provided a more effective use of regulatory resources. The number of critical control points (CCPs) in HACCP plans typically decreased over the course of the pilot (one establishment went from 80 CCPs to 2). Industry participants felt that management and line employees gained a better understanding of the hazards unique to the establishment's products and processes. While most benefits to industry are intangible (e.g., more efficient and effective operation, higher level of confidence in food safety, and greater customer satisfaction), most participating establishments plan to expand their use of HACCP to other product lines and establishments, and to require that their suppliers implement HACCP.

Juice HACCP

In the wake of highly publicized death and illness attributed to unpasteurized juice products, FDA published two proposed rules: "Hazard Analysis and Critical Control Point (HACCP); Procedures for the Safe and Sanitary Processing and Importing of Juice" and "Food Labeling: Warning and Notice Statements; Labeling of Juice Products" (FDA, 1998a and 1998b). The first proposed rule would mandate, along the lines of the seafood HACCP rule, the application of sanitation standard operating procedures (SSOPs) and HACCP principles to the processing of fruit and vegetable juices and juice products.

The juice HACCP proposal sets forth a specific requirement for use of a validated technology or practice to achieve a minimum 5-log reduction of the most resistant microorganism of public health significance likely to occur in juice products. This proposal does not apply to juice products already subject to the FDA acidified or low-acid canned foods regulations.

In the interim period before implementation of a final HACCP regulation, FDA mandated that juices not processed to achieve a 5-log reduction must bear a warning label on the product information panel or the principal display panel (or for the first year, at the point of purchase). The warning would note that the product has not been pasteurized and, therefore, may contain harmful bacteria that can cause serious illness. This final rule on juice labeling became effective on September 8, 1998 for apple juice and cider, and on November 8 for all other juices (FDA, 1998c).

Fresh Produce

A number of outbreaks, including one from *Cyclospora* in raspberries in 1996 and another in 1997, began to focus attention on the increase in foodborne disease associated with consumption of fresh produce. To date, the consensus of industry and government is that HACCP seems inappropriate for application to this industry segment. Rather, a more useful approach currently would involve the development and application of Good Agricultural Practices (GAPs) and Good Manufacturing Practices (GMPs).

FDA announced the availability of a guide for growers, packers and shippers of fresh fruits and vegetables, which provides information on agricultural and management practices they may apply in order to enhance the safety of their fresh produce (FDA, 1998d). The document, titled "Guidance for Industry: Guide to Minimize Microbial Food Safety Hazards for Fresh Fruits and Vegetables," was prepared in consultation with the USDA. The guide is intended for use by both domestic producers of raw agricultural products and foreign producers who would export such products to the United States.

The document addresses various categories of production practices such as control of water, manure and biosolids, worker health and hygiene, field and facility sanitation, and transportation. The guidance also includes suggestions on how to maintain records to aid in tracing food items back to the source to help identify and eliminate the pathway of a pathogen associated with a foodborne illness outbreak.

Eggs

Eggs contaminated with *Salmonella enterica* serotype Enteritidis (SE) are associated with a significant number of human illnesses in the U.S. USDA/FSIS and FDA share regulatory responsibility for eggs; the regulation of shell eggs is primarily the responsibility of FDA, and egg products are the responsibility of USDA/FSIS. For several years USDA/FSIS has been indicating that a proposal to mandate HACCP for egg products was "imminent," however at this point it is not clear when a proposal will be issued. USDA/FSIS must deal with the problems of meat and poultry HACCP implementation, as well as the need for major regulatory reform to make current regulations compatible with HACCP.

Retail

The retail sector provides some very unique challenges in the application of HACCP, since retail businesses can range from restaurants and grocery stores to camps and day-care centers to mobile food carts and roadside stands. Many of these businesses lack a corporate support structure; have little capital to work with; have employees with a broad range of educational levels and communication skills; have a high employee turnover rate; and have a large number of products and processes that may change frequently.

FDA recently released a document "Managing Food Safety: A HACCP Principles Guide for Operators of Food Establishments at the Retail Level" (FDA, 1998e). The guide is intended to assist the retail industry in the voluntary implementation of HACCP principles, and it emphasizes that the Food Code is a fundamental program prerequisite to implementing HACCP (Food Code, 1999). The Food Code is an FDA-developed model code that provides a HACCP-based prescriptive approach to food safety at retail. It is neither federal law nor regulation. The Food Code may be adopted in whole or in part by state and local governments, or may simply be used as guidance on what is scientifically appropriate and necessary for food safety at retail. Under the Food Code, the only instance in which a HACCP plan is required is when an establishment packages food using a reduced-oxygen packaging method.

INTERNATIONAL TRADE— HACCP AND CODEX ALIMENTARIUS

The Codex Alimentarius Commission's Committee on Food Hygiene has played an active role in formulation, refinement, and encouragement of HACCP as a consensus international mechanism for assuring the production of safe food products. The document, "General HACCP Definitions and Procedures for Use by Codex," was introduced at the 25th session (Oct–Nov, 1991) of the Codex Committee on Food Hygiene. The committee agreed that HACCP should be incorporated into Codex Codes of Practice and the General Principles. In 1997, the Codex HACCP guidelines, "Hazard Analysis and Critical Control Point (HACCP) System and Guidelines for its Application," were adopted by the Codex Commission as an Annex to the General Principles for Food Hygiene (Codex, 1997). (Appendix A contains a reprint of this Codex HACCP document.) Codex involvement brings even greater potential for international harmonization and understanding of the HACCP principles. The process of incorporating HACCP into specific codes of practice is underway, with much initial effort associated with codes for products falling within the terms of reference of the Codex Committee on Fish and Fishery Products.

Other International bodies, including the Food and Agriculture Organization of the United Nations (FAO) and the World Health Organization (WHO), have continued to sponsor international consultations on the topic of HACCP and its key elements. The purpose of these consultations is to further the international understanding of HACCP and to help develop training materials and expertise that can be made available to all nations, including developing countries.

FUTURE USES OF HACCP

The precise manner in which HACCP will be applied to additional segments of the food industry is not yet clear. What is clear, however, is that many establishments are voluntarily implementing HACCP programs on their own initiative. In fact, many establishments are requiring their suppliers and co-packers to develop and implement HACCP plans as a requisite for doing business. The extent of this is a clear indication of the benefits that establishments perceive from the use of the best system available today for assuring the safety of their products.

SUMMARY

This chapter provides only a snapshot of the current regulatory environment for HACCP. The evolving U.S. approach to HACCP seems to be, "if there is a food safety problem, apply HACCP." But it should be recognized that HACCP is not a silver bullet, it will not solve all food safety problems, and it must rest on a solid foundation of prerequisite programs including training, glass control programs, allergen control programs, etc. HACCP is an industry program, and HACCP plans should be establishment, product and line specific. The appropriate role for regulators is to verify that industry has developed and implemented appropriate plans; their role is neither to dictate plan content, nor to specify CCPs and critical limits. While the process has experienced some problems, a cooperative effort between the industry and the Agencies should allow for successful implementation. It is likely that the U.S. approach to food safety will be undergoing some fundamental changes in the future. However, HACCP likely will remain as the risk management strategy of choice for much of the food industry.

REFERENCES

Codex. 1997. Hazard Analysis and Critical Control Point (HACCP) System and Guidelines for its Application. Alinorm 97/13A. Codex Alimentarius Committee on Food Hygiene, Rome.

FDA. 1994a. Development of Hazard Analysis Critical Control Points for the food industry; request for comments. *Federal Register* 59 (149): 39888. (August 4)

FDA. 1994b. Hazard Analysis Critical Control Point systems; Invitation to participate in a voluntary HACCP pilot program for the food manufacturing industry. *Federal Register* 59 (149): 39771. (August 4)

FDA. 1995. Procedures for the safe and sanitary processing and importing of fish and fishery products; final rule. *Federal Register* 60 (242): 63096. (December 18)

FDA. 1996. *HACCP Pilot Program: Interim Report of Observations and Comments.* Food and Drug Administration, Washington, D.C.

FDA. 1997. *HACCP Pilot Program: Second Interim Report of Observations and Comments.* Food and Drug Administration, Washington, D.C.

FDA. 1998a. Hazard Analysis and Critical Control Point (HACCP); Procedures for the safe and sanitary processing and importing of juice. *Federal Register* 63 (79): 20450. (April 24)

FDA. 1998b. Food labeling: Warning and notice statements; Labeling of juice products. Federal Register 63 (79): 20486. (April 24)

FDA. 1998c. Food labeling: Warning and notice statements; Labeling of juice products; final rule. *Federal Register* 63 (130): 37029. (July 8)

FDA. 1998d. *Guidance for Industry-Guide to Minimize Microbial Food Safety Hazards for Fresh Fruits and Vegetables.* Food and Drug Administration. Washington, DC.

FDA. 1998e. *Managing Food Safety: A HACCP Principles Guide for Operators of Food Establishments at the Retail Level.* Food and Drug Administration, Washington D.C. (The document is available on the following FDA website: *http://vm.cfsan.fda.gov/~dms/hret-toc.html*)

NACMCF. 1998. Hazard analysis and critical control point principles and application guidelines. *J. Food Protect.* 61:1246.

USDA/FSIS. 1996. Pathogen reduction; Hazard Analysis and Critical Control Point (HACCP) system; final rule. *Federal Register* 61 (144): 38806. (July 25)

USDA/FSIS. 1999. Hazard analysis and critical control point (HACCP) systems. Title 9, *Code of Federal Regulations*, Parts 416 & 417. U.S. Government Printing Office, Washington, D.C. (Published annually)

Chapter 18

HACCP TRAINING

By Jon-Mikel Woody, Robert B. Gravani, and
Dane T. Bernard

INTRODUCTION

The success of the HACCP system within a food processing establishment depends on everyone who works in the facility. Every person in the establishment needs to be properly informed about his or her role within the HACCP system. Employees must first understand what HACCP is, learn the skills necessary to make it function properly, and then be aware of what is expected of them and their roles within the HACCP system.

As discussed in Chapter 16 on organizing and managing HACCP programs, management must be committed to providing adequate time and resources to thoroughly educate and train supervisors, plant workers and technical personnel about their role within the HACCP system. It is important to view this management commitment as an on-going process. Even after an initial period of HACCP training, additional training needs may be identified once the implementation phase begins. For example, there may be a line employee who is not on the HACCP team, but has been given responsibility for monitoring a CCP, performing any necessary corrective actions and record-keeping procedures. This employee will need training to understand

not only what his or her responsibilities are, but also why these responsibilities are important. Therefore, management should commit time and necessary resources before any formal HACCP training is conducted. This commitment must be maintained through plan development, implementation, and reassessment of the HACCP plan if the program is to be successful.

ADULT LEARNING

While developing a HACCP education and training program, it is important to understand how adults learn and to incorporate these learning styles into the training program. Compared to children, adults possess a number of distinct traits that can influence the way in which they learn:

- Adults are more goal oriented.
- Adults need to know why they are learning something.
- Adults tend to be more practical and problem-solvers.
- Adults have accumulated life experiences.

These unique characteristics should be taken into consideration in order to design effective training programs that meet the needs of adult learners.

It is very difficult to hold audience attention by lecturing alone. Most adults can listen at a rate of about 500 words per minute, while the average speaker talks at a rate of about 125 words per minute. This 375 word per minute difference leaves the audience with 75% of their "mental time" free to either absorb the message or to pursue other activities. A speaker must motivate and involve the audience or they will use this "free time" to daydream and forget what is being said. Programs that involve case studies, group exercises, and other hands-on activities are most useful for reaching adult learners. The instructor's role is to draw from the participant's experiences, facilitate discussions, and keep the participants "on-track", rather than to lecture. The method of instruction used also influences the retention rate of the participants as illustrated in Table 18-1. It is imperative that instructional methods be used that inform the audience and involve them through actually participating in the training program.

PREPARING THE PROGRAM

It takes considerable time and effort to prepare an effective HACCP training program. When designing the program, consideration should be given to who your audience will be (e.g., executives, QA managers, plant personnel, etc.) and their expected level of knowledge regarding the subject matter. Whenever possible, it is a good idea to send out a pre-program survey to the participants in order to more effectively gauge their knowledge of HACCP. The survey should include questions on the participant's job responsibilities, the types of products their company produces (if not already known), and how the participant would rate his or her own knowledge of HACCP. This information can then be used to more effectively tailor the program to the participant's needs.

Audiovisuals

As mentioned earlier, adults learn more effectively through visual images rather than words alone, so audiovisuals should be incorporated into the training activities to keep participant's interest. The audiovisuals may take on a variety of forms, from overhead transparencies and slides, to videotape programs and teleconferencing.

Videotape training programs have become popular to use in educational settings and are available to meet most training needs. Videotapes should be reviewed in advance to be sure the content and message are appropriate for the educational situation and the groups' needs. Probably the worst way to use a videotape in an educational program is to play a long tape from start to finish with little or no audience interaction. An instructor should regularly interrupt a videotape of any appreciable length to emphasize important points just shown, or to conduct a short learning activity with the audience that reinforces the material presented in the tape. This avoids mesmerization and inattentiveness caused by passive "TV watching."

PREPARING THE SETTING

One of the most important aspects of a training program is to plan the physical environment where the program will take place. Is the training room large enough? Are there enough tables and comfortable chairs? Is there a workable public address system? Is all necessary audiovisual equipment present and in working order? Are temperature and ventilation comfortable? Are there outside distractions (e.g., plant noise, paging systems) which need to be taken into consideration? Are there restrooms and telephones nearby? Careful planning prior to the day of the training can alleviate much of the stress associated with conducting such a program. Instructors should arrive early to the training room to allow time to make any last minute changes/room modifications/equipment checks, etc. that may be needed. It is a good idea to prepare a checklist to assist in planning a training program. A sample checklist can be found in Appendix 18-A.

PREPARING THE AUDIENCE

The beginning of a training program is perhaps the most critical part of the session. The instructor must take time to set the climate of the program. Plan to spend an adequate amount of time (10-15 minutes) briefly discussing the day's schedule, general "housekeeping" details, handouts and other course materials, and anticipate common questions that people usually have, including:

- What topics are going to be covered?
- When are the breaks scheduled?
- What time is lunch and where will it be served?
- Where are the telephones? Restrooms? Smoking areas?
- When will the program be finished?

Participants will naturally come into the program with these questions in mind and the instructor should address these concerns early to put the audience at ease. After the climate of the program has been established, explain the goals and objectives of the program and the purpose of the information being presented. Each person in the audience will be thinking about

Table 18-1.—METHOD OF INSTRUCTION ON RETENTION RATE OF ADULT LEARNERS

Method of Instruction	Recall 3 Hours Later (%)	Recall 3 Days Later (%)
Lecturing alone	70	10
Demonstrating alone	72	20
Lecturing and Demonstrating together	85	65

how this information will benefit them, so it is a good idea to tell them how they will benefit.

Instructors should consider conducting a brief "ice-breaker" activity that involves audience participation. This may take the form of a simple exercise that asks participants to get together in small groups and write down several questions they have regarding HACCP. This allows participants to interact with one another and identify others with similar questions. Also, it is another way for the instructor to gauge the audience's knowledge of HACCP and ensure that pertinent questions that the audience may have will be answered during the program. By encouraging participants to interact early on in the program, they will feel relaxed and comfortable and will be more focused on listening to and learning the material.

CONDUCTING THE PROGRAM

There are numerous methods for conducting HACCP workshops and there is certainly more than one correct way. However, one pattern that seems to have emerged among training organizations is the use of working groups. Building on the concept that adults learn better through "hands-on" activities, working groups guide participants through various stages of HACCP plan development. For example, an instructor at a HACCP workshop designed to teach participants the seven principles of HACCP may present a relatively short lecture on conducting a hazard analysis and determining critical control points (CCPs). Participants are then divided into working groups and proceed through the process of conducting a hazard analysis and determining CCPs for a chosen food product. Once all the working groups have completed the exercise, each group reports on their hazard analysis and what CCPs they have identified. Fellow participants as well as the instructors have the opportunity to provide feedback following the reports. The interaction that occurs between group members during the exercise and in the subsequent discussions following the group reports results in better understanding of the concepts being taught than lecturing alone can accomplish.

REGULATORY REQUIREMENTS REGARDING HACCP TRAINING

Current federal requirements for HACCP training are contained in 21 *CFR* 123.10 for FDA's seafood HACCP rule and 9 *CFR* 417.7 for the USDA/FSIS rule on HACCP for meat and poultry products (Appendices B and C). Both regulations stipulate that the individual developing, reassessing and modifying the HACCP plan must have successfully completed a course of instruction in the application of the seven HACCP principles to:

- Meat or poultry product processing, including a segment on the development of a HACCP plan for a specific product and on record review (USDA/FSIS) and/or.
- Fish and fishery products (FDA).

FDA's seafood HACCP rule also states that job experience may qualify an individual to perform these functions in lieu of attending a HACCP training course. Both regulations state the HACCP-trained individual does not need to be an employee of the establishment.

HACCP ALLIANCES AND TRAINING

The tremendous interest in HACCP over the past several years has led to a number of different organizations offering HACCP training. In response to this demand, several HACCP Alliances have been formed in an effort to provide standardized curricula and accreditation for HACCP courses. The International HACCP Alliance, formerly the International Meat and Poultry HACCP Alliance, is one such Alliance that has worked cooperatively with USDA/FSIS and other regulatory agencies. To date, the International HACCP Alliance has developed five standardized curricula and accredited over 25 training programs. Another group, the Seafood HACCP Alliance has worked closely with the FDA and the Association of Food and Drug Officials (AFDO) to develop a standardized education and training program for the seafood industry to facilitate a more uniform implementation of HACCP within this industry.

There are a number of industry associations, educational foundations, universities, and third party/private companies offering HACCP training. A number of these organizations are well established and have been conducting HACCP training for many years, but some have not. It is a good idea to do a little research on any organization being considered for HACCP training to determine if their program matches the participant's training needs. Find out if the organization is accredited by the International HACCP Alliance and/or registered with AFDO and if possible, talk to individuals who have taken courses from the training organization in the past.

SUMMARY

Adequate HACCP training of supervisors, plant workers and technical personnel is essential for the proper development, implementation and maintenance of the HACCP system. Management must be committed to providing the time and resources for this training. HACCP programs should involve working groups, case studies and other group exercises that draw on the strengths and experiences of adult learners.

REFERENCES

Cantor, Jeffrey A. 1992. *Delivering Instruction to Adult Learners*. Wall and Emerson, Toronto, Canada.
Gravani, R. B., and D. L. Scott. 1997. *Planning A HACCP Education and Training Program*
  For Food Processing Plant Workers. Institute of Food Science, Cornell University, Ithaca, NY.

Appendix 18-A
Example HACCP Workshop Administrative Checklist

Equipment/Room Needs

	Slide projector with remote slide changer and/or video projector
	2 slide carousels
	Overhead projector, acetates, and markers
	Secured extension cord
	Screenpodium or lectern
	Lavaliere microphone
	Small table in front for teaching materials
	Instructor's table in back of room
	Breakout rooms — 1 per working group (can include main room)
	Flip charts, easels, markers, and masking tape for each working group

Registration Needs

Before workshop	
	Confirmation letter with course location and times sent to attendees & instructors
	Name tags and holders
	Sign-in sheets/list of attendees
After workshop	
	Certificates distributed to attendees after workshop completion
	Follow-up handouts & overheads distributed to attendees after workshop completion
	Evaluation summary and overhead copies distributed to instructors

Materials

	HACCP manuals
	Workbooks
	Teaching Bag

HAZARD ANALYSIS AND CRITICAL CONTROL POINT (HACCP) SYSTEM AND GUIDELINES FOR ITS APPLICATION

Annex to CAC/RCP 1-1969, Rev. 3 (1997)

Preamble

The first section of this document sets out the principles of the Hazard Analysis and Critical Control Point (HACCP) system adopted by the Codex Alimentarius Commission. The second section provides general guidance for the application of the system while recognizing that the details of application may vary depending on the circumstances of the food operation.[1]

The HACCP system, which is science based and systematic, identifies specific hazards and measures for their control to ensure the safety of food. HACCP is a tool to assess hazards and establish control systems that focus on prevention rather than relying mainly on end-product testing. Any HACCP system is capable of accommodating change, such as advances in equipment design, processing procedures or technological developments.

HACCP can be applied throughout the food chain from primary production to final consumption and its implementation should be guided by scientific evidence of risks to human health. As well as enhancing food safety, implementation of HACCP can provide other significant benefits. In addition, the application of HACCP systems can aid inspection by regulatory authorities and promote international trade by increasing confidence in food safety.

The successful application of HACCP requires the full commitment and involvement of management and the work force. It also requires a multidisciplinary approach; this multidisciplinary approach should include, when appropriate, expertise in agronomy, veterinary health, production, microbiology, medicine, public health, food technology, environmental health, chemistry and engineering, according to the particular study. The application of HACCP is compatible with the implementation of quality management systems, such as the ISO 9000 series, and is the system of choice in the management of food safety within such systems.

---

[1]The Principles of HACCP set the basis for the requirements for the application of HACCP, while the Guidelines provide general guidance for practical application.

While the application of HACCP to food safety was considered here, the concept can be applied to other aspects of food quality.

Definitions

Control (verb): To take all necessary actions to ensure and maintain compliance with criteria established in the HACCP plan.

Control (noun): The state wherein correct procedures are being followed and criteria are being met.

Control measure: Any action and activity that can be used to prevent or eliminate a food safety hazard or reduce it to an acceptable level.

Corrective action: Any action to be taken when the results of monitoring at the CCP indicate a loss of control.

Critical Control Point (CCP): A step at which control can be applied and is essential to prevent or eliminate a food safety hazard or reduce it to an acceptable level.

Critical limit (CL): A criterion which separates acceptability from unacceptability.

Deviation: Failure to meet a CL.

Flow diagram: A systematic representation of the sequence of steps or operations used in the production or manufacture of a particular food item.

HACCP: A system which identifies, evaluates, and controls hazards which are significant for food safety.

HACCP plan: A document prepared in accordance with the principles of HACCP to ensure control of hazards which are significant for food safety in the segment of the food chain under consideration.

Hazard: A biological, chemical or physical agent in, or condition of, food with the potential to cause an adverse health effect.

Hazard analysis: The process of collecting and evaluating information on hazards and conditions leading to their presence to decide which are significant for food safety and therefore should be addressed in the HACCP plan.

Monitor: The act of conducting a planned sequence of observations or measurements of control parameters to assess whether a CCP is under control.

Step: A point, procedure, operation or step in the food chain including raw materials, from primary production to final consumption.

Validation: Obtaining evidence that the elements of the HACCP plan are effective.

Verification: The application of methods, procedures, tests and other evaluations, in addition to monitoring to determine compliance with the HACCP plan.

Principles of the HACCP System

The HACCP system consists of the following seven principles:

Principle 1

Conduct a hazard analysis.

Principle 2

Determine the Critical Control Points (CCPs).

Principle 3

Establish critical limit(s) (CLs).

Principle 4

Establish a system to monitor control of the CCP.

Principle 5

Establish the corrective action to be taken when monitoring indicates that a particular CCP is not under control.

Principle 6

Establish procedures for verification to confirm that the HACCP system is working effectively.

Principle 7

Establish documentation concerning all procedures and records appropriate to these principles and their application.

Guidelines for the Application of the HACCP System

Prior to application of HACCP to any sector of the food chain, that sector should be operating according to the Codex General Principles of Food Hygiene, the appropriate Codex Codes of Practice, and appropriate food safety legislation. Management commitment is necessary for implementation of an effective HACCP system. During hazard identification, evaluation, and subsequent operations in designing and applying HACCP systems, consideration must be given to the impact of raw materials, ingredients, food manufacturing practices, role of manufacturing processes to control hazards, likely end-use of the product, categories of consumers of concern, and epidemiological evidence relative to food safety.

The intent of the HACCP system is to focus control at CCPs. Redesign of the operation should be considered if a hazard which must be controlled is identified but no CCPs are found.

HACCP should be applied to each specific operation separately. CCPs identified in any given example in any Codex Code of Hygienic Practice might not be the only ones identified for a specific application or might be of a different nature.

The HACCP application should be reviewed and necessary changes made when any modification is made in the product, process, or any step.

It is important when applying HACCP to be flexible where appropriate, given the context of the application taking into account the nature and the size of the operation.

Application

The application of HACCP principles consists of the following tasks as identified in the Logic Sequence for Application of HACCP (Figure 1).

Figure 1—Logic Sequence for Application of HACCP

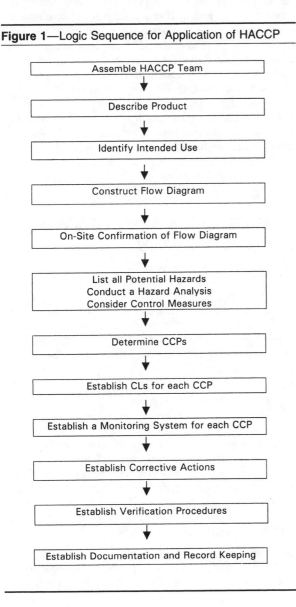

1. Assemble HACCP Team

The food operation should assure that the appropriate product specific knowledge and expertise is available for the development of an effective HACCP plan. Optimally, this may be accomplished by assembling a multidisciplinary team. Where such expertise is not available on site, expert advice should be obtained from other sources. The scope of the HACCP plan should be identified. The scope should describe which segment of the food chain is involved and the general classes of hazards to be addressed (e.g., does it cover all classes of hazards or only selected classes).

2. Describe Product

A full description of the product should be drawn up, including relevant safety information such as: composition, physical/chemical structure (including a_w, pH, etc.), microcidal/static treatments (heat treatment, freezing, brining, smoking, etc.), packaging, durability and storage conditions and method of distribution.

3. Identify Intended Use

The intended use should be based on the expected uses of the product by the end user or consumer. In specific cases, vulnerable groups of the population, e.g., institutional feeding, may have to be considered.

4. Construct Flow Diagram

The flow diagram should be constructed by the HACCP team. The flow diagram should cover all steps in the operation. When applying HACCP to a given operation, consideration should be given to steps preceding and following the specified operation.

5. On-site Confirmation of Flow Diagram

The HACCP team should confirm the processing operation against the flow diagram during all stages and hours of operation and amend the flow diagram where appropriate.

6. List All Potential Hazards Associated with Each Step, Conduct a Hazard Analysis, and Consider Any Measures to Control Identified Hazards (See Principle 1)

The HACCP team should list all of the hazards that may be reasonably expected to occur at each step from primary production, processing, manufacture, and distribution until the point of consumption.

The HACCP team should next conduct a hazard analysis to identify for the HACCP plan which hazards are of such a nature that their elimination or reduction to acceptable levels is essential to the production of a safe food.

In conducting the hazard analysis, wherever possible the following should be included:

* the likely occurrence of hazards and severity of their adverse health effects;
* the qualitative and/or quantitative evaluation of the presence of hazards;
* survival or multiplication of microorganisms of concern;
* production or persistence in foods of toxins, chemicals or physical agents: and,
* conditions leading to the above.

The HACCP team must then consider what control measures, if any, exist which can be applied for each hazard.

More than one control measure may be required to control a specific hazard(s) and more than one hazard may be controlled by a specified control measure.

7. Determine Critical Control Points (See Principle 2)[2]

There may be more than one CCP at which control is applied to address the same hazard. The determination of a CCP in the HACCP system can be facilitated by the application of a decision tree (e.g. Figure 2), which indicates a logic reasoning approach. Application of a decision tree should be flexible, given whether the operation is for production, slaughter, processing, storage, distribution or other. It should be used for guidance when determining CCPs. This example of a decision tree may not be applicable to all situations and other approaches may be used. Training in the application of the decision tree is recommended.

If a hazard has been identified at a step where control is necessary for safety, and no control measure exists at that step, or any other, then the product or process should be modified at that step, or at any earlier or later stage, to include a control measure.

8. Establish Critical Limits for Each CCP (See Principle 3)

Critical limits must be specified and validated if possible for each CCP. In some cases more than one CL will be elaborated at a particular step. Criteria often

used include measurements of temperature, time, moisture level, pH, a_w, available chlorine, and sensory parameters such as visual appearance and texture.

9. Establish a Monitoring System for Each CCP (See Principle 4)

Monitoring is the scheduled measurement or observation of a CCP relative to its CLs. The monitoring procedures must be able to detect loss of control at the CCP. Further, monitoring should ideally provide this information in time to make adjustments to ensure control of the process to prevent violating the critical limits. Where possible, process adjustments should be made when monitoring results indicate a trend towards loss of control at a CCP. The adjustments should be taken before a deviation occurs. Data derived from monitoring must be evaluated by a designated person with knowledge and authority to carry out corrective actions when indicated. If monitoring is not continuous, then the amount or frequency of monitoring must be sufficient to guarantee the CCP is in control. Most monitoring procedures for CCPs will need to be done rapidly because they relate to on-line processes and there will not be time for lengthy analytical testing. Physical and chemical measurements are often preferred to microbiological testing because they may be done rapidly and can often indicate the microbiological control of the product. All records and documents associated with monitoring CCPs must be signed by the person(s) doing the monitoring and by a responsible reviewing official(s) of the company.

10. Establish Corrective Actions (See Principle 5)

Specific corrective actions must be developed for each CCP in the HACCP system in order to deal with deviations when they occur.

The actions must ensure that the CCP has been brought under control. Actions taken must also include proper disposition of the affected product. Deviation and product disposition procedures must be documented in the HACCP record keeping.

11. Establish Verification Procedures (See Principle 6)

Establish procedures for verification. Verification and auditing methods, procedures and tests, including random sampling and analysis, can be used to determine if the HACCP system is working correctly. The frequency of verification should be sufficient to confirm that the HACCP system is working effectively. Examples of verification activities include:

* Review of the HACCP system and its records:
* Review of deviations and product dispositions;
* Confirmation that CCPs are kept under control.

---

[2]Since the publication of the decision tree by Codex, its use has been implemented many times for training purposes. In many instances, while this tree has been useful to explain the logic and depth of understanding needed to determine CCPs it is not specific to all food operations. e.g., slaughter, and therefore it should be used in conjunction with professional judgment, and modified in some cases.

Figure 2—Example of Decision Tree to Identify CCPS

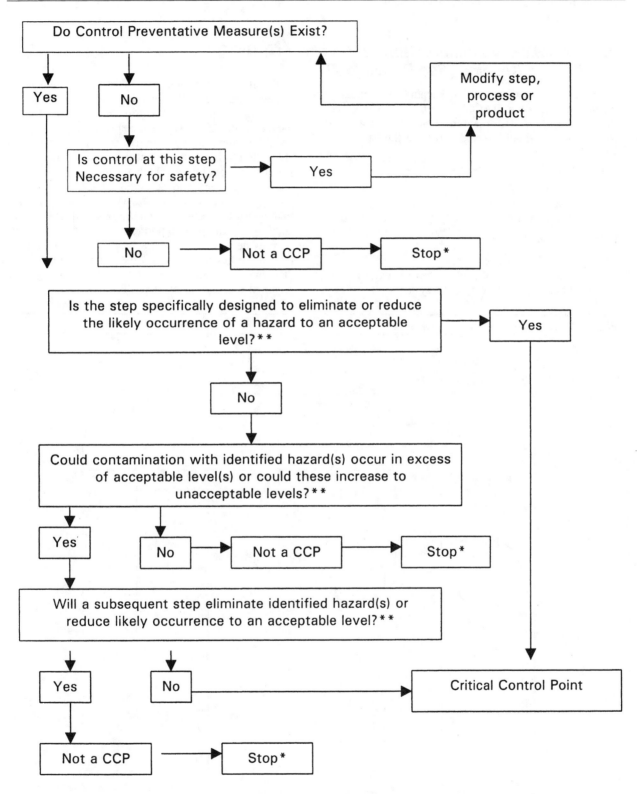

*   Proceed to the next identified hazard in the described process.
** Acceptable and unacceptable levels need to be defined within the overall objectives in identifying the CCPs of HACCP plan.

Where possible, validation activities should include actions to confirm the efficacy of all elements of the HACCP plan.

12. Establish Documentation and Record Keeping (See Principle 7)

Efficient and accurate record keeping is essential to the application of a HACCP system. HACCP procedures should be documented. Documentation and record keeping should be appropriate to the nature and size of the operation.

Documentation examples are:

• Hazard analysis;
• CCP determination;
• CL determination.

Record examples are:

• CCP monitoring activities;
• Deviations and associated corrective actions;
• Modifications to the HACCP system.

An example of a HACCP worksheet is attached as Figure 3.

Training

Training of personnel in industry, government and academia in HACCP principles and applications, and increasing awareness of consumers are essential elements for the effective implementation of HACCP. As an aid in developing specific training to support a HACCP plan, working instructions and procedures should be developed which define the tasks of the operating personnel to be stationed at each CCP.

Cooperation between primary producers, industry, trade groups, consumer organizations, and a responsible authority is of vital importance. Opportunities should be provided for the joint training of industry and control authorities to encourage and maintain a continuous dialogue and create a climate of understanding in the practical application of HACCP.

Figure 3—Example of a HACCP Worksheet

| Describe Product |

| Diagram Process Flow |

LIST							
Step	Hazard(s)	Control Measures	CCPs	Critical Limits	Monitoring Procedures	Corrective Actions	Record(s)

| Verification |

CODE OF FEDERAL REGULATIONS TITLE 9, PARTS 416 AND 417

Hazard Analysis and Critical Control Point (HACCP) Systems (USDA/FSIS Meat and Poultry HACCP Regulation)

Part 416—Sanitation

Section
416.11 General rules.
416.12 Development of sanitation SOP's.
416.13 Implementation of SOP's.
416.14 Maintenance of sanitation SOP's.
416.15 Corrective actions.
416.16 Recordkeeping Requirements.
416.17 Agency verification.

[Authority: 21 U.S.C. 451-470, 601-695; 7 U.S.C. 450, 1901-1906; 7 CFR 2.18, 2.53.]

[Source: 61 FR 38868, July 25, 1996, unless otherwise noted.]

Part 417—Hazard Analysis and Critical Control Point (HACCP) Systems

Section
417.1 Definitions.
417.2 Hazard analysis and HACCP plan.

417.3 Corrective actions.
417.4 Validation, verification, reassessment.
417.5 Records.
417.6 Inadequate HACCP Systems.
417.7 Training.
417.8 Agency verification.

[Authority: 7 U.S.C. 450; 21 U.S.C. 451-470, 601-695; 7 U.S.C. 1901-1906; 7 CFR 2.18, 2.53.]

[Source: 61 FR 38868, July 25, 1996, unless otherwise noted.]

Part 416—Sanitation

§ 416.11 General Rules

Each official establishment shall develop, implement, and maintain written standard operating procedures for sanitation (Sanitation SOP's) in accordance with the requirements of this part.

§ 416.12 Development of Sanitation SOP's

(a) The Sanitation SOP's (SSOPs) shall describe all procedures an official establishment will conduct daily, before and during operations, sufficient to prevent direct contamination or adulteration of product(s).

(b) The SSOPs shall be signed and dated by the individual with overall authority on-site or a higher level official of the establishment. This signature shall signify that the establishment will implement the SSOPs as specified and will maintain the SSOPs in accordance with the requirements of this part. The SSOPs shall be signed and dated upon initially implementing the SSOPs and upon any modification to the SSOPs.

(c) Procedures in the SSOPs that are to be conducted prior to operations shall be identified as such, and shall address, at a minimum, the cleaning of food contact surfaces of facilities, equipment, and utensils.

(d) The SSOPs shall specify the frequency with which each procedure in the SSOPs is to be conducted and identify the establishment employee(s) responsible for the implementation and maintenance of such procedure(s).

§ 416.13 Implementation of SOP's

(a) Each official establishment shall conduct the pre-operational procedures in the SSOPs before the start of operations.

(b) Each official establishment shall conduct all other procedures in the SSOPs at the frequencies specified.

(c) Each official establishment shall monitor daily the implementation of the procedures in the SSOPs.

§ 416.14 Maintenance of Sanitation SOP's

Each official establishment shall routinely evaluate the effectiveness of the SSOPs and the procedures therein in preventing direct contamination or adulteration of product(s)and shall revise both as necessary to keep them effective and current with respect to changes in facilities, equipment, utensils, operations, or personnel.

§ 416.15 Corrective Actions

(a) Each official establishment shall take appropriate corrective action(s)when either the establishment or FSIS determines that the establishment's SSOPs or the procedures specified therein, or the implementation or maintenance of the SSOPs, may have failed to prevent direct contamination or adulteration of product(s).

(b) Corrective actions include procedures to ensure appropriate disposition of product(s) that may be contaminated, restore sanitary conditions, and prevent the recurrence of direct contamination or adulteration of product(s), including appropriate reevaluation and modification of the SSOPs and the procedures specified therein or appropriate improvements in the execution of the SSOPs or the procedures specified therein.

[61 FR 38868, July 25, 1996, as amended at 62 FR 26219, May 13, 1997]

§ 416.16 Recordkeeping Requirements

(a) Each official establishment shall maintain daily records sufficient to document the implementation and monitoring of the SSOPs and any corrective actions taken. The establishment employee(s) specified in the SSOPs as being responsible for the implementation and monitoring of the procedure(s) specified in the SSOPs shall authenticate these records with his or her initials and the date.

(b) Records required by this part may be maintained on computers provided the establishment implements appropriate controls to ensure the integrity of the electronic data.

(c) Records required by this part shall be maintained for at least 6 months and made accesable [sic] available to FSIS. All such records shall be maintained at the official establishment for 48 hours following completion, after which they may be maintained off-site provided such records can be made available to FSIS within 24 hours of request.

§ 416.17 Agency Verification

FSIS shall verify the adequacy and effectiveness of the SSOPs and the procedures specified therein by determining that they meet the requirements of this part. Such verification may include:

(a) Reviewing the SSOPs;

(b) Reviewing the daily records documenting the implementation of the SSOPs and the procedures specified therein and any corrective actions taken or required to be taken;

(c) Direct observation of the implementation of the SSOPs and the procedures specified therein and any corrective actions taken or required to be taken; and

(d) Direct observation or testing to assess the sanitary conditions in the establishment.

Part 417—Hazard Analysis and Critical Control Point (HACCP) Systems

§ 417.1 Definitions

For purposes of this part, the following definitions shall apply:

Corrective action. Procedures to be followed when a deviation occurs.

Critical control point (CCP). A point, step, or procedure in a food process at which control can be applied and, as a result, a food safety hazard can be prevented, eliminated, or reduced to acceptable levels.

Critical limit. The maximum or minimum value to which a physical, biological, or chemical hazard must be controlled at a CCP to prevent, eliminate, or reduce to an acceptable level the occurrence of the identified food safety hazard.

Food safety hazard. Any biological, chemical, or physical property that may cause a food to be unsafe for human consumption.

HACCP System. The HACCP plan in operation, including the HACCP plan itself.

Hazard. See Food Safety Hazard.

Preventive measure. Physical, chemical, or other means that can be used to control an identified food safety hazard.

Process-monitoring instrument. An instrument or device used to indicate conditions during processing at a critical control point.

Responsible establishment official. The individual with overall authority on-site or a higher level official of the establishment.

§ 417.2 Hazard Analysis and HACCP Plan

(a) **Hazard analysis.**

(1) Every official establishment shall conduct, or have conducted for it, a hazard analysis to determine the food safety hazards reasonably likely to occur in the production process and identify the preventive measures the establishment can apply to control those hazards. The hazard analysis shall include food safety hazards that can occur before, during, and after entry into the establishment. A food safety hazard that is reasonably likely to occur is one for which a prudent establishment would establish controls because it historically has occurred, or because there is a reasonable possibility that it will occur in the particular type of product being processed, in the absence of those controls.

(2) A flow chart describing the steps of each process and product flow in the establishment shall be prepared, and the intended use or consumers of the finished product shall be identified.

(3) Food safety hazards might be expected to arise from the following:

(i)   Natural toxins;

(ii)   Microbiological contamination;

(iii)   Chemical contamination;

(iv)   Pesticides;

(v)   Drug residues;

(vi)   Zoonotic diseases;

(vii)   Decomposition;

(viii) Parasites;

(ix)   Unapproved use of direct or indirect food or color additives; and

(x)   Physical hazards.

(b) **The HACCP plan.**

(1) Every establishment shall develop and implement a written HACCP plan covering each product produced by that establishment whenever a hazard analysis reveals one or more food safety hazards that are reasonably likely to occur, based on the hazard analysis conducted in accordance with paragraph (a) of this section, including products in the following processing categories:

(i)   Slaughter—all species.

(ii)   Raw product—ground.

(iii)   Raw product—not ground.

(iv)   Thermally processed—commercially sterile.

(v)   Not heat treated—shelf stable.

(vi)   Heat treated—shelf stable.

(vii)   Fully cooked—not shelf stable.

(viii) Heat treated but not fully cooked—not shelf stable.

(ix)   Product with secondary inhibitors—not shelf stable.

(2) A single HACCP plan may encompass multiple products within a single processing category identified in this paragraph, if the food safety hazards, CCPs, CLs, and procedures required to be identified and performed in paragraph (c) of this section are essentially the same, provided that any required features of the plan that are unique to a specific product are clearly delineated in the plan and are observed in practice.

(3) HACCP plans for thermally processed/commercially sterile products do not have to address the food safety hazards associated with microbiological contamination if the product is produced in accordance with the requirements of part 318, subpart G, or part 381, subpart X, of this chapter.

(c) **The contents of the HACCP plan.** The HACCP plan shall, at a minimum:

(1) List the food safety hazards identified in accordance with paragraph (a) of this section, which must be controlled for each process.

(2) List the CCPs for each of the identified food safety hazards, including, as appropriate:

    (i) CCPs designed to control food safety hazards that could be introduced in the establishment, and

    (ii) CCPs designed to control food safety hazards introduced outside the establishment, including food safety hazards that occur before, during, and after entry into the establishment;

(3) List the CLs that must be met at each of the critical control points. CLs shall, at a minimum, be designed to ensure that applicable targets or performance standards established by FSIS, and any other requirement set forth in this chapter pertaining to the specific process or product, are met;

(4) List the procedures, and the frequency with which those procedures will be performed, that will be used to monitor each of the CCPs to ensure compliance with the CLs;

(5) Include all corrective actions that have been developed in accordance with § 417.3(a) of this part, to be followed in response to any deviation from a critical limit at a critical control point; and

(6) Provide for a recordkeeping system that documents the monitoring of the CCPs. The records shall contain the actual values and observations obtained during monitoring.

(7) List the verification procedures, and the frequency with which those procedures will be performed, that the establishment will use in accordance with § 417.4 of this part.

(d) **Signing and dating the HACCP plan.**

(1) The HACCP plan shall be signed and dated by the responsible establishment individual. This signature shall signify that the establishment accepts and will implement the HACCP plan.

(2) The HACCP plan shall be dated and signed:

    (i) Upon initial acceptance;

    (ii) Upon any modification; and

    (iii) At least annually, upon reassessment, as required under § 417.4(a)(3)of this part.

(e) Pursuant to 21 U.S.C. 456, 463, 608, and 621, the failure of an establishment to develop and implement a HACCP plan that complies with this section, or to operate in accordance with the requirements of this part, may render the products produced under those conditions adulterated.

[61 FR 38868, July 25, 1996, as amended at 62 FR 61009, Nov. 14, 1997]

§ 417.3 Corrective Actions

(a) The written HACCP plan shall identify the corrective action to be followed in response to a deviation from a CL. The HACCP plan shall describe the corrective action to be taken, and assign responsibility for taking corrective action, to ensure:

(1) The cause of the deviation is identified and eliminated;

(2) The CCP will be under control after the corrective action is taken;

(3) Measures to prevent recurrence are established; and

(4) No product that is injurious to health or otherwise adulterated as a result of the deviation enters commerce.

(b) If a deviation not covered by a specified corrective action occurs, or if another unforeseen hazard arises, the establishment shall:

(1) Segregate and hold the affected product, at least until the requirements of paragraphs (b)(2) and (b)(3)of this section are met;

(2) Perform a review to determine the acceptability of the affected product for distribution;

(3) Take action, when necessary, with respect to the affected product to ensure that no product that is injurious to health or otherwise adulterated, as a result of the deviation, enters commerce;

(4) Perform or obtain reassessment by an individual trained in accordance with § 417.7 of this part, to determine whether the newly identified deviation or other unforeseen hazard should be incorporated into the HACCP plan.

(c) All corrective actions taken in accordance with this section shall be documented in records that are subject to verification in accordance with § 417.4(a)(2)(iii) and the recordkeeping requirements of § 417.5 of this part.

§ 417.4 Validation, Verification, Reassessment

(a) Every establishment shall validate the HACCP plan's adequacy in controlling the food safety hazards identified during the hazard analysis, and shall verify that the plan is being effectively implemented.

(1) **Initial validation.** Upon completion of the hazard analysis and development of the HACCP plan, the establishment shall conduct activities designed to determine that the HACCP plan is functioning as intended. During this HACCP

plan validation period, the establishment shall repeatedly test the adequacy of the CCP's, CLs, monitoring and recordkeeping procedures, and corrective actions set forth in the HACCP plan. Validation also encompasses reviews of the records themselves, routinely generated by the HACCP system, in the context of other validation activities.

(2) **Ongoing verification activities.** Ongoing verification activities include, but are not limited to:

    (i) The calibration of process-monitoring instruments;

    (ii) Direct observations of monitoring activities and corrective actions; and

    (iii) The review of records generated and maintained in accordance with § 417.5(a)(3) of this part.

(3) **Reassessment of the HACCP plan.** Every establishment shall reassess the adequacy of the HACCP plan at least annually and whenever any changes occur that could affect the hazard analysis or alter the HACCP plan. Such changes may include, but are not limited to, changes in: raw materials or source of raw materials; product formulation; slaughter or processing methods or systems; production volume; personnel; packaging; finished product distribution systems; or, the intended use or consumers of the finished product. The reassessment shall be performed by an individual trained in accordance with § 417.7 of this part. The HACCP plan shall be modified immediately whenever a reassessment reveals that the plan no longer meets the requirements of § 417.2(c) of this part.

(b) **Reassessment of the hazard analysis.** Any establishment that does not have a HACCP plan because a hazard analysis has revealed no food safety hazards that are reasonably likely to occur shall reassess the adequacy of the hazard analysis whenever a change occurs that could reasonably affect whether a food safety hazard exists. Such changes may include, but are not limited to, changes in: raw materials or source of raw materials; product formulation; slaughter or processing methods or systems; production volume; packaging; finished product distribution systems; or, the intended use or consumers of the finished product.

§ 417.5 Records

(a) The establishment shall maintain the following records documenting the establishment's HACCP plan:

(1) The written hazard analysis prescribed in § 417.2(a) of this part, including all supporting documentation.

(2) The written HACCP plan, including decision-making documents associated with the selection and development of CCP's and CLs, and documents supporting both the monitoring and verification procedures selected and the frequency of those procedures.

(3) Records documenting the monitoring of CCP's and their CLs, including the recording of actual times, temperatures, or other quantifiable values, as prescribed in the establishment's HACCP plan; the calibration of process-monitoring instruments; corrective actions, including all actions taken in response to a deviation; verification procedures and results; product code(s), product name or identity, or slaughter production lot. Each of these records shall include the date the record was made.

(b) Each entry on a record maintained under the HACCP plan shall be made at the time the specific event occurs and include the date and time recorded, and shall be signed or initialed by the establishment employee making the entry.

(c) Prior to shipping product, the establishment shall review the records associated with the production of that product, documented in accordance with this section, to ensure completeness, including the determination that all CLs were met and, if appropriate, corrective actions were taken, including the proper disposition of product. Where practicable, this review shall be conducted, dated, and signed by an individual who did not produce the record(s), preferably by someone trained in accordance with § 417.7 of this part, or the responsible establishment official.

(d) **Records maintained on computers.** The use of records maintained on computers is acceptable, provided that appropriate controls are implemented to ensure the integrity of the electronic data and signatures.

(e) **Record retention.**

(1) Establishments shall retain all records required by paragraph (a)(3) of this section as follows: for slaughter activities, for at least one year; for refrigerated product, for at least one year; for frozen, preserved, or shelf-stable products, for at least two years.

(2) Off-site storage of records required by paragraph (a)(3) of this section is permitted after six months, if such records can be retrieved and provided, on-site, within 24 hours of an FSIS employee's request.

(f) **Official review.** All records required by this part and all plans and procedures required by this part shall be available for official review and copying.

§ 417.6 Inadequate HACCP Systems

A HACCP system may be found to be inadequate if:

(a) The HACCP plan in operation does not meet the requirements set forth in this part;

(b) Establishment personnel are not performing tasks specified in the HACCP plan;

(c) The establishment fails to take corrective actions, as required by § 417.3 of this part;

(d) HACCP records are not being maintained as required in § 417.5 of this part; or

(e) Adulterated product is produced or shipped.

§ 417.7 Training

(a) Only an individual who has met the requirements of paragraph (b) of this section, but who need not be an employee of the establishment, shall be permitted to perform the following functions:

(1) Development of the HACCP plan, in accordance with § 417.2(b) of this part, which could include adapting a generic model that is appropriate for the specific product; and

(2) Reassessment and modification of the HACCP plan, in accordance with § 417.3 of this part.

(b) The individual performing the functions listed in paragraph (a) of this section shall have successfully completed a course of instruction in the application of the seven HACCP principles to meat or poultry product processing, including a segment on the development of a HACCP plan for a specific product and on record review.

§ 417.8 Agency Verification

FSIS will verify the adequacy of the HACCP plan(s) by determining that each HACCP plan meets the requirements of this part and all other applicable regulations. Such verification may include:

(a) Reviewing the HACCP plan;

(b) Reviewing the CCP records;

(c) Reviewing and determining the adequacy of corrective actions taken when a deviation occurs;

(d) Reviewing the CLs;

(e) Reviewing other records pertaining to the HACCP plan or system;

(f) Direct observation or measurement at a CCP;

(g) Sample collection and analysis to determine the product meets all safety standards; and

(h) On-site observations and record review.

Appendix C

CODE OF FEDERAL REGULATIONS TITLE 21, PART 123

Procedures for the Safe & Sanitary Processing and Importing of Fish and Fisheries Products (FDA Seafood HACCP Regulation)

Subpart A—General Provisions

Subpart B—Smoked and Smoke-Flavored Fishery Products

Subpart C—Raw Molluscan Shellfish

[Authority: Secs. 201, 402, 403, 406, 409, 701, 704, 721, 801, 903 of the Federal Food, Drug, and Cosmetic Act (21 U.S.C. 321, 342, 343, 346, 348, 371, 374, 379e, 381, 393); secs. 301, 307, 361 of the Public Health Service Act (42 U.S.C. 241, 242l, 264).]

[Source: 60 FR 65197, Dec. 18, 1995, unless otherwise noted.]

[Effective Date Note: At 60 FR 65197, Dec. 18, 1995, part was added, effective December 18, 1997.]

Subpart A—General Provisions

§ 123.3 Definitions

The definitions and interpretations of terms in section 201 of the Federal Food, Drug, and Cosmetic Act (the act) and in part 110 of this chapter are applicable to such terms when used in this part, except where they are herein redefined. The following definitions shall also apply:

(a) **Certification number** means a unique combination of letters and numbers assigned by a shellfish control authority to a molluscan shellfish processor.

(b) **Critical control point (CCP)** means a point, step, or procedure in a food process at which control can be applied, and a food safety hazard can as a result be prevented, eliminated, or reduced to acceptable levels.

(c) **Critical limit (CL)** means the maximum or minimum value to which a physical, biological, or chemical parameter must be controlled at a CCP to prevent, eliminate, or reduce to an acceptable level the occurrence of the identified food safety hazard.

(d) **Fish** means fresh or saltwater finfish, crustaceans, other forms of aquatic animal life (including, but not limited to, alligator, frog, aquatic turtle, jellyfish, sea cucumber, and sea urchin and the roe of such animals) other than birds or mammals, and all mollusks, where such animal life is intended for human consumption.

(e) **Fishery product** means any human food product in which fish is a characterizing ingredient.

(f) **Food safety hazard** means any biological, chemical, or physical property that may cause a food to be unsafe for human consumption.

(g) **Importer** means either the U.S. owner or consignee at the time of entry into the United States, or the U.S. agent or representative of the foreign owner or consignee at the time of entry into the United States, who is responsible for ensuring that goods being offered for entry into the United States are in compliance with all laws affecting the importation. For the purposes of this definition, ordinarily the importer is not the custom house broker, the freight forwarder, the carrier, or the steamship representative.

(h) **Molluscan shellfish** means any edible species of fresh or frozen oysters, clams, mussels, or scallops, or edible portions of such species, except when the product consists entirely of the shucked adductor muscle.

(i) **Preventive measure** means physical, chemical, or other factors that can be used to control an identified food safety hazard.

(j) **Process-monitoring instrument** means an instrument or device used to indicate conditions during processing at a CCP.

(k) (1) **Processing** means, with respect to fish or fishery products: Handling, storing, preparing, heading, eviscerating, shucking, freezing, changing into different market forms, manufacturing, preserving, packing, labeling, dockside unloading, or holding.

(2) The regulations in this part do not apply to:

(i) Harvesting or transporting fish or fishery products, without otherwise engaging in processing.

(ii) Practices such as heading, eviscerating, or freezing intended solely to prepare a fish for holding on board a harvest vessel.

(iii) The operation of a retail establishment.

(l) **Processor** means any person engaged in commercial, custom, or institutional processing of fish or fishery products, either in the United States or in a foreign country. A processor includes any person engaged in the production of foods that are to be used in market or consumer tests.

(m) **Scombroid toxin-forming species** means tuna, bluefish, mahi mahi, and other species, whether or not in the family Scombridae, in which significant levels of histamine may be produced in the fish flesh by decarboxylation of free histidine as a result of exposure of the fish after capture to temperatures that permit the growth of mesophilic bacteria.

(n) **Shall** is used to state mandatory requirements.

(o) **Shellfish control authority** means a Federal, State, or foreign agency, or sovereign tribal government, legally responsible for the administration of a program that includes activities such as classification of molluscan shellfish growing areas, enforcement of molluscan shellfish harvesting controls, and certification of molluscan shellfish processors.

(p) **Shellstock** means raw, in-shell molluscan shellfish.

(q) **Should** is used to state recommended or advisory procedures or to identify recommended equipment.

(r) **Shucked shellfish** means molluscan shellfish that have one or both shells removed.

(s) **Smoked or smoke-flavored fishery products** means the finished food prepared by:

(1) Treating fish with salt (sodium chloride), and

(2) Subjecting it to the direct action of smoke from burning wood, sawdust, or similar material and/or imparting to it the flavor of smoke by a means such as immersing it in a solution of wood smoke.

(t) **Tag** means a record of harvesting information attached to a container of shellstock by the harvester or processor.

§ 123.5 Current Good Manufacturing Practices

(a) Part 110 of this chapter applies in determining whether the facilities, methods, practices, and controls used to process fish and fishery products are safe, and whether these products have been processed under sanitary conditions.

(b) The purpose of this part is to set forth requirements specific to the processing of fish and fishery products.

§ 123.6 Hazard Analysis and Hazard Analysis Critical Control Point (HACCP) Plan

(a) **Hazard analysis.** Every processor shall conduct, or have conducted for it, a hazard analysis to determine whether there are food safety hazards that are reasonably likely to occur for each kind of fish and fishery product processed by that processor and to identify the preventive measures that the processor can apply to control those hazards. Such food safety hazards can be introduced both within and outside the processing plant environment, including food safety hazards that can occur before, during, and after harvest. A food safety hazard that is reasonably likely to occur is one for which a prudent processor would establish controls because experience, illness data, scientific reports, or other information provide a basis to conclude that there is a reasonable possibility that it will occur in the particular type of fish or fishery product being processed in the absence of those controls.

(b) **The HACCP plan.** Every processor shall have and implement a written HACCP plan whenever a hazard analysis reveals one or more food safety hazards that are reasonably likely to occur, as described in paragraph (a) of this section. A HACCP plan shall be specific to:

(1) Each location where fish and fishery products are processed by that processor; and

(2) Each kind of fish and fishery product processed by the processor. The plan may group kinds of fish and fishery products together, or group kinds of production methods together, if the food safety hazards, CCPs, CLs, and procedures required to be identified and performed in paragraph (c) of this section are identical for all fish and fishery products so grouped or for all production methods so grouped.

(c) **The contents of the HACCP plan.** The HACCP plan shall, at a minimum:

(1) List the food safety hazards that are reasonably likely to occur, as identified in accordance with paragraph (a) of this section, and that thus must be controlled for each fish and fishery product. Consideration should be given to whether any food safety hazards are reasonably likely to occur as a result of the following:

(i) Natural toxins;

(ii) Microbiological contamination;

(iii) Chemical contamination;

(iv) Pesticides;

(v) Drug residues;

(vi) Decomposition in scombroid toxin-forming species or in any other species where a food safety hazard has been associated with decomposition;

(vii) Parasites, where the processor has knowledge or has reason to know that the parasite-containing fish or fishery product will be consumed without a process sufficient to kill the parasites, or where the processor represents, labels, or intends for the product to be so consumed;

(viii) Unapproved use of direct or indirect food or color additives; and

(ix) Physical hazards;

(2) List the CCPs for each of the identified food safety hazards, including as appropriate:

(i) CCPs designed to control food safety hazards that could be introduced in the processing plant environment; and

(ii) CCPs designed to control food safety hazards introduced outside the processing plant environment, including food safety hazards that occur before, during, and after harvest;

(3) List the CLs that must be met at each of the CCPs;

(4) List the procedures, and frequency thereof, that will be used to monitor each of the critical control points to ensure compliance with the CLs;

(5) Include any corrective action plans that have been developed in accordance with § 123.7(b), to be followed in response to deviations from CLs at CCPs;

(6) List the verification procedures, and frequency thereof, that the processor will use in accordance with § 123.8(a);

(7) Provide for a recordkeeping system that documents the monitoring of the CCPs. The records shall contain the actual values and observations obtained during monitoring.

(d) **Signing and dating the HACCP plan.**
   (1) The HACCP plan shall be signed and dated, either by the most responsible individual onsite at the processing facility or by a higher level official of the processor. This signature shall signify that the HACCP plan has been accepted for implementation by the firm.
   (2) The HACCP plan shall be dated and signed:
      (i)   Upon initial acceptance;
      (ii) Upon any modification; and
      (iii) Upon verification of the plan in accordance with § 123.8(a)(1).

(e) **Products subject to other regulations.** For fish and fishery products that are subject to the requirements of part 113 or 114 of this chapter, the HACCP plan need not list the food safety hazard associated with the formation of *Clostridium botulinum* toxin in the finished, hermetically sealed container, nor list the controls to prevent that food safety hazard. A HACCP plan for such fish and fishery products shall address any other food safety hazards that are reasonably likely to occur.

(f) **Sanitation.** Sanitation controls may be included in the HACCP plan. However, to the extent that they are monitored in accordance with § 123.11(b) they need not be included in the HACCP plan, and vice versa.

(g) **Legal basis.** Failure of a processor to have and implement a HACCP plan that complies with this section whenever a HACCP plan is necessary, otherwise operate in accordance with the requirements of this part, shall render the fish or fishery products of that processor adulterated under section 402(a)(4) of the act. Whether a processor's actions are consistent with ensuring the safety of food will be determined through an evaluation of the processors overall implementation of its HACCP plan, if one is required.

§ 123.7 Corrective Actions

(a) Whenever a deviation from a CL occurs, a processor shall take corrective action either by:
   (1) Following a corrective action plan that is appropriate for the particular deviation, or
   (2) Following the procedures in paragraph (c) of this section.

(b) Processors may develop written corrective action plans, which become part of their HACCP plans in accordance with § 123.6(c)(5), by which they predetermine the corrective actions that they will take whenever there is a deviation from a CL. A corrective action plan that is appropriate for a particular deviation is one that describes the steps to be taken and assigns responsibility for taking those steps, to ensure that:
   (1) No product enters commerce that is either injurious to health or is otherwise adulterated as a result of the deviation; and
   (2) The cause of the deviation is corrected.

(c) When a deviation from a CL occurs and the processor does not have a corrective action plan that is appropriate for that deviation, the processor shall:
   (1) Segregate and hold the affected product, at least until the requirements of paragraphs (c)(2) and (c)(3) of this section are met;
   (2) Perform or obtain a review to determine the acceptability of the affected product for distribution. The review shall be performed by an individual or individuals that have adequate training or experience to perform such a review. Adequate training may or may not include training in accordance with § 123.10;
   (3) Take corrective action, when necessary, with respect to the affected product to ensure that no product enters commerce that is either injurious to health or is otherwise adulterated as a result of the deviation;
   (4) Take corrective action, when necessary, to correct the cause of the deviation;
   (5) Perform or obtain timely reassessment by an individual or individuals who have been trained in accordance with § 123.10, to determine whether the HACCP plan needs to be modified to reduce the risk of recurrence of the deviation, and modify the HACCP plan as necessary.

(d) All corrective actions taken in accordance with this section shall be fully documented in records that are subject to verification in accordance with § 123.8(a)(3)(ii) and the recordkeeping requirements of § 123.9.

§ 123.8 Verification

(a) **Overall verification.** Every processor shall verify that the HACCP plan is adequate to control food safety hazards that are reasonably likely to occur, and that the plan is being effectively implemented. Verification shall include, at a minimum:
   (1) **Reassessment of the HACCP plan.** A reassessment of the adequacy of the HACCP plan whenever any changes occur that could affect the hazard analysis or alter the HACCP plan in any way or at least annually. Such changes may include changes in the following: Raw materials or source of raw materials, product formulation, processing methods or systems, finished product distribution systems, or the intended use or con-

sumers of the finished product. The reassessment shall be performed by an individual or individuals that have been trained in accordance with § 123.10. The HACCP plan shall be modified immediately whenever a reassessment reveals that the plan is no longer adequate to fully meet the requirements of § 123.6(c).

(2) **Ongoing verification activities.** Ongoing verification activities including:

(i) A review of any consumer complaints that have been received by the processor to determine whether they relate to the performance of CCPs or reveal the existence of unidentified CCPs;

(ii) The calibration of process-monitoring instruments; and,

(iii) At the option of the processor, the performing of periodic end-product or in-process testing.

(3) **Records review.** A review, including signing and dating, by an individual who has been trained in accordance with § 123.10, of the records that document:

(i) The monitoring of CCPs. The purpose of this review shall be, at a minimum, to ensure that the records are complete and to verify that they document values that are within the CLs. This review shall occur within 1 week of the day that the records are made;

(ii) The taking of corrective actions. The purpose of this review shall be, at a minimum, to ensure that the records are complete and to verify that appropriate corrective actions were taken in accordance with § 123.7. This review shall occur within 1 week of the day that the records are made; and

(iii) The calibrating of any process control instruments used at CCPs and the performing of any periodic end-product or in-process testing that is part of the processor's verification activities. The purpose of these reviews shall be, at a minimum, to ensure that the records are complete, and that these activities occurred in accordance with the processor's written procedures. These reviews shall occur within a reasonable time after the records are made.

(b) **Corrective actions.** Processors shall immediately follow the procedures in § 123.7 whenever any verification procedure, including the review of a con-

sumer complaint, reveals the need to take a corrective action.

(c) **Reassessment of the hazard analysis.** Whenever a processor does not have a HACCP plan because a hazard analysis has revealed no food safety hazards that are reasonably likely to occur, the processor shall reassess the adequacy of that hazard analysis whenever there are any changes that could reasonably affect whether a food safety hazard now exists. Such changes may include, but are not limited to changes in: Raw materials or source of raw materials, product formulation, processing methods or systems, finished product distribution systems, or the intended use or consumers of the finished product. The reassessment shall be performed by an individual or individuals that have been trained in accordance with § 123.10.

(d) **Recordkeeping.** The calibration of process-monitoring instruments, and the performing of any periodic end-product and in-process testing, in accordance with paragraphs (a)(2)(ii) through (iii) of this section shall be documented in records that are subject to the recordkeeping requirements of § 123.9.

§ 123.9 Records

(a) **General requirements.** All records required by this part shall include:

(1) The name and location of the processor or importer;

(2) The date and time of the activity that the record reflects;

(3) The signature or initials of the person performing the operation; and

(4) Where appropriate, the identity of the product and the production code, if any. Processing and other information shall be entered on records at the time that it is observed.

(b) **Record retention.**

(1) All records required by this part shall be retained at the processing facility or importer's place of business in the United States for at least 1 year after the date they were prepared in the case of refrigerated products and for at least 2 years after the date they were prepared in the case of frozen, preserved, or shelf-stable products.

(2) Records that relate to the general adequacy of equipment or processes being used by a processor, including the results of scientific studies and evaluations, shall be retained at the processing facility or the importer's place of business in the United States for at least 2 years after their

applicability to the product being produced at the facility.

(3) If the processing facility is closed for a prolonged period between seasonal packs, or if record storage capacity is limited on a processing vessel or at a remote processing site, the records may be transferred to some other reasonably accessible location at the end of the seasonal pack but shall be immediately returned for official review upon demand.

(c) **Official review.** All records required by this part and all plans and procedures required by this part shall be available for official review and copying at reasonable times.

(d) **Public disclosure.**

(1) Subject to the limitations in paragraph (d)(2) of this section, all plans and records required by this part are not available for public disclosure unless they have been previously disclosed to the public as defined in § 20.81 of this chapter or they relate to a product or ingredient that has been abandoned and they no longer represent a trade secret or confidential commercial or financial information as defined in § 20.61 of this chapter.

(2) However, these records and plans may be subject to disclosure to the extent that they are otherwise publicly available, or that disclosure could not reasonably be expected to cause a competitive hardship, such as generic-type HACCP plans that reflect standard industry practices.

(e) **Tags.** Tags as defined in § 123.3(t) are not subject to the requirements of this section unless they are used to fulfill the requirements of § 123.28(c).

(f) **Records maintained on computers.** The maintenance of records on computers is acceptable, provided that appropriate controls are implemented to ensure the integrity of the electronic data and signatures.

§ 123.10 Training

At a minimum, the following functions shall be performed by an individual who has successfully completed training in the application of HACCP principles to fish and fishery product processing at least equivalent to that received under standardized curriculum recognized as adequate by the U.S. Food and Drug Administration or who is otherwise qualified through job experience to perform these functions. Job experience will qualify an individual to perform these functions if it has provided knowledge at least equivalent to that provided through the standardized curriculum.

(a) Developing a HACCP plan, which could include adapting a model or generic-type HACCP plan, that

is appropriate for a specific processor, in order to meet the requirements of § 123.6(b);

(b) Reassessing and modifying the HACCP plan in accordance with the corrective action procedures specified in § 123.7(c)(5), the HACCP plan in accordance with the verification activities specified in § 123.8(a)(1), and the hazard analysis in accordance with the verification activities specified in § 123.8(c); and

(c) Performing the record review required by § 123.8(a)(3); the trained individual need not be an employee of the processor.

§ 123.11 Sanitation Control Procedures

(a) **Sanitation SOP.** Each processor should have and implement a written sanitation standard operating procedure (herein referred to as SSOP) or similar document that is specific to each location where fish and fishery products are produced. The SSOP should specify how the processor will meet those sanitation conditions and practices that are to be monitored in accordance with paragraph (b) of this section.

(b) **Sanitation monitoring.** Each processor shall monitor the conditions and practices during processing with sufficient frequency to ensure, at a minimum, conformance with those conditions and practices specified in part 110 of this chapter that are both appropriate to the plant and the food being processed and relate to the following:

(1) Safety of the water that comes into contact with food or food contact surfaces, or is used in the manufacture of ice;

(2) Condition and cleanliness of food contact surfaces, including utensils, gloves, and outer garments;

(3) Prevention of cross-contamination from unsanitary objects to food, food packaging material, and other food contact surfaces, including utensils, gloves, and outer garments, and from raw product to cooked product;

(4) Maintenance of hand washing, hand sanitizing, and toilet facilities;

(5) Protection of food, food packaging material, and food contact surfaces from adulteration with lubricants, fuel, pesticides, cleaning compounds, sanitizing agents, condensate, and other chemical, physical, and biological contaminants;

(6) Proper labeling, storage, and use of toxic compounds;

(7) Control of employee health conditions that could result in the microbiological contamination of

food, food packaging materials, and food contact surfaces; and

(8) Exclusion of pests from the food plant.

The processor shall correct in a timely manner, those conditions and practices that are not met.

(c) **Sanitation control records.** Each processor shall maintain sanitation control records that, at a minimum, document the monitoring and corrections prescribed by paragraph (b) of this section. These records are subject to the requirements of § 123.9.

(d) **Relationship to HACCP plan.** Sanitation controls may be included in the HACCP plan, required by § 123.6(b). However, to the extent that they are monitored in accordance with paragraph (b) of this section they need not be included in the HACCP plan, and vice versa.

§ 123.12 Special Requirements for Imported Products

This section sets forth specific requirements for imported fish and fishery products.

(a) **Importer verification.** Every importer of fish or fishery products shall either:

(1) Obtain the fish or fishery product from a country that has an active memorandum of understanding (MOU) or similar agreement with the Food and Drug Administration, that covers the fish or fishery product and documents the equivalency or compliance of the inspection system of the foreign country with the U.S. system, accurately reflects the current situation between the signing parties, and is functioning and enforceable in its entirety; or

(2) Have and implement written verification procedures for ensuring that the fish and fishery products that they offer for import into the United States were processed in accordance with the requirements of this part. The procedures shall list at a minimum:

  (i) Product specifications that are designed to ensure that the product is not adulterated under section 402 of the Federal Food, Drug, and Cosmetic Act because it may be injurious to health or have been processed under unsanitary conditions, and,

  (ii) Affirmative steps that may include any of the following:

    (A) Obtaining from the foreign processor the HACCP and sanitation monitoring records required by this part that relate to the specific lot of fish or fishery products being offered for import;

    (B) Obtaining either a continuing or lot-by-lot certificate from an appropriate foreign government inspection authority or competent third party certifying that the imported fish or fishery product is or was processed in accordance with the requirements of this part;

    (C) Regularly inspecting the foreign processor's facilities to ensure that the imported fish or fishery product is being processed in accordance with the requirements of this part;

    (D) Maintaining on file a copy, in English, of the foreign processor's HACCP plan, and a written guarantee from the foreign processor that the imported fish or fishery product is processed in accordance with the requirements of the part;

    (E) Periodically testing the imported fish or fishery product, and maintaining on file a copy, in English, of a written guarantee from the foreign processor that the imported fish or fishery product is processed in accordance with the requirements of this part or,

    (F) Other such verification measures as appropriate that provide an equivalent level of assurance of compliance with the requirements of this part.

(b) **Competent third party.** An importer may hire a competent third party to assist with or perform any or all of the verification activities specified in paragraph (a)(2) of this section, including writing the importer's verification procedures on the importer's behalf.

(c) **Records.** The importer shall maintain records, in English, that document the performance and results of the affirmative steps specified in paragraph (a)(2)(ii) of this section. These records shall be subject to the applicable provisions of § 123.9.

(d) **Determination of compliance.** There must be evidence that all fish and fishery products offered for entry into the United States have been processed under conditions that comply with this part. If assurances do not exist that the imported fish or fishery product has been processed under conditions that are equivalent to those required of domestic processors under this part, the product will appear to be adulterated and will be denied entry.

Subpart B—Smoked and Smoke-Flavored Fishery Products

§ 123.15 General

This subpart augments subpart A of this part by setting forth specific requirements for processing smoked and smoke-flavored fishery products.

§ 123.16 Process Controls

In order to meet the requirements of subpart A of this part, processors of smoked and smoke-flavored fishery products, except those subject to the requirements of part 113 or 114 of this chapter, shall include in their HACCP plans how they are controlling the food safety hazard associated with the formation of toxin by *Clostridium botulinum* for at least as long as the shelf life of the product under normal and moderate abuse conditions.

Subpart C—Raw Molluscan Shellfish

§ 123.20 General

This subpart augments subpart A of this part by setting forth specific requirements for processing fresh or frozen molluscan shellfish, where such processing does not include a treatment that ensures the destruction of vegetative cells of microorganisms of public health concern.

§ 123.28 Source Controls

(a) In order to meet the requirements of subpart A of this part as they apply to microbiological contamination, chemical contamination, natural toxins, and related food safety hazards, processors shall include in their HACCP plans how they are controlling the origin of the molluscan shellfish they process to ensure that the conditions of paragraphs (b), (c), and (d) of this section are met.

(b) Processors shall only process molluscan shellfish harvested from growing waters approved for harvesting by a shellfish control authority. In the case of molluscan shellfish harvested from U.S. Federal waters, the requirements of this paragraph will be met so long as the shellfish have not been harvested from waters that have been closed to harvesting by an agency of the Federal government.

(c) To meet the requirements of paragraph (b) of this section, processors who receive shellstock shall accept only shellstock from a harvester that is in compliance with such licensure requirements as may apply to the harvesting of molluscan shellfish or from a processor that is certified by a shellfish control authority, and that has a tag affixed to each container of shellstock. The tag shall bear, at a minimum, the information required in § 1240.60(b) of this chapter. In place of the tag, bulk shellstock shipments may be accompanied by a bill of lading or similar shipping document that contains the information required in § 1240.60(b) of this chapter. Processors shall maintain records that document that all shellstock have met the requirements of this section. These records shall document:

(1) The date of harvest;

(2) The location of harvest by State and site;

(3) The quantity and type of shellfish;

(4) The date of receipt by the processor; and

(5) The name of the harvester, the name or registration number of the harvester's vessel, or an identification number issued to the harvester by the shellfish control authority.

(d) To meet the requirements of paragraph (b) of this section, processors who receive shucked molluscan shellfish shall accept only containers of shucked molluscan shellfish that bear a label that complies with § 1240.60(c) of this chapter. Processors shall maintain records that document that all shucked molluscan shellfish have met the requirements of this section. These records shall document:

(1) The date of receipt;

(2) The quantity and type of shellfish; and

(3) The name and certification number of the packer or repacker of the product.

APPENDIX D

Side-By-Side Comparison of USDA/FSIS Meat and Poultry HACCP Rule and FDA Seafood HACCP Rule

Element	USDA/FSIS Mega-Reg	FDA Seafood HACCP Regulation
Title of Rule	PATHOGEN REDUCTION; HAZARD ANALYSIS AND CRITICAL CONTROL POINT (HACCP) SYSTEMS	PROCEDURES FOR THE SAFE AND SANITARY PROCESSING AND IMPORTING OF FISH AND FISHERY PRODUCTS
CFR Part	9 CFR PART 417—HAZARD ANALYSIS AND CRITICAL CONTROL POINT (HACCP) SYSTEMS	21 CFR PART 123—FISH AND FISHERY PRODUCTS
Index	417.1 Definitions. 17.2 Hazard analysis and HACCP plan. 417.3 Corrective actions. 417.4 Validation, verification, reassessment. 417.5 Records. 417.6 Inadequate HACCP Systems. 417.7 Training. 417.8 Agency verification. **NOTE: Pathogen reduction and sanitation components of the Mega-Reg are not covered in this comparison.**	123.3 Definitions. 123.5 Current good manufacturing practice. 123.6 Hazard Analysis and Hazard Analysis Critical Control Point (HACCP) plan. 123.7 Corrective actions. 123.8 Verification. 123.9 Records. 123.10 Training. 123.11 Sanitation control procedures. (not discussed here) 123.12 Special requirements for imported products. Subpart B—Smoked and Smoke-Flavored Fishery Products Subpart C—Raw Molluscan Shellfish **NOTE: 123.11, Subpart B, and Subpart C are not covered in this comparison.**
Definitions	**§417.1 Definitions.** For purposes of this part, the following definitions shall apply:	**§123.3 Definitions.** The definitions and interpretations of terms in section 201 of the Federal Food, Drug, and Cosmetic Act (the act) and in part 110 of this chapter are applicable to such terms when used in this part, except where they are herein redefined. The following definitions shall also apply:

Element	USDA/FSIS Mega-Reg	FDA Seafood HACCP Regulation
Certification number	NA	. . . a unique combination of letters and numbers assigned by a shellfish control authority to a molluscan shellfish processor.
Corrective action	Procedures to be followed when a deviation occurs	NA
Critical control point	A point, step, or procedure in a food process at which control can be applied and, as a result, a food safety hazard can be prevented, eliminated, or reduced to acceptable levels.	. . . a point, step, or procedure in a food process at which control can be applied, and a food safety hazard can as a result be prevented, eliminated, or reduced to acceptable levels.
Critical limit	The maximum or minimum value to which a physical, biological, or chemical hazard must be controlled at a critical control point to prevent, eliminate, or reduce to an acceptable level the occurrence of the identified food safety hazard.	. . . the maximum or minimum value to which a physical, biological, or chemical parameter must be controlled at a critical control pint to prevent, eliminate, or reduce to an acceptable level the occurrence of the identified food safety hazard.
Fish	NA	. . . fresh or saltwater finfish, crustaceans, other forms of aquatic animal life (including, but not limited to, alligator, frog, aquatic turtle, jellyfish, sea cucumber, and sea urchin and the roe of such animals) other than birds or mammals, and all mollusks, where such animal life is intended for human consumption.
Fishery product	NA	. . . any human food product in which fish is a characterizing ingredient.
Food safety hazard	Any biological, chemical, or physical property that may cause a food to be unsafe for human consumption.	. . . any biological, chemical, or physical property that may cause a food to be unsafe for human consumption.
HACCP System	The HACCP plan in operation, including the HACCP plan itself	NA
Hazard	See Food Safety Hazard.	NA
Importer	NA	. . . either the U.S. owner or consignee at the time of entry into the United States, or the U.S. agent or representative of the foreign owner or consignee at the time of entry into the United States, who is responsible for ensuring that goods being offered for entry into the United States are in compliance with all laws affecting the importation. For the purposes of this definition, ordinarily the importer is not the custom house broker, the freight forwarder, the carrier, or the steamship representative.
Molluscan shellfish	NA	. . . any edible species of fresh or frozen oysters, clams, mussels, or scallops, or edible portions of such species, except when the product consists entirely of the shucked adductor muscle.
Preventive measure	Physical, chemical, or other means that can be used to control an identified food safety hazard.	. . . physical, chemical, or other factors that can be used to control an identified food safety hazard.
Process-monitoring instrument	An instrument or device used to indicate conditions during processing at a critical control point.	. . . an instrument or device used to indicate conditions during processing at a critical control point.
Processing		(1) . . . with respect to fish or fishery products: Handling, storing, preparing, heading, eviscerating, shucking, freezing, changing into different market forms, manufacturing, preserving, packing, labeling, dockside unloading, or holding. (2) The regulations in this part do not apply to: (i) Harvesting or transporting fish or fishery products, without otherwise engaging in processing. (ii) Practices such as heading, eviscerating, or freezing intended solely to prepare a fish for holding on board a harvest vessel. (iii) The operation of a retail establishment.
Processor	NA	. . . any person engaged in commercial, custom, or institutional processing of fish or fishery products, either in the United States or in a foreign country. A processing includes any person engaged in the production of foods that are to be used in market or consumer tests.
Responsible establishment official	The individual with overall authority on-site or a higher level official of the establishment.	NA
Scombroid toxin-forming species	NA	. . . tuna, bluefish, mahi mahi, and other species, whether or not in the family Scombridae, in which significant levels of histamine may be produced in the fish flesh by decarboxylation of free histidine as a result of exposure of the fish after capture to temperatures that permit the growth of mesophilic bacteria.
Shall	NA	. . . is used to state mandatory requirements.

Continued next page

Appendix D, cont.

Element	USDA/FSIS Mega-Reg	FDA Seafood HACCP Regulation
Shellfish control authority	NA	. . . a Federal, State, or foreign agency, or sovereign tribal government, legally responsible for the administration of a program that includes activities such as classification of molluscan shellfish growing areas, enforcement of molluscan shellfish harvesting controls, and certification of molluscan shellfish processors.
Shellstock	NA	. . . raw, in-shell molluscan shellfish.
Should	NA	. . . is used to state recommended or advisory procedures or to identify recommended equipment.
Shucked shellfish	NA	. . . molluscan shellfish that have one or both shells removed.
Smoked or smoke-flavored fishery products	NA	. . . the finished food prepared by: (1) Treating fish with salt (sodium chloride), and (2) Subjecting it to the direct action of smoke from burning wood, sawdust, or similar material and/or imparting to it the flavor of smoke by a means such as immersing it in a solution of wood smoke.
Tag	NA	. . . a record of harvesting information attached to a container of shellstock by the harvester or processor.
Current Good Manufacturing Practice	NA	**§ 123.5 Current Good Manufacturing Practice.** (a) Part 110 of this chapter applies in determining whether the facilities, methods, practices, and controls used to process fish and fishery products are safe, and whether these products have been processed under sanitary conditions.
		(b) The purpose of this part is to set forth requirements specific to the processing of fish and fishery products.
Hazard Analysis and HACCP Plan.	**§ 417.2 Hazard Analysis and HACCP Plan.**	**§ 123.6 Hazard Analysis and Hazard Analysis Critical Control Point (HACCP) Plan.**
Hazard analysis	(a) *Hazard analysis.* (1) Every official establishment shall conduct, or have conducted for it, a hazard analysis to determine the food safety hazards reasonably likely to occur in the production process and identify the preventive measures the establishment can apply to control those hazards. The hazard analysis shall include food safety hazards that can occur before, during, and after entry into the establishment. A food safety hazard that is reasonably likely to occur is one for which a prudent establishment would establish controls because it historically has occurred, or because there is a reasonable possibility that it will occur in the particular type of product being processed, in the absence of those controls.	(a) *Hazard analysis.* Every processor shall conduct, or have conducted for it, a hazard analysis to determine whether there are food safety hazards that are reasonably likely to occur for each kind of fish and fishery product processed by that processor and to identify the preventive measures that the processor can apply to control those hazards. Such food safety hazards can be introduced both within and outside the processing plant environment, including food safety hazards that can occur before, during, and after harvest. A food safety hazard that is reasonably likely to occur is one for which a prudent processor would establish controls because experience, illness data, scientific reports, or other information provide a basis to conclude that there is a reasonable possibility that it will occur in the particular type of fish or fishery product being processed in the absence of those controls.
	(2) A flow chart describing the steps of each process and product flow in the establishment shall be prepared, and the intended use or consumers of the finished product shall be identified.	
	(3) Food safety hazards might be expected to arise from the following: (i) Natural toxins. (ii) Microbiological contamination. (iii) Chemical contamination. (iv) Pesticides. (v) Drug residues. (vi) Zoonotic diseases. (vii) Decomposition. (viii) Parasites. (ix) Unapproved use of direct or indirect food or color additives. (x) Physical hazards.	[§ 123.6(c)(1)] Consideration should be given to whether any food safety hazards are reasonably likely to occur as a result of the following: (i) Natural toxins. (ii) Microbiological contamination. (iii) Chemical contamination. (iv) Pesticides. (v) Drug residues. (vi) Decomposition in scombroid toxin-forming species or in any other species where a food safety hazard has been associated with decomposition; (vii) Parasites, where the processor has knowledge or has reason to know that the parasite-containing fish or fishery product will be consumed without a process sufficient to kill the parasites, or where the processor represents, labels, or intends for the product to be so consumed; (viii) Unapproved use of direct or indirect food or color additives; and (ix) Physical hazards;

Element	USDA/FSIS Mega-Reg	FDA Seafood HACCP Regulation
The HACCP plan	(b) *The HACCP plan.* (1) Every establishment shall develop and implement a written HACCP plan covering each product produced by that establishment whenever a hazard analysis reveals one or more food safety hazards that are reasonably likely to occur, based on the hazard analysis conducted in accordance with paragraph (a) of this section, including products in the following processing categories: (i) Slaughter—all species. (ii) Raw product—ground. (iii) Raw product—not ground. (iv) Thermally processed—commercially sterile. (v) Not heat treated—shelf stable. (vi) Heat treated—shelf stable. (vii) Fully cooked—not shelf stable. (viii) Heat treated but not fully cooked—not shelf stable. (ix) Product with secondary inhibitors—not shelf stable.	(b) *The HACCP plan.* Every processor shall have and implement a written HACCP plan whenever a hazard analysis reveals one or more food safety hazards that are reasonably likely to occur, as described in paragraph (a) of this section. A HACCP plan shall be specific to: (1) Each location where fish and fishery products are processed by that processor; and (2) Each kind of fish and fishery product processed by the processor.
	(2) A single HACCP plan may encompass multiple products within a single processing category identified in this paragraph, if the food safety hazards, critical control points, critical limits, and procedures required to be identified and performed in paragraph (c) of this section are essentially the same, provided that any required features of the plan that are unique to a specific product are clearly delineated in the plan and are observed in practice.	[§ 123.6 (b)(2) continued] The plan may group kinds of fish and fishery products together, or group kinds of production methods together, if the food safety hazards, critical control points, critical limits, and procedures required to be identified and performed in paragraph (c) of this section are identical for all fish and fishery products so grouped or for all production methods so grouped.
Thermally processed foods	(3) HACCP plans for thermally processed/commercially sterile products do not have to address the food safety hazards associated with microbiological contamination if the product is produced in accordance with the requirements of part 318, subpart G, or part 381, subpart X, of this chapter.	(e) *Products subject to other regulations.* For fish and fishery products that are subject to the requirements of part 113 or 114 of this chapter, the HACCP plan need not list the food safety hazard associated with the formation of *Clostridium botulinum* toxin in the finished, hermetically sealed container, nor list the controls to prevent that food safety hazard. A HACCP plan for such fish and fishery products shall address any other food safety hazards that are reasonably likely to occur.
The contents of the HACCP plan	(c) *The contents of the HACCP plan.* The HACCP plan shall, at a minimum:	(c) *The contents of the HACCP plan.* The HACCP plan shall, at a minimum:
	(1) List the food safety hazards identified in accordance with paragraph (a) of this section, which must be controlled for each process.	(1) List the food safety hazards that are reasonably likely to occur, as identified in accordance with paragraph (a) of this section, and that thus must be controlled for each fish and fishery product.
	(2) List the critical control points for each of the identified food safety hazards, including, as appropriate: (i) Critical control points designed to control food safety hazards that could be introduced in the establishment, and (ii) Critical control points designed to control food safety hazards introduced outside the establishment, including food safety hazards that occur before, during, and after entry into the establishment;	(2) List the critical control points for each of the identified food safety hazards, including as appropriate: (i) Critical control points designed to control food safety hazards that could be introduced in the processing plant environment; and (ii) Critical control points designed to control food safety hazards introduced outside the processing plant environment, including food safety hazards that occur before, during, and after harvest;
	(3) List the critical limits that must be met at each of the critical control points. Critical limits shall, at a minimum, be designed to ensure that applicable targets or performance standards established by FSIS, and any other requirement set forth in this chapter pertaining to the specific process or product, are met;	(3) List the critical limits that must be met at each of the critical control points;
	(4) List the procedures, and the frequency with which those procedures will be performed, that will be used to monitor each of the critical control points to ensure compliance with the critical limits;	(4) List the procedures, and frequency thereof, that will be used to monitor each of the critical control points to ensure compliance with the critical limits;
	(5) Include all corrective actions that have been developed in accordance with § 417.3(a) of this part, to be followed in response to any deviation from a critical limit at a critical control point; and	(5) Include any corrective action plans that have been developed in accordance with § 123.7(b), to be followed in response to deviations from critical limits at critical control points;
	(6) Provide for a recordkeeping system that documents the monitoring of the critical control points. The records shall contain the actual values and observations obtained during monitoring.	(6) Provide for a recordkeeping system that documents the monitoring of the critical control points. The records shall contain the actual values and observations obtained during monitoring.
	(7) List the verification procedures, and the frequency with which those procedures will be performed, that the establishment will use in accordance with § 417.4 of this part.	(7) List the verification procedures, and frequency thereof, that the processor will use in accordance with § 123.8(a);

Continued next page

Appendix D, cont.

Element	USDA/FSIS Mega-Reg	FDA Seafood HACCP Regulation
		(f) *Sanitation.* Sanitation controls may be included in the HACCP plan. However, to the extent that they are monitored in accordance with § 123.11(b) they need not be included in the HACCP plan, and vice versa.
Signing and dating the HACCP plan.	(d) *Signing and dating the HACCP plan.* (1) The HACCP plan shall be signed and dated by the responsible establishment individual. This signature shall signify that the establishment accepts and will implement the HACCP plan.	(d) *Signing and dating the HACCP plan.* (1) The HACCP plan shall be signed and dated either by the most responsible individual onsite at the processing facility or by a higher level official of the processor. This signature shall signify that the HACCP plan has been accepted for implementation by the firm.
	(2) The HACCP plan shall be dated and signed: (i) Upon initial acceptance; (ii) Upon any modification; and (iii) At least annually, upon reassessment, as required under § 417.4(a)(3) of this part.	(2) The HACCP plan shall be dated and signed: (i) Upon initial acceptance; (ii) Upon any modification; and (iii) Upon verification of the plan in accordance with § 123.8(a)(1)
Failure to develop and implement a HACCP plan	(e) Pursuant to 21 U.S.C. 608 and 621, the failure of an establishment to develop and implement a HACCP plan that complies with this section, or to operate in accordance with the requirements of this part, may render the products produced under those conditions adulterated.	(g) *Legal basis.* Failure of a processor to have and implement a HACCP plan that complies with this section whenever a HACCP plan is necessary, otherwise operate in accordance with the requirements of this part, shall render the fish or fishery products of that processor adulterated under section 402(a)(4) of the act. Whether a processor's actions are consistent with ensuring the safety of food will be determined through an evaluation of the processors overall implementation of its HACCP plan, if one is required.
Corrective actions	**§ 417.3 Corrective actions.**	**§ 123.7 Corrective Actions**
	(a) The written HACCP plan shall identify the corrective action to be followed in response to a deviation from a critical limit. The HACCP plan shall describe the corrective action to be taken, and assign responsibility for taking corrective action, to ensure:	(a) Whenever a deviation from a critical limit occurs, a processor shall take corrective action either by: (1) Following a corrective action plan that is appropriate for the particular deviation, or (2) Following the procedures in paragraph (c) of this section. (b) Processors may develop written corrective action plans, which become part of their HACCP plans in accordance with § 123.6(c)(5), by which they predetermine the corrective actions that they will take whenever there is a deviation from a critical limit. A corrective action plan that is appropriate for a particular deviation is one that describes the steps to be taken and assigns responsibility for taking those steps, to ensure that:
	(1) The cause of the deviation is identified and eliminated;	(2) The cause of the deviation is corrected.
	(2) The CCP will be under control after the corrective action is taken;	
	(3) Measures to prevent recurrence are established; and	
	(4) No product that is injurious to health or otherwise adulterated as a result of the deviation enters commerce.	(1) No product enters commerce that is either injurious to health or is otherwise adulterated as a result of the deviation; and
	(b) If a deviation not covered by a specified corrective action occurs, or if another unforeseen hazard arises, the establishment shall:	(c) When a deviation from a critical limit occurs and the processor does not have a corrective action plan that is appropriate for that deviation, the processor shall:
	(1) Segregate and hold the affected product, at least until the requirements of paragraphs (b)(2) and (b)(3) of this section are met;	(1) Segregate and hold the affected product, at least until the requirements of paragraphs (c)(2) and (c)(3) of this section are met;
	(2) Perform a review to determine the acceptability of the affected product for distribution;	(2) Perform or obtain a review to determine the acceptability of the affected product for distribution. The review shall be performed by an individual or individuals who have adequate training or experience to perform such a review. Adequate training may or may not include training in accordance with § 123.10;
	(3) Take action, when necessary, with respect to the affected product to ensure that no product that is injurious to health or otherwise adulterated, as a result of the deviation, enters commerce;	(3) Take corrective action, when necessary, with respect to the affected product to ensure that no product enters commerce that is either injurious to health or is otherwise adulterated as a result of the deviation;
		(4) Take corrective action, when necessary, to correct the cause of the deviation;
	(4) Perform or obtain reassessment by an individual trained in accordance with § 417.7 of this part, to determine whether the newly identified deviation or other unforeseen hazard should be incorporated into the HACCP plan.	(5) Perform or obtain timely reassessment by an individual or individuals who have been trained in accordance with § 123.10, to determine whether the HACCP plan needs to be modified to reduce the risk of recurrence of the deviation, and modify the HACCP plan as necessary.

Element	USDA/FSIS Mega-Reg	FDA Seafood HACCP Regulation
	(c) All corrective actions taken in accordance with this section shall be documented in records that are subject to verification in accordance with § 417.4(a)(2)(iii) and the recordkeeping requirements of § 417.5 of this part.	(d) All corrective actions taken in accordance with this section shall be fully documented in records that are subject to verification in accordance with § 123.8(a)(3)(ii) and the recordkeeping requirements of § 123.9.
Validation, Verification, Reassessment.	**§417.4 Validation, Verification, Reassessment.**	**§ 123.8 Verification.**
	(a) Every establishment shall validate the HACCP plan's adequacy in controlling the food safety hazards identified during the hazard analysis, and shall verify that the plan is being effectively implemented.	(a) *Overall verification.* Every processor shall verify that the HACCP plan is adequate to control food safety hazards that are reasonably likely to occur, and that the plan is being effectively implemented. Verification shall include, at a minimum:
	(1) *Initial validation.* Upon completion of the hazard analysis and development of the HACCP plan, the establishment shall conduct activities designed to determine that the HACCP plan is functioning as intended. During this HACCP plan validation period, the establishment shall repeatedly test the adequacy of the CCP's, critical limits, monitoring and recordkeeping procedures, and corrective actions set forth in the HACCP plan. Validation also encompasses reviews of the records themselves, routinely generated by the HACCP system, in the context of other validation activities.	
	(2) *Ongoing verification activities.* Ongoing verification activities include, but are not limited to:	(2) *Ongoing verification activities.* Ongoing verification activities including:
		(i) A review of any consumer complaints that have been received by the processor to determine whether they relate to the performance of critical control points or reveal the existence of unidentified critical control points;
	(i) The calibration of process-monitoring instruments;	(ii) The calibration of process-monitoring instruments; and,.
		(iii) At the option of the processor, the performing of periodic end-product or in-process testing.
	(ii) Direct observations of monitoring activities and corrective actions; and	
		(d) *Recordkeeping.* The calibration of process-monitoring instruments, and the performing of any periodic end-product and in- process testing, in accordance with paragraphs (a)(2)(ii) through (iii) of this section shall be documented in records that are subject to the recordkeeping requirements of § 123.9.
	(iii) The review of records generated and maintained in accordance with § 417.5(a)(3) of this part.	(3) *Records review.* A review, including signing and dating, by an individual who has been trained in accordance with § 123.10, of the records that document: (i) The monitoring of critical control points. The purpose of this review shall be, at a minimum, to ensure that the records are complete and to verify that they document values that are within the critical limits. This review shall occur within 1 week of the day that the records are made; (ii) The taking of corrective actions. The purpose of this review shall be, at a minimum, to ensure that the records are complete and to verify that appropriate corrective actions were taken in accordance with § 123.7. This review shall occur within 1 week of the day that the records are made; and (iii) The calibrating of any process control instruments used at critical control points and the performing of any periodic end-product or in-process testing that is part of the processor's verification activities. The purpose of these reviews shall be, at a minimum, to ensure that the records are complete, and that these activities occurred in accordance with the processor's written procedures. These reviews shall occur within a reasonable time after the records are made.

Continued next page

Appendix D, cont.

Element	USDA/FSIS Mega-Reg	FDA Seafood HACCP Regulation
	(3) *Reassessment of the HACCP plan.* Every establishment shall reassess the adequacy of the HACCP plan at least annually and whenever any changes occur that could affect the hazard analysis or alter the HACCP plan. Such changes may include, but are not limited to, changes in: raw materials or source of raw materials; product formulation; slaughter or processing methods or systems; production volume; personnel; packaging; finished product distribution systems; or, the intended use or consumers of the finished product. The reassessment shall be performed by an individual trained in accordance with § 417.7 of this part. The HACCP plan shall be modified immediately whenever a reassessment reveals that the plan no longer meets the requirements of § 417.2(c) of this part.	(1) *Reassessment of the HACCP plan.* A reassessment of the adequacy of the HACCP plan whenever any changes occur that could affect the hazard analysis or alter the HACCP plan in any way or at least annually. Such changes may include changes in the following: raw materials or source of raw materials, product formulation, processing methods or systems, finished product distribution systems, or the intended use or consumers of the finished product. The reassessment shall be performed by an individual or individuals who have been trained in accordance with § 123.10. The HACCP plan shall be modified immediately whenever a reassessment reveals that the plan is no longer adequate to fully meet the requirements of § 123.6(c).
		(b) *Corrective actions.* Processors shall immediately follow the procedures in § 123.7 whenever any verification procedure, including the review of a consumer complaint, reveals the need to take a corrective action.
	(b) *Reassessment of the hazard analysis.* Any establishment that does not have a HACCP plan because a hazard analysis has revealed no food safety hazards that are reasonably likely to occur shall reassess the adequacy of the hazard analysis whenever a change occurs that could reasonably affect whether a food safety hazard exists. Such changes may include, but are not limited to, changes in: raw materials or source of raw materials; product formulation; slaughter or processing methods or systems; production volume; packaging; finished product distribution systems; or, the intended use or consumers of the finished product.	(c) *Reassessment of the hazard analysis.* Whenever a processor does not have a HACCP plan because a hazard analysis has revealed no food safety hazards that are reasonably likely to occur, the processor shall reassess the adequacy of that hazard analysis whenever there are any changes that could reasonably affect whether a food safety hazard now exists. Such changes may include, but are not limited to changes in: Raw materials or source of raw materials, product formulation, processing methods or systems, finished product distribution systems, or the intended use or consumers of the finished product. The reassessment shall be performed by an individual or individuals who have been trained in accordance with § 123.10.
Records	**§417.5 Records.**	**§ 123.9 Records.**
	(a) The establishment shall maintain the following records documenting the establishment's HACCP plan:	(a) *General requirements.* All records required by this part shall include:
	(1) The written hazard analysis prescribed in § 417.2(a) of this part, including all supporting documentation;	
	(2) The written HACCP plan, including decisionmaking documents associated with the selection and development of CCP's and critical limits, and documents supporting both the monitoring and verification procedures selected and the frequency of those procedures.	
	(3) Records documenting the monitoring of CCP's and their critical limits, including the recording of actual times, temperatures, or other quantifiable values, as prescribed in the establishment's HACCP plan; the calibration of process-monitoring instruments; corrective actions, including all actions taken in response to a deviation; verification procedures and results; product code(s), product name or identity, or slaughter production lot. Each of these records shall include the date the record was made.	
	(b) Each entry on a record maintained under the HACCP plan shall be made at the time the specific event occurs and include the date and time recorded, and shall be signed or initialed by the establishment employee making the entry.	(1) The name and location of the processor or importer; (2) The date and time of the activity that the record reflects; (3) The signature or initials of the person performing the operation; and (4) Where appropriate, the identity of the product and the production code, if any. Processing and other information shall be entered on records at the time that it is observed.
	(c) Prior to shipping product, the establishment shall review the records associated with the production of that product, documented in accordance with this section, to ensure completeness, including the determination that all critical limits were met and, if appropriate, corrective actions were taken, including the proper disposition of product. Where practicable, this review shall be conducted, dated, and signed by an individual who did not produce the record(s), preferably by someone trained in accordance with § 417.7 of this part, or the responsible establishment official.	[see § 123.8 (a)(3)]

Element	USDA/FSIS Mega-Reg	FDA Seafood HACCP Regulation
	(d) *Records maintained on computers.* The use of records maintained on computers is acceptable, provided that appropriate controls are implemented to ensure the integrity of the electronic data and signatures.	(f) *Records maintained on computers.* The maintenance of records on computers is acceptable, provided that appropriate controls are implemented to ensure the integrity of the electronic data and signatures.
Record Retention	(e) *Record retention.* (1) Establishments shall retain all records required by paragraph (a)(3) of this section as follows: • For slaughter activities for at least one year. • For refrigerated product, for at least one year. • For frozen, preserved, or shelf-stable products, for at least two years.	(b) *Record retention.* (1) All records required by this part shall be retained at the processing facility or importer's place of business in the United States for at least 1 year after the date they were prepared in the case of refrigerated products and for at least 2 years after the date they were prepared in the case of frozen, preserved, or shelf-stable products. (2) Records that relate to the general adequacy of equipment or processes being used by a processor, including the results of scientific studies and evaluations, shall be retained at the processing facility or the importer's place of business in the United States for at least 2 years after their applicability to the product being produced at the facility.
	(2) Off-site storage of records required by paragraph (a)(3) of this section is permitted after six months, if such records can be retrieved and provided, on-site, within 24 hours of an FSIS employee's request.	(3) If the processing facility is closed for a prolonged period between seasonal packs, or if record storage capacity is limited on a processing vessel or at a remote processing site, the records may be transferred to some other reasonably accessible location at the end of the seasonal pack but shall be immediately returned for official review upon demand.
	(f) *Official review.* All records required by this part and all plans and procedures required by this part shall be available for official review and copying.	(c) *Official review.* All records required by this part and all plans and procedures required by this part shall be available for official review and copying at reasonable times.
		(d) *Public disclosure.* (1) Subject to the limitations in paragraph (d)(2) of this section, all plans and records required by this part are not available for public disclosure unless they have been previously disclosed to the public as defined in § 20.81 of this chapter or they relate to a product or ingredient that has been abandoned and they no longer represent a trade secret or confidential commercial or financial information as defined in § 20.61 of this chapter. (2) However, these records and plans may be subject to disclosure to the extent that they are otherwise publicly available, or that disclosure could not reasonably be expected to cause a competitive hardship, such as generic-type HACCP plans that reflect standard industry practices.
		(e) *Tags.* Tags as defined in § 123.3(t) are not subject to the requirements of this section unless they are used to fulfill the requirements of § 123.28(c).
Inadequate HACCP Systems	§ 417.6 Inadequate HACCP Systems.	
	A HACCP system may be found to be inadequate if:	
	(a) The HACCP plan in operation does not meet the requirements set forth in this part;	
	(b) Establishment personnel are not performing tasks specified in the HACCP plan;	
	(c) The establishment fails to take corrective actions, as required by § 417.3 of this part;	
	(d) HACCP records are not being maintained as required in § 417.5 of this part; or	
	(e) Adulterated product is produced or shipped.	

Continued next page

Appendix D, cont.

Element	USDA/FSIS Mega-Reg	FDA Seafood HACCP Regulation
Training	**§ 417.7 Training.**	**§ 123.10 Training.**
	(a) Only an individual who has met the requirements of paragraph (b) of this section, but who need not be an employee of the establishment, shall be permitted to perform the following functions:	At a minimum, the following functions shall be performed by an individual who has successfully completed training in the application of HACCP principles to fish and fishery product processing at least equivalent to that received under standardized curriculum recognized as adequate by the U.S. Food and Drug Administration or who is otherwise qualified through job experience to perform these functions. Job experience will qualify an individual to perform these functions if it has provided knowledge at least equivalent to that provided through the standardized curriculum. (Copied from §123.10c below) The trained individual need not be an employee of the processor.
	(1) Development of the HACCP plan, in accordance with § 417.2(b) of this part, which could include adapting a generic model that is appropriate for the specific product; and	(a) Developing a HACCP plan, which could include adapting a model or generic-type HACCP plan, that is appropriate for a specific processor, in order to meet the requirements of § 123.6(b);
	(2) Reassessment and modification of the HACCP plan, in accordance with § 417.3 of this part.	(b) Reassessing and modifying the HACCP plan in accordance with the corrective action procedures specified in § 123.7(c)(5), the HACCP plan in accordance with theverification activities specified in § 123.8(a)(1), and the hazard analysis in accordance with the verification activities specified in § 123.8(c); and
		(c) Performing the record review required by § 123.8(a)(3); The trained individual need not be an employee of the processor.
	(b) The individual performing the functions listed in paragraph (a) of this section shall have successfully completed a course of instruction in the application of the seven HACCP principles to meat or poultry product processing, including a segment on the development of a HACCP plan for a specific product and on record review.	(Copied from §123.10 introduction above) in the application of HACCP principles to fish and fishery product processing at least equivalent to that received under standardized curriculum recognized as adequate by the U.S. Food and Drug Administration or who is otherwise qualified through job experience to perform these functions. Job experience will qualify an individual to perform these functions if it has provided knowledge at least equivalent to that provided through the standardized curriculum.
Agency verification	**§ 417.8 Agency verification.**	
	FSIS will verify the adequacy of the HACCP plan(s) by determining that each HACCP plan meets the requirements of this part and all other applicable regulations. Such verification may include: (a) Reviewing the HACCP plan; (b) Reviewing the CCP records; (c) Reviewing and determining the adequacy of corrective actions taken when a deviation occurs; (d) Reviewing the critical limits; (e) Reviewing other records pertaining to the HACCP plan or system; (f) Direct observation or measurement at a CCP; (g) Sample collection and analysis to determine the product meets all safety standards; and (h) On-site observations and record review.	

Element	USDA/FSIS Mega-Reg	FDA Seafood HACCP Regulation
Imported Products		**§ 123.12 Special requirements for imported products.** This section sets forth specific requirements for imported fish and fishery products. (a) *Importer verification.* Every importer of fish or fishery products shall either: (1) Obtain the fish or fishery product from a country that has an active memorandum of understanding (MOU) or similar agreement with the Food and Drug Administration, that covers the fish or fishery product and documents the equivalency or compliance of the inspection system of the foreign country with the U.S. system, accurately reflects the current situation between the signing parties, and is functioning and enforceable in its entirety; or (2) Have and implement written verification procedures for ensuring that the fish and fishery products that they offer for import into the United States were processed in accordance with the requirements of this part. The procedures shall list at a minimum: (i) Product specifications that are designed to ensure that the product is not adulterated under section 402 of the Federal Food, Drug, and Cosmetic Act because it may be injurious to health or have been processed under insanitary conditions, and, (ii) Affirmative steps that may include any of the following: (A) Obtaining from the foreign processor the HACCP and sanitation monitoring records required by this part that relate to the specific lot of fish or fishery products being offered for import; (B) Obtaining either a continuing or lot-by-lot certificate from an appropriate foreign government inspection authority or competent third party certifying that the imported fish or fishery product is or was processed in accordance with the requirements of this part; (C) Regularly inspecting the foreign processor's facilities to ensure that the imported fish or fishery product is being processed in accordance with the requirements of this part; (D) Maintaining on file a copy, in English, of the foreign processor's HACCP plan, and a written guarantee from the foreign processor that the imported fish or fishery product is processed in accordance with the requirements of the part; (E) Periodically testing the imported fish or fishery product, and maintaining on file a copy, in English, of a written guarantee from the foreign processor that the imported fish or fishery product is processed in accordance with the requirements of this part or, (F) Other such verification measures as appropriate that provide an equivalent level of assurance of compliance with the requirements of this part. (b) *Competent third party.* An importer may hire a competent third party to assist with or perform any or all of the verification activities specified in paragraph (a)(2) of this section, including writing the importer's verification procedures on the importer's behalf. (c) *Records.* The importer shall maintain records, in English, that document the performance and results of the affirmative steps specified in paragraph (a)(2)(ii) of this section. These records shall be subject to the applicable provisions of § 123.9. (d) *Determination of compliance.* There must be evidence that all fish and fishery products offered for entry into the United States have been processed under conditions that comply with this part. If assurances do not exist that the imported fish or fishery product has been processed under conditions that are equivalent to those required of domestic processors under this part, the product will appear to be adulterated and will be denied entry.

HACCP Models

INTRODUCTION

Appendix E contains model HACCP plans for the following four products: cheddar cheese, frozen breaded fish sticks, frozen raw beef patties, and all-beef hot dogs. These four models are designed to demonstrate the thought process involved with conducting a hazard analysis and subsequently developing a HACCP plan. The models are based on the HACCP principles as outlined in the National Advisory Committee on Microbiological Criteria For Foods (NACMCF) HACCP document, adopted by the committee in 1997, and may not reflect current regulatory Agency positions on HACCP. The HACCP models are intended to be used for training purposes only and are not intended to replace a processor's hazard analysis and HACCP plan development.

PREREQUISITE PROGRAMS

The development of the HACCP models was based on implementation of well-developed prerequisite programs that provide a solid foundation for environmental and operational control. This foundation is essential for the development of an effective HACCP plan. The following are examples of prerequisite programs that may influence the outcome of a hazard analysis:

- Facilities maintained to meet cGMP regulations.
- Continuing supplier guarantee program.
- Written specifications for all ingredients and packaging materials.
- Antibiotic residue screening program.
- Established and documented preventive maintenance and calibration schedules.
- Sanitation program with written sanitation standard operating procedures (SSOPs).
- Documented employee training programs in personal hygiene and plant operations.
- Pest control program.
- Procedures for proper receiving, storing and shipping of materials and finished products.
- Effective product coding and recall systems.
- Plant-wide temperature control SOPs.

CHEDDAR CHEESE

Description of Product and Process Flow

Cheddar cheese is prepared from a blend of milk and non-fat dry milk (NFDM), starter culture, rennet, calcium chloride (CaCl₂), annatto, and salt. The cheese is formulated and aged up to 12 months to meet customer specifications. The materials used are waxed, wooden boxes and plastic shrink-wrap film supplied in rollstock.

Cheddar cheese is distributed in 40-pound shrink-wrapped blocks. The cheese may be consumed without further preparation. The product is aged and stored at 40–45°F and shipped refrigerated at 35–40°F. The product is intended for the food service and retail deli trade or as an ingredient for further processing.

Raw milk is received in refrigerated tanker trucks. Prior to use, the milk is stored in silos at refrigerated temperatures of 40–45°F. The other ingredients are received and warehoused at ambient temperatures.

Cream is separated from the raw milk and a portion, along with the NFDM, is blended back into the raw milk to meet formulation specifications. The raw milk blend is pre-heated, pasteurized and cooled through a high-temperature short-time (HTST) plate heat exchanger.

The pasteurized milk blend and the prepared starter culture are then mixed with rotating stainless steel paddles in temperature controlled cheese vats.

The blend is heated at 86–88°F to ripen and to increase the acidity level. The ripening process is watched closely to ensure adequate acid formation. Annatto, rennet, and CaCl₂ are added to the blend when the titratable acidity reaches 0.02%.

The batch is held for curd formation. After forming, the curd is cut with wire knives. The whey is expressed and drained out by heating the curd to 95°F. The remaining curd is cheddared, then mechanically milled in the cheese vats. The pH of the curd and time for acid development is monitored and controlled at this point. Vats which have a high pH or which were slow in acid development provide the environment for *Staphylococcus aureus* growth and subsequent enterotoxin development.

After salting, the curd is conveyed from the cheese vats, through a metal detector and is filled into waxed wooden boxes. The boxes hold 640 pounds of product.

Pressure is applied to the boxes and the cheese is aged at 40–45°F for 4 to 12 months. After aging, the cheese is sawed into 40 pound block portions and shrink wrapped.

The blocks continue to age to meet customer specifications. After aging, the blocks of cheddar cheese are stored and distributed at refrigerated temperatures of 35–40°F.

This generic HACCP plan was developed for training purposes only and is not intended to replace the processor's hazard analysis and HACCP plan development.

Cheddar Cheese

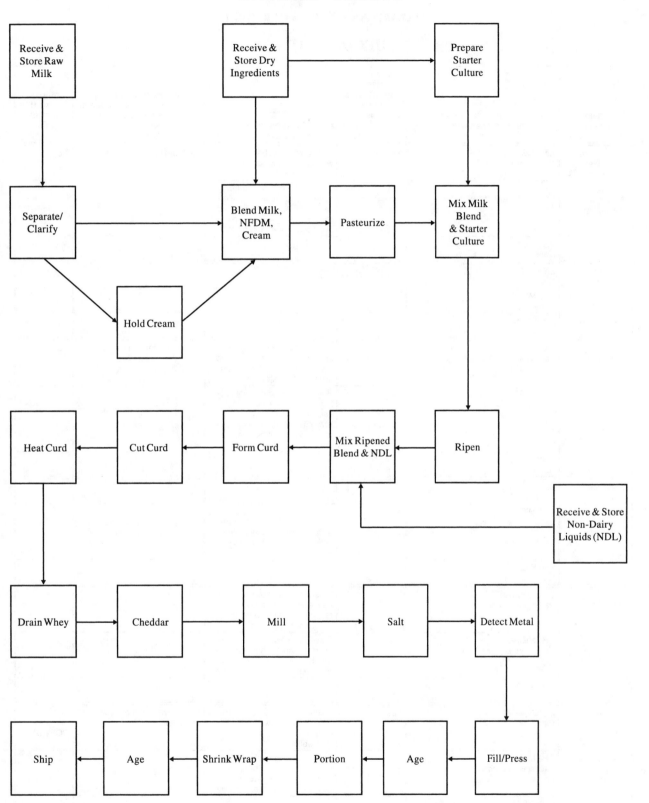

Example: For Training Purposes Only

HAZARD ANALYSIS WORKSHEET

CHEDDAR CHEESE

Ingredient or Processing Step	Potential hazards introduced, controlled or enhanced at this step.	Does this potential hazard need to be addressed in HACCP plan? (Yes/No)	WHY? (Justification for decision made in previous column)	What measures can be applied to prevent, eliminate or reduce the hazards being addressed in your HACCP plan?	Is this step a critical control point (CCP)?
Receive and Store Dry Ingredients (NFDM, starter, salt, packaging)	BIOLOGICAL Salmonella	Yes	*Salmonella* has been associated with non-fat dry milk (NFDM).	Pasteurization at later step	No
	CHEMICAL Non-food grade ingredient	No	Ingredients purchased from company approved suppliers who meet specifications for ingredients. Unlikely to receive non-food grade ingredients.		
	PHYSICAL None				
Receive & Store Non-Dairy Liquids (Annatto, rennet, CaCl₂)	BIOLOGICAL None				
	CHEMICAL None				
	PHYSICAL None				
Receive & Store Raw Milk	BIOLOGICAL Pathogens (Enteric pathogens and *Salmonella*)	Yes	Pathogens have been associated with raw milk and may grow due to temperature abuse during storage.	Pasteurization at later step	No
	CHEMICAL Antibiotic residues	No	Regular residue screening is part of a prerequisite program associated with purchasing raw milk. Not reasonably likely to receive raw milk with hazardous residue levels.		
	PHYSICAL None				
Separate/ Clarify	BIOLOGICAL None				
	CHEMICAL Excessive sanitizers	No	Sanitizer levels controlled by effective sanitation program with SSOPs. Reasonably unlikely to result in illness or injury.		
	PHYSICAL None				
Blend Ingredients	BIOLOGICAL Pathogens (growth)	No	Potential for temperature abuse at this step not reasonably likely to occur due to brief duration.		
	CHEMICAL Excessive sanitizers	No	Sanitizer levels controlled by effective sanitation program with SSOPs. Not reasonably likely to result in illness or injury.		
	PHYSICAL None				
Pasteurize	BIOLOGICAL Pathogens	Yes	This is the only step where heat is applied with sufficient control for pathogen destruction.	Pasteurization to destroy pathogens	Yes CCP1(B)
	CHEMICAL Excessive sanitizers	No	Sanitizer levels controlled by effective sanitation program with SSOPs. Not reasonably likely to result in illness or injury.		
	PHYSICAL None				

Continued next page

Ingredient or Processing Step	Potential hazards introduced, controlled or enhanced at this step.	Does this potential hazard need to be addressed in HACCP plan? (Yes/No)	WHY? (Justification for decision made in previous column)	What measures can be applied to prevent, eliminate or reduce the hazards being addressed in your HACCP plan?	Is this step a critical control point (CCP)?
Prepare Starter Culture	BIOLOGICAL None				
	CHEMICAL Excessive sanitizers	No	Sanitizer levels controlled by effective sanitation program with SSOPs. Not reasonably likely to result in illness or injury.		
	PHYSICAL None				
Mix Milk Blend & Starter Culture	BIOLOGICAL Staphylococcus aureus	Yes	Recontamination with S. aureus and subsequent enterotoxin development is a potential hazard.	Proper acid development will control the growth of S. aureus. Monitored at a later step in process.	No
	CHEMICAL Excessive sanitizers	No	Sanitizer levels controlled by effective sanitation program with SSOPs. Not reasonably likely to result in illness or injury.		
	PHYSICAL None				
Ripen	BIOLOGICAL Staphylococcus aureus	Yes	Growth of S. aureus and subsequent enterotoxin development is a potential hazard.	Proper acid development will control the growth of S. aureus. Controlled at a later step in process.	
	CHEMICAL None				
	PHYSICAL None				
Mix Ripened Blend & Non-Dairy Liquids	BIOLOGICAL None				
	CHEMICAL None				
	PHYSICAL None				
Form Curd	BIOLOGICAL None				
	CHEMICAL None				
	PHYSICAL None				
Cut Curd	BIOLOGICAL None				
	CHEMICAL None				
	PHYSICAL Metal	Yes	Metal from cutting wires may be introduced into product.	Metal detection at later step	No
Heat Curd	BIOLOGICAL Staphylococcus aureus	Yes	Growth of S. aureus and subsequent enterotoxin development is a potential hazard.	Proper acid development will control the growth of S. aureus. Controlled at a later step in process.	
	CHEMICAL None				
	PHYSICAL None				
Drain Whey	BIOLOGICAL None				
	CHEMICAL None				
	PHYSICAL None				

Ingredient or Processing Step	Potential hazards introduced, controlled or enhanced at this step.	Does this potential hazard need to be addressed in HACCP plan? (Yes/No)	WHY? (Justification for decision made in previous column)	What measures can be applied to prevent, eliminate or reduce the hazards being addressed in your HACCP plan?	Is this step a critical control point (CCP)?
Cheddar	BIOLOGICAL None				
	CHEMICAL None				
	PHYSICAL None				
Mill	BIOLOGICAL Staphylococcus aureus	Yes	Growth of S. aureus and subsequent enterotoxin development is a potential hazard.	Proper acid development will control the growth of S. aureus. Controlled at this step in process.	Yes CCP2(B)
	CHEMICAL None				
	PHYSICAL Metal	Yes	Metal from milling equipment may be introduced into product.	Metal detection at later step	No
Salt	BIOLOGICAL None				
	CHEMICAL None				
	PHYSICAL None				
Detect Metal	BIOLOGICAL None				
	CHEMICAL None				
	PHYSICAL Metal	Yes	The potential for metal contamination from the equipment exists. The risk for additional metal contamination after this step is low.	Operable metal detector/reject mechanism	Yes CCP3(P)
Fill/Press	BIOLOGICAL None				
	CHEMICAL None				
	PHYSICAL None				
Age	BIOLOGICAL None				
	CHEMICAL None				
	PHYSICAL None				
Portion	BIOLOGICAL S. aureus (recontamination)	No	The acid content will inhibit the growth of S. aureus.		
	CHEMICAL None				
	PHYSICAL Metal	No	The existence of an effective and documented preventative maintenance program has resulted in the unlikely occurrence of metal being introduced at this step.		
Shrink Wrap	BIOLOGICAL None				
	CHEMICAL None				
	PHYSICAL None				

Continued next page

Ingredient or Processing Step	Potential hazards introduced, controlled or enhanced at this step.	Does this potential hazard need to be addressed in HACCP plan? (Yes/No)	WHY? (Justification for decision made in previous column)	What measures can be applied to prevent, eliminate or reduce the hazards being addressed in your HACCP plan?	Is this step a critical control point (CCP)?
Age	BIOLOGICAL None				
	CHEMICAL None				
	PHYSICAL None				
Ship	BIOLOGICAL None				
	CHEMICAL None				
	PHYSICAL None				

Example: For Training Purposes Only

HACCP Plan Form

CHEDDAR CHEESE

Critical Control Point (CCP)	Hazard(s) to be Addressed in HACCP Plan	Critical Limits for each Control Measure	Monitoring				Corrective Action	Verification Activities	Record-keeping Procedures
			What	How	Frequency	Who			
CCP1(B) Pasteurize	Pathogens (destruction)	Product temperature ≥ 161°F for ≥ 15 seconds.	Temperature of milk at exit of hold tube.	Temperature recorder at end of hold tube, automatic low temperature divert valve.	Continual recording.	Pasteurizer operator.	Recalibrate and reseal pump if seal is broken. Milk will be automatically diverted if temperature at end of hold tube is low; milk will be repasteurized.	QA checks positive displacement pump RPM daily and enters on pasteurization log. Maintenance calibrates divert valve and thermometers monthly.	Pasteurizer log. Calibration records. QA flow verification log. Corrective action logs.
			Seal on timing pump.	Visual check of seal.	At start-up.	Pasteurizer operator.	If divert valve fails to work, product will be retained and repasteurized. If indicating thermometer and recorder don't agree, adjustments are made to thermometers; affected product placed on hold for evaluation.	Pasteurizer operator compares indicating thermometer and recorder twice daily. QA manager will review and initial records daily. Hold tube length and diameter are tested once per year with salt tracer test to validate the residence time.	
CCP2(B) Mill	S. aureus	pH ≤ 5.60 within 8 hours after the start of the culture process.	pH of blend in vats.	pH meter.	Prior to adding salt to each batch.	Cheese maker.	Segregate product, resample for S. aureus after Press step. If S. aureus counts ≥ 10⁴, test for staphylococcal enterotoxin; if enterotoxin present destroy product; if enterotoxin absent divert cheese to thermally processed product.	QA calibrates pH meter at the start of each shift. Cheese maker calibrate pH meter before each use. QA manager will review and initial records daily.	Batch records with time and pH readings. Corrective action reports.
CCP3(P) Detect Metal	Metal	Operable metal detector on. No metal detected.	Ferrous and non-ferrous metal.	Automatic screening.	All product prior to Fill step.	Fill operator checks to ensure detector is on.	If metal is detected, line is stopped; product diverted for inspection. If detector is not on or fails sensitivity check, all product since last acceptable check is held and rechecked for metal after the aging process.	Fill operator to run test material with metal of appropriate size to check sensitivity hourly[1]. QA manager will review and initial records daily. QA verifies sensitivity of detector weekly.	Fill operator log. Deviation reports with results of evaluation and disposition of product. Detector calibration logs.

[1]The sensitivity of the metal detector is set at 2mm even though the HACCP team has determined that metal smaller than 7mm is not a health hazard (see chapter 7 for more information). Metal of any size in the product can be determined to be an adulterant.

FROZEN BREADED FISH STICKS

Description of Product and Process Flow

Frozen breaded fish sticks are prepared from blocks of frozen minced fish; batter and breading prepared from pre-blended mixes of wheat and corn flour, modified corn starch, spices and seasonings, egg whites, and food additives; and vegetable oil (blend of canola, cottonseed and/or soybean.) The packaging materials used are PET trays, plastic shrink-wrap film supplied in rollstock, and corrugated shipping cartons for consumer packages; polyethylene film liners and corrugated cartons for food service packages; and package labels.

The breaded fish sticks are not fully cooked and require cooking prior to consumption. The fish sticks are distributed for retail sales (packaged in 8 or 22 oz. PET tray with a heat-sealed plastic film lid) or food service use (packaged in polyethylene film lined, 10 pound food service cartons). There is no atmosphere modification. Each package is labeled with a "use by" date, cooking instructions and the phrase, "keep frozen." The product is intended for the general public. The product is stored at −10°F and shipped on freezer trucks to retail or food service distribution centers.

Frozen minced fish (either pollock or haddock), purchased from an importer, is received in frozen blocks via freezer truck. The blocks are transferred to frozen storage, the freezer is set at −0°F and monitored by a recording chart and alarm system. Dry ingredients (batter, breading) and packaging materials are delivered to the plant by truck. Dry goods are placed in dry, cold storage.

The fish blocks are removed from the freezer, one pallet at a time, for processing. Cases are opened and blocks unwrapped. Blocks are cut into pre-formed fish sticks with a saw. As sticks proceed on a conveyor belt, they are culled for uniformity and then battered and breaded, twice each. Batter is kept chilled to 45°F to prevent potential growth of pathogenic microorganisms. Batter temperature is monitored periodically throughout the day.

From the last breading application, the sticks pass though a fryer containing vegetable oil for less than one minute at 400°F. This fryer sets the batter/breading but does not cook the fish.

The fish sticks exit the fryer and enter a nitrogen tunnel for individual quick freezing. The nitrogen tunnel freezer is set at temperatures equivalent to −120°F; the exposure time is 6–10 minutes.

As the fish sticks exit the freezer, they are culled for breading uniformity, packaged into either consumer packages or food service cartons, and then labeled. Packages are cased, palletized, and stored in the freezer at −10°F. Product is shipped on freezer trucks to retail or food service distribution centers.

This generic HACCP plan was developed for training purposes only and is not intended to replace the processor's hazard analysis and HACCP plan development. This model may not reflect all concerns outlined in FDA's Fish and Fisheries Products Hazards and Controls Guide: Second Edition.

Frozen Breaded Fish Sticks

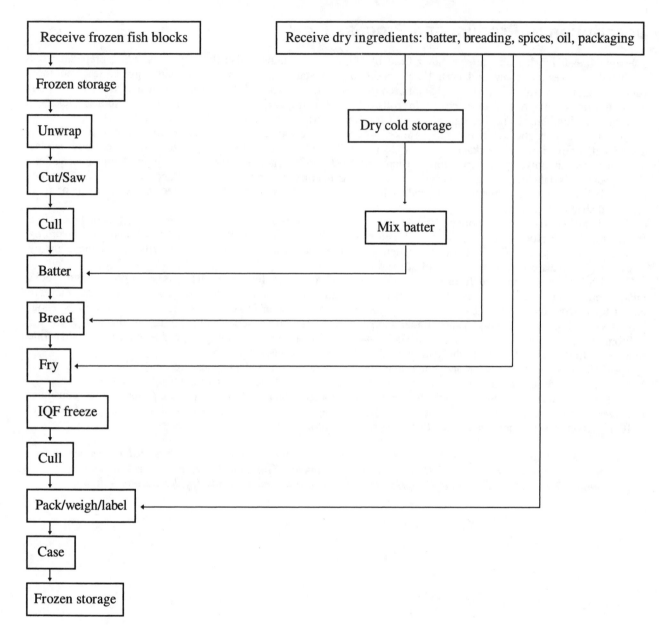

Example: For Training Purposes Only

HAZARD ANALYSIS WORKSHEET

FROZEN BREADED FISH STICKS

Ingredient or Processing Step	Potential hazards introduced, controlled or enhanced at this step.	Does this potential hazard need to be addressed in HACCP plan? (Yes/No)	WHY? (Justification for decision made in previous column)	What measures can be applied to prevent, eliminate or reduce the hazards being addressed in your HACCP plan?	Is this step a critical control point (CCP)?
Receive frozen fish blocks	BIOLOGICAL Pathogens Parasites	No	Product is not ready to eat. Product is intended to be fully cooked prior to consumption.		
	CHEMICAL None				
	PHYSICAL Bones	No	This inherent defect is not reasonably likely to result in the food being unsafe for consumption.		
Frozen storage	BIOLOGICAL Pathogens	No	Product is frozen so opportunity for pathogen growth or contamination is not reasonably likely to occur.		
	CHEMICAL None				
	PHYSICAL None				
Unwrap	BIOLOGICAL Pathogens	No	Period of time at this step is short; product remains frozen; opportunity of pathogen growth not reasonably likely to occur.		
	CHEMICAL None				
	PHYSICAL None				
Cut/Saw	BIOLOGICAL Pathogens	No	Period of time at this step is short; product remains frozen; opportunity of pathogen growth not reasonably likely to occur.		
	CHEMICAL None				
	PHYSICAL Metal fragments	Yes	Potential for saw blade to break and contaminate product is reasonably likely to occur.	Periodic inspection of equipment.	Yes CCP1(P)
Cull	BIOLOGICAL Pathogens	No	Period of time at this step is short; product remains frozen; pathogen growth not reasonably likely to occur.		
	CHEMICAL None				
	PHYSICAL None				
Receive dry ingredients	BIOLOGICAL Pathogens	No	Possibility of pathogen contamination is remote as documented by past experience of compliance with purchase specifications.		
	CHEMICAL None				
	PHYSICAL None				

Ingredient or Processing Step	Potential hazards introduced, controlled or enhanced at this step.	Does this potential hazard need to be addressed in HACCP plan? (Yes/No)	WHY? (Justification for decision made in previous column)	What measures can be applied to prevent, eliminate or reduce the hazards being addressed in your HACCP plan?	Is this step a critical control point (CCP)?
Dry cold storage	BIOLOGICAL None				
	CHEMICAL None				
	PHYSICAL None				
Mix batter	BIOLOGICAL Pathogens	No	Risk is low due to short mixing time; potable water is used.		
	CHEMICAL None				
	PHYSICAL None				
Batter	BIOLOGICAL Growth of *Staphylococcus aureus* with toxin formation	Yes[1]	Potential for *S. aureus* growth if batter held too long at elevated temperature.	Keep temperature low.	Yes CCP2(B)
	CHEMICAL None				
	PHYSICAL Metal fragments	Yes	Potential for metal fragments from wire-mesh conveyor contaminating product.	Periodic inspection of equipment.	Yes CCP3(P)
Bread	BIOLOGICAL Pathogens	No	Application of dry breading does not promote pathogen growth.		
	CHEMICAL None				
	PHYSICAL Metal fragments	Yes	Potential for metal fragments from wire-mesh conveyor contaminating product.	Periodic inspection of equipment.	Yes CCP3(P)
Fry	BIOLOGICAL None				
	CHEMICAL Rancid cooking oil	No	Potential for toxic compounds from cooking oil is not reasonably likely to occur.		
	PHYSICAL None				
IQF freeze	BIOLOGICAL Pathogens	No	Product is frozen within minutes of frying, making pathogen growth not reasonably likely to occur.		
	CHEMICAL None				
	PHYSICAL None				
Cull	BIOLOGICAL Pathogens	No	Period of time at this step is short; product remains frozen; pathogen growth not reasonably likely to occur.		
	CHEMICAL None				
	PHYSICAL None				
Pack/weigh/ label	BIOLOGICAL None				
	CHEMICAL None				
	PHYSICAL None				

Continued next page

Ingredient or Processing Step	Potential hazards introduced, controlled or enhanced at this step.	Does this potential hazard need to be addressed in HACCP plan? (Yes/No)	WHY? (Justification for decision made in previous column)	What measures can be applied to prevent, eliminate or reduce the hazards being addressed in your HACCP plan?	Is this step a critical control point (CCP)?
Case	BIOLOGICAL Pathogens	No	Period of time at this step is short; product remains frozen; pathogen growth not reasonably likely to occur.		
	CHEMICAL None				
	PHYSICAL None				
Frozen storage	BIOLOGICAL Pathogens	No	Product stored and distributed frozen so pathogen growth not reasonably likely to occur.		
	CHEMICAL None				
	PHYSICAL None				

[1]Based on the manufacturing practices in place, firms may be able to show that this hazard is not reasonably likely to occur, thus eliminating this step as a CCP.

Example: For Training Purposes Only

HACCP PLAN FORM

FROZEN BREADED FISH STICKS

Critical Control Point (CCP)	Hazard(s) to be Addressed in HACCP Plan	Critical Limits for each Control Measure	Monitoring				Corrective Action	Verification Activities	Record-keeping Procedures
			What	How	Frequency	Who			
CCP1(P) Cut/Saw and CCP3(P) Batter/Bread	Metal fragments	No broken or missing metal parts from sawblade or mesh conveyor belt.	Presence of broken or missing metal parts from sawblade or conveyor belt.	Visually check sawblade or conveyor belt for broken or missing parts.	Prior to start-up. End of operations. After sawblade or conveyor belt malfunction.	Saw operator (CCP1). Batter/bread operator (CCP3).	Stop production. Adjust or modify equipment to reduce risk of recurrence. Hold product from last acceptable check. Run product through operable metal detector.	QA to inspect sawblade (CCP1) and conveyor belt (CCP3) once per personnel shift. QA supervisor or designated employee to review monitoring and corrective action records daily.	Sawblade inspection log (CCP1). Batter/breading inspection log (CCP3). Corrective Action log. QA verification log.
CCP2(B) Batter	*Staphylococcus aureus* toxin formation.	Hydrated batter temperature should not exceed 50°F for more than 12 hours. And should not exceed 70°F for more than 3 hours.	Temperature of hydrated batter. (exposure time will be monitored by frequency of checks).	Manually check temperature in hold tank with digital indicating thermometer.	Every 2 hours.	Batter operator.	Cool batter if temperature exceeds 70°F; determine exposure time. Monitor exposure time if temperature exceeds 50°F, cool batter. Dump batter and clean batter storage tank if temperature is over 50°F for more than 12 hours or over 70°F for more than 3 hours. Make repairs to batter refrigeration equipment. Hold product involved since last good check to evaluate the total time/temperature exposure.	QA personnel verify batter temperature once per personnel shift. QA supervisor or designated employee to review monitoring and corrective action records daily. Calibrate digital indicating thermometer weekly.	Batter/breading inspection log (CCP3). Corrective Action log. Thermometer calibration log. QA verification log.

FROZEN RAW BEEF PATTIES

Description of Product and Process Flow

Frozen raw beef patties are prepared from a blend of boneless beef primal cuts and trimmings. The patties are formulated to a specified fat content to meet customer specifications. The materials used are corrugated boxes and polyethylene film liners.

The frozen raw beef patties are distributed in corrugated boxes lined with polyethylene film. The product is intended to be fully cooked prior to consumption. The product is stored and distributed at 0°F or lower. The raw beef patties are intended for the food service trade for serving to the general public.

The boneless beef is purchased from several USDA-inspected establishments. The fresh beef is received in 2000-pound combos. At receipt the combos are inspected to ensure compliance with temperature and quality specifications. The combos are held at refrigerated temperatures of 30–35°F for short-term storage. The packaging materials are warehoused at ambient temperatures.

The beef is coarse ground, blended to meet fat content specifications and chilled to 30°F with carbon dioxide. The chilled beef blend is reground at final size. A bone collection system is installed at the final grinder which diverts any bone fragments remaining in the beef. The ground beef is automatically formed into patties, then frozen in a spiral freezer. After freezing, individual frozen patties pass through a metal detector before being packaged into polyethylene film lined corrugated boxes. The finished product is stored at 0 to −10°F.

This generic HACCP plan was developed for training purposes only and is not intended to replace the processor's hazard analysis and HACCP plan development. This model may not reflect the current USDA/FSIS position on the contents of a HACCP plan.

Frozen Raw Beef Patties

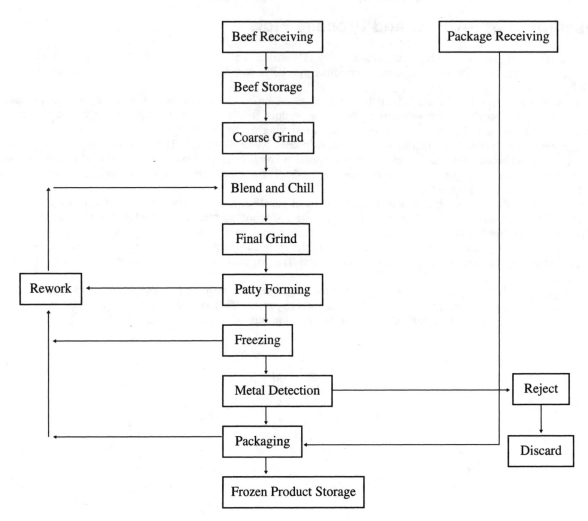

Example: For Training Purposes Only

HAZARD ANALYSIS WORKSHEET

FROZEN RAW BEEF PATTIES

Ingredient or Processing Step	Potential hazards introduced, controlled or enhanced at this step.	Does this potential hazard need to be addressed in HACCP plan? (Yes/No)	WHY? (Justification for decision made in previous column)	What measures can be applied to prevent, eliminate or reduce the hazards being addressed in your HACCP plan?	Is this step a critical control point (CCP)?
Beef Receiving (primal cuts, trimmings)	BIOLOGICAL Enteric pathogens such as salmonellae and *E. coli* O157:H7	No	Existing prerequisite program which emphasizes a microbial testing program to qualify suppliers has demonstrated that the hazard is not reasonably likely to occur in this establishment.		
	CHEMICAL Antibiotics Growth hormones Sanitizers Lubricants	No	All beef purchased from USDA-inspected establishments with validated HACCP plans. Not reasonably likely for beef to have violative levels of chemical contaminants.		
	PHYSICAL Metal	Yes	History has shown that incoming beef may be contaminated with metal, which could end up in the finished product.	Metal detector at a later step.	No
	Bone	No	Although the incoming beef may contain some bone fragments, the final grinder is equipped with a bone collection system. The grinder will not function without the bone collection system in place.		
Package Receiving	BIOLOGICAL None				
	CHEMICAL Non-food grade materials used in packaging materials	No	Packaging materials purchased from company approved suppliers who meet specifications for food contact packaging materials. Not reasonably likely to receive non-food grade materials.		
	PHYSICAL None				
Beef Storage	BIOLOGICAL Enteric pathogens could increase in number	No	Historical microbiological data has shown that pathogen growth is not reasonably likely to occur due to adherence to plant-wide temperature control SOPs.[1]		
	CHEMICAL None				
	PHYSICAL None				

Ingredient or Processing Step	Potential hazards introduced, controlled or enhanced at this step.	Does this potential hazard need to be addressed in HACCP plan? (Yes/No)	WHY? (Justification for decision made in previous column)	What measures can be applied to prevent, eliminate or reduce the hazards being addressed in your HACCP plan?	Is this step a critical control point (CCP)?
Coarse Grind	BIOLOGICAL Enteric pathogens could increase in number	No	Historical microbiological data has shown that pathogen growth is not reasonably likely to occur due to adherence to plant-wide temperature control SOPs.[1]		
	CHEMICAL Excessive sanitizers	No	Sanitizer levels controlled by effective sanitation program with SSOPs. Not reasonably likely to result in illness or injury.		
	PHYSICAL Metal Fragments	Yes	The potential for metal contamination from grinder exists.	Metal detector at a later step.	No
	Bone	No	The final grinder is equipped with a bone collection system. The grinder will not function without the bone collection system in place.		
Blend and Chill	BIOLOGICAL Enteric pathogens could increase in number	No	Historical microbiological data has shown that pathogen growth is not reasonably likely to occur due to adherence to plant-wide temperature control SOPs.[1]		
	CHEMICAL Excessive sanitizers	No	Sanitizer levels controlled by effective sanitation program with SSOPs. Reasonably unlikely to result in illness or injury.		
	PHYSICAL Metal	Yes	The potential for metal contamination from blender exists.		
Final Grind	BIOLOGICAL Enteric pathogens could increase in number	No	Historical microbiological data has shown that pathogen growth is not reasonably likely to occur due to adherence to plant-wide temperature control SOPs.[1]		
	CHEMICAL Excessive sanitizers	No	Sanitizer levels controlled by effective sanitation program with SSOPs. Reasonably unlikely to result in illness or injury.		
	PHYSICAL Metal fragments	Yes	The potential for metal contamination from grinder exists.	Metal detector at a later step.	No
	Bone	No	The final grinder is equipped with a bone collection system. The grinder will not function without the bone collection system in place.		
Patty Forming	BIOLOGICAL Enteric pathogens could increase in number	No	Historical microbiological data has shown that pathogen growth is not reasonably likely to occur due to adherence to plant-wide temperature control SOPs.[1]		
	CHEMICAL Excessive sanitizers	No	Sanitizer levels controlled by effective sanitation program with SSOPs. Reasonably unlikely to result in illness or injury.		
	PHYSICAL Metal	Yes	The potential for metal contamination from grinder exists.	Metal detector at a later step.	No

Continued next page

Ingredient or Processing Step	Potential hazards introduced, controlled or enhanced at this step.	Does this potential hazard need to be addressed in HACCP plan? (Yes/No)	WHY? (Justification for decision made in previous column)	What measures can be applied to prevent, eliminate or reduce the hazards being addressed in your HACCP plan?	Is this step a critical control point (CCP)?
Freezing	BIOLOGICAL Enteric pathogens could increase in number	No	Total time to freeze product is very short, pathogen growth not reasonably likely to occur.		
	CHEMICAL None				
	PHYSICAL None				
Metal Detection	BIOLOGICAL None				
	CHEMICAL None				
	PHYSICAL Metal (controlled at this step)	Yes	The potential for metal contamination from supplier and production equipment exists.	Operable metal detector/reject mechanism.	Yes CCP1(P)
Packaging	BIOLOGICAL Enteric pathogens could increase in number	No	Total time at this step is very short, pathogen growth not reasonably likely to occur.		
	CHEMICAL None				
	PHYSICAL None				
Rework	BIOLOGICAL Enteric pathogens could increase in number	No	Historical microbiological data has shown that pathogen growth is not reasonably likely to occur due to adherence to rework SOPs which stipulates reworking products within a 2-hour timeframe.[2]		
	CHEMICAL None				
	PHYSICAL Metal				
Frozen Product Storage	BIOLOGICAL Enteric pathogens could increase in number	No	Pathogen growth not reasonably likely to occur due to adherence to plant-wide temperature control SOPs.		
	CHEMICAL None				
	PHYSICAL None				

[1]USDA/FSIS has indicated an expectation that establishments that grind beef should reassess their hazard analysis if they do not have a CCP that addresses pathogen control during processing. This implies that the Agency may expect a CCP for temperature control. Establishments should develop data that demonstrates little or no microbial growth under normal conditions of operation. Temperature control records and microbial data will be necessary as part of the hazard analysis to demonstrate that this hazard is not reasonably likely to occur.
[2]Rework SOP includes a record-keeping system which documents time, quantity, the original batch code and the code of the receiving batch. Product which can not be reworked within the 2 hour timeframe is diverted to a ready-to-eat product line.

Example: For Training Purposes Only

HACCP PLAN FORM

FROZEN RAW BEEF PATTIES

Critical Control Point (CCP)	Hazard(s) to be Addressed in HACCP Plan	Critical Limits for each Control Measure	Monitoring				Corrective Action	Verification Activities	Record-keeping Procedures
			What	How	Frequency	Who			
CCP1(P) Metal Detection	Metal	Patties pass through functioning detector.	Patties conveyed through metal detector.	Visual observation to ensure detector is on and patties conveyed through detector.	Once every 2 hours.	Packaging operator.	If detector not operational or not operating within specification, product retained until detector repaired.	QA personnel checks sensitivity by running test material with metal of appropriate size once per shift.	Packaging line production form. Corrective action reports with results of evaluation and disposition of product.
			Metal detector is functioning.	Challenge with sample seeded with appropriate size metal.	Once every 2 hours.	Packaging operator.	Adjust metal detector to obtain required sensitivity. Patties from last acceptable monitoring check will be held until they can be rescanned. Requirements of 9 *CFR* 417.3 will be followed.	QA manager will conduct preshipment review of monitoring, corrective action and applicable verification records. Maintenance calibrates metal detector monthly.	Metal detector calibration logs.

ALL-BEEF HOT DOGS

Description of Product and Process Flow

All-beef hot dogs are prepared from a blend of beef and other non-beef ingredients (i.e., water, flavorings, corn syrup, salt, dextrose, ascorbic acid, and sodium nitrite.) The non-food materials used are shirred cellulose casings, plastic film comprised of a coextrusion of various plastics supplied in rollstock and corrugated shipping cartons.

All-beef hot dogs are distributed in corrugated shipping cartons. Product is stored and distributed at 40°F; shelf-life is expected to be at least 60 days. The product is intended for the general public and is intended to be reheated prior to use. Although the package lists reheating instructions, some consumers may eat the product without reheating.

Fresh boneless beef is purchased from several USDA-inspected establishments. The beef is received in 2000-pound combos. At receipt the combos are inspected to ensure compliance with temperature and quality specifications. The combos are held at refrigerated temperatures of 30–35°F for short-term storage and staging. The non-meat ingredients and materials are purchased from approved suppliers and warehoused at ambient temperatures.

The beef is coarse ground then blended to meet fat content specifications. The beef is ground then mixed with the remaining ingredients in a blender. The blend is chopped in a vacuum chopper, pumped to an emulsifier then to the stuffing hopper. The emulsified blend is automatically stuffed into casings, linked, hung on smoke sticks and placed on oven racks. The racks are manually pushed into a smoke house.

The hot dogs are cooked to a specific internal temperature that is greater than USDA/FSIS's requirements for cooked sausage. After cooking, the hot dogs are cooled immediately by showering with chilled water, blast-chilling and transferring to a holding cooler. Prior to packaging the hot dogs are peeled and collated. The product is vacuum packaged, cased and palletized for storage and shipment. The finished product is stored at 40°F or lower.

This generic HACCP plan was developed for training purposes only and is not intended to replace the processor's hazard analysis and HACCP plan development. This model may not reflect the current USDA/FSIS position on the contents of a HACCP plan.

All-Beef Hot Dogs

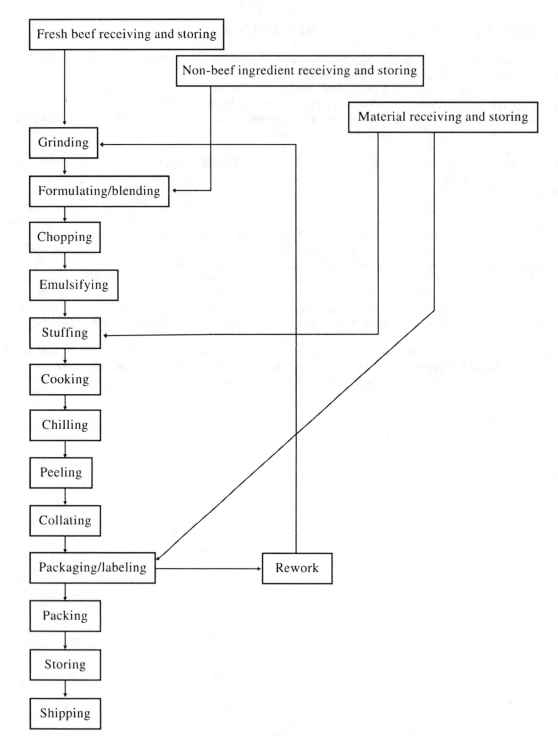

Example: For Training Purposes Only

HAZARD ANALYSIS WORKSHEET

ALL-BEEF HOT DOGS

Ingredient or Processing Step	Potential hazards introduced, controlled or enhanced at this step.	Does this potential hazard need to be addressed in HACCP plan? (Yes/No)	WHY? (Justification for decision made in previous column)	What measures can be applied to prevent, eliminate or reduce the hazards being addressed in your HACCP plan?	Is this step a critical control point (CCP)?
Fresh Beef Receiving and Storing	**BIOLOGICAL** **Vegetative pathogens** (*Salmonella*, *E. coli* O157:H7, and other enteric pathogens, *Listeria monocytogenes*) from raw beef	Yes	Raw beef is a known source of vegetative pathogens.	Proper cooking at later step	No
	Sporeforming pathogens (C. perfringens and others) from raw beef	Yes	Raw beef is know source of sporeforming pathogens.	Proper chilling after the cooking step	No
	CHEMICAL Excessive antibiotic and hormone residues in beef	No	Not reasonably likely to receive beef trim with hazardous residue levels due to prerequisite programs, purchasing from USDA inspected suppliers with HACCP plans and USDA tissue-residue monitoring activities.		
	Allergen from species contamination	No	Research has indicated that allergenic reactions to species contamination is relatively mild. Allergens present in meat are unstable to heat. Not reasonably likely to cause illness in consumer.		
	PHYSICAL Bone chips	No	Although the incoming beef may contain some bone fragments, the final grinder is equipped with a bone collection system. The grinder will not function without the bone collection system in place.		
	Plastic Wood Metal	No	The potential exists for plastic, wood and metal to contaminate the fresh beef. However, this hazard is not reasonably likely to occur in the finished product due to the emulsification step later in the process which reduces the size of any foreign object to below that determined by USDA/FSIS Public Health Hazard Analysis Board to present a risk.		
Non-beef Ingredient Receiving and Storing (flavorings, corn syrup, salt, dextrose, ascorbic acid, sodium nitrite preblend)	**BIOLOGICAL** Sporeforming pathogens (*C. perfringens* and others) from spices	Yes	Spices are known sources of sporeforming pathogens.	Proper chilling after the cooking step	No
	CHEMICAL Excessive levels of sodium nitrite in pre-blend	No	Not reasonably likely to receive pre-blend with excessive levels of sodium nitrite due to purchasing from approved suppliers with verified HACCP plan.		
	Non-food grade ingredient	No	Ingredients purchased from company approved suppliers who meet specifications for ingredients. Not reasonably likely to receive non-food grade ingredients.		
	PHYSICAL None				

Ingredient or Processing Step	Potential hazards introduced, controlled or enhanced at this step.	Does this potential hazard need to be addressed in HACCP plan? (Yes/No)	WHY? (Justification for decision made in previous column)	What measures can be applied to prevent, eliminate or reduce the hazards being addressed in your HACCP plan?	Is this step a critical control point (CCP)?
Material Receiving and Storing (casings, packaging materials)	BIOLOGICAL None				
	CHEMICAL Non-food grade materials	No	Materials purchased from company approved suppliers who meet specifications for materials. Not reasonably likely to receive non-food grade ingredients.		
	PHYSICAL None				
Grinding	BIOLOGICAL Vegetative pathogens (growth)	No	Period of time at this step is short; opportunity for pathogen growth not reasonably likely to occur.		
	CHEMICAL Excessive sanitizers	No	Sanitizer levels controlled by effective sanitation program with SSOPs. Not reasonably likely to result in illness or injury.		
	Allergen from species contamination	No	Research has indicated that allergenic reactions to species contamination is relatively mild. Allergens present in meat are unstable to heat. Not reasonably likely to cause illness if consumed. Established rework SOP has historically prevented the mixing of other species into all-beef products.		
	PHYSICAL Bone chips	No	The final grinder is equipped with a bone collection system. The grinder will not function without the bone collection system in place.		
	Metal fragments	Yes	The potential for metal contamination from grinder exists.	Periodic inspection of equipment	Yes CCP1(P)
Formulating/ Blending	BIOLOGICAL Vegetative pathogens (growth)	No	Period of time at this step is short; opportunity for pathogen growth not reasonably likely to occur.		
	CHEMICAL Excessive sanitizers	No	Sanitizer levels controlled by effective sanitation program with SSOPs. Not reasonably likely to result in illness or injury.		
	Allergen from species contamination	No	Research has indicated that allergenic reactions to species contamination is relatively mild. Allergens present in meat are unstable to heat. Not reasonably likely to cause illness in consumer.		
	PHYSICAL Metal fragments	Yes	The potential for metal contamination from blender exists.	Periodic inspection of equipment	Yes CCP1(P)
Chopping	BIOLOGICAL Pathogens (growth)	No	Period of time at this step is short; opportunity for pathogen growth not reasonably likely to occur.		
	CHEMICAL Excessive sanitizers	No	Sanitizer levels controlled by effective sanitation program with SSOPs. Not reasonably likely to result in illness or injury.		
	PHYSICAL Metal fragments	Yes	The potential for metal contamination from chopper exists.	Periodic inspection of equipment	Yes CCP1(P)

Continued next page

Ingredient or Processing Step	Potential hazards introduced, controlled or enhanced at this step.	Does this potential hazard need to be addressed in HACCP plan? (Yes/No)	WHY? (Justification for decision made in previous column)	What measures can be applied to prevent, eliminate or reduce the hazards being addressed in your HACCP plan?	Is this step a critical control point (CCP)?
Emulsifying	BIOLOGICAL Pathogen (growth)	No	Period of time at this step is short; opportunity for pathogen growth not reasonably likely to occur.		
	CHEMICAL Excessive sanitizers	No	Sanitizer levels controlled by effective sanitation program with SSOPs. Not reasonably likely to result in illness or injury.		
	PHYSICAL Metal fragments	Yes	The potential for metal contamination from chopper exists.	Periodic inspection of equipment	Yes CCP1(P)
Stuffing	BIOLOGICAL Pathogen (growth)	No	Period of time at this step is short; opportunity for pathogen growth not reasonably likely to occur.		
	CHEMICAL Excessive sanitizers	No	Sanitizer levels controlled by effective sanitation program with SSOPs. Not reasonably likely to result in illness or injury.		
	PHYSICAL None				
Cooking	BIOLOGICAL Vegetative pathogens (*Salmonella, E. coli O157:H7,* and other enteric pathogens, *Listeria monocytogenes*)	Yes	This is the only step where heat is applied sufficient to destroy vegetative pathogens.	Cooking to destroy pathogens	Yes CCP2(B)
	CHEMICAL None				
	PHYSICAL None				
Chilling	BIOLOGICAL Sporeforming pathogens (*C. perfringens* and others)	Yes	Sporeforming pathogens are not completely destroyed with the cook and may grow if not rapidly chilled.	Rapid cooling of product to prevent growth of sporeforming pathogens	Yes CCP3(B)
	Listeria monocytogenes (recontamination)	No	Not reasonably likely to recontaminate the product with *L. monocytogenes* due to effective plant-wide prerequisite programs such as GMPs, sanitation, and training.[1]		
	CHEMICAL None				
	PHYSICAL None				
Peeling	BIOLOGICAL *Listeria monocytogenes* (recontamination)	No	Not reasonably likely to recontaminate the product with *L. monocytogenes* due to effective plant-wide prerequisite programs such as GMPs, sanitation, and training.[1]		
	CHEMICAL None				
	PHYSICAL None				
Collating	BIOLOGICAL *Listeria monocytogenes* (recontamination)	No	Not reasonably likely to recontaminate the product with *L. monocytogenes* due to effective plant-wide prerequisite programs such as GMPs, sanitation, and training.[1]		
	CHEMICAL None				
	PHYSICAL None				

Ingredient or Processing Step	Potential hazards introduced, controlled or enhanced at this step.	Does this potential hazard need to be addressed in HACCP plan? (Yes/No)	WHY? (Justification for decision made in previous column)	What measures can be applied to prevent, eliminate or reduce the hazards being addressed in your HACCP plan?	Is this step a critical control point (CCP)?
Packaging/ Labeling	BIOLOGICAL Listeria monocytogenes (recontamination)	No	Not reasonably likely to recontaminate the product with L. monocytogenes due to effective plant-wide prerequisite programs such as GMPs, sanitation, and training.[1]		
	CHEMICAL None				
	PHYSICAL None				
Rework	BIOLOGICAL Pathogens (growth)	Yes	Although reworked product is maintained at low temperatures, it is reasonably likely that some pathogen growth may occur prior to rework.	Proper cooking and cooling at later steps	No
	CHEMICAL Allergen from species contamination	No	Research has indicated that allergenic reactions to species contamination is relatively mild. Allergens present in meat are unstable to heat. Not reasonably likely to cause illness in consumer.		
	PHYSICAL None				
Packing	BIOLOGICAL Sporeforming pathogens (growth)	No	Growth of sporeforming pathogens not reasonably likely to occur because the product will support the growth of spoilage organisms which will inhibit the germination of spores.		
	CHEMICAL None				
	PHYSICAL None				
Storing	BIOLOGICAL Sporeforming pathogens (growth)	No	Growth of sporeforming pathogens not reasonably likely to occur because the product will support the growth of spoilage organisms which will inhibit the germination of spores.		
	CHEMICAL None				
	PHYSICAL None				
Shipping	BIOLOGICAL Sporeforming pathogens (growth)	No	Growth of sporeforming pathogens not reasonably likely to occur because the product will support the growth of spoilage organisms which will inhibit the germination of spores.		
	CHEMICAL None				
	PHYSICAL None				

[1]On May 25, 1999, USDA/FSIS published a notice in the Federal Register (64 Fed. Reg. 28351) stating its position that Listeria monocytogenes is a food safety hazard that is reasonably likely to occur in ready-to-eat livestock and poultry products. Establishments manufacturing these products were given 30 days to reassess their HACCP plans to determine if this hazard is adequately addressed in the plans. Unless the establishment can show that the pathogen is not likely to occur in its products (including from post-process recontamination) a CCP specific for this hazard will be expected. See the USDA/FSIS publication "Listeria Guidelines for Industry," May, 1999, for additional advice on L. monocytogenes control. The document may be accessed at the following website: http://www.fsis.usda.gov/index.htm.

Example: For Training Purposes Only

HACCP PLAN FORM

ALL-BEEF HOT DOGS

Critical Control Point (CCP)	Hazard(s) to be Addressed in HACCP Plan	Critical Limits for each Control Measure	Monitoring				Corrective Action	Verification Activities	Record-keeping Procedures
			What	How	Frequency	Who			
CCP1(P) Grinding, blending, chopping, emulsifying[1]	Metal	No broken or missing metal parts from grinder, blender, chopper, emulsifier.	Presence of broken or missing metal parts from equipment.	Visually check equipment for broken or missing parts.	Prior to start-up. End of operations. After grinder, blender, chopper, or emulsifier malfunction.	Production supervisor.	Hold product from last acceptable check for evaluation. Run affected product through operable metal detector. Requirements of 9 *CFR* 417.3 will be met.	QA personnel check sensitivity of corrective action metal detector once every 2 hours. QA manager will review monitoring, corrective action and applicable verification records daily.	Equipment inspection log. Deviation reports with results of evaluation and disposition of product. Metal detector calibration log. QA verification log.
CCP2(B) Cooking	Vegetative pathogens	Minimum internal product temperature 148°F[2].	Temperature of product.	Manual thermometer.	Once per batch.	Oven operator.	Continue cooking batch until critical limit is met. If cook cannot be completed, hold product. Evaluate safety of product. Requirements of 9 *CFR* 417.3 will be met.	QA manager will conduct preshipment review of monitoring, corrective action and applicable verification records. QA verifies accuracy of manual thermometer prior to production start-up. Outside consultant to validate operation of oven at least once per year.	Oven log. Calibration records. Oven validation report. Corrective action logs.
CCP3(B) Chilling	Spore-forming pathogens	Chill to ≤ 50°F within 4 hours after completion of cook.	Temperature of product.	Manual thermometer.	Every 2 hours.	Cooler operator.	Retain product from last good check. Requirements of 9 *CFR* 417.3 will be met.	QA manager will conduct preshipment review of monitoring, corrective action and applicable verification records. QA verifies accuracy of manual thermometer prior to production start-up. Outside consultant to validate operation of blast chiller every two years.	Cooling log book. Calibration records. Oven validation report. Corrective action logs.

[1] The HACCP team has decided that the appropriate control measure for metal contamination is the inspection of the equipment. All product is routinely passed through a metal detector set at a detection sensitivity of 2 mm.
[2] Critical limit is based on USDA/FSIS Directive 7370.2. Establishment has collected data which validates that this critical limit is adequate for the destruction of the pathogens of concern.

REFERENCES

Bernard, D.T., W.R. Cole, D.E. Gombas, M. Pierson, R. Savage, R.B. Tompkin, and R.P. Wooden. 1997. Beef franks. *Dairy, Food Env. Sanit.* 17:417.

Bernard, D.T., W.R. Cole, D.E. Gombas, M. Pierson, R. Savage, R.B. Tompkin, and R.P. Wooden. 1997. Bulk cheddar cheese for food service or further processing. *Dairy, Food Env. Sanit.* 17:344.

Bernard, D.T., W.R. Cole, D.E. Gombas, M. Pierson, R. Savage, R.B. Tompkin, and R.P. Wooden. 1997. Frozen, raw beef patties for food service. *Dairy, Food Env. Sanit.* 17:427.

National Seafood HACCP Alliance for Training and Education. 1997. Appendix V: Models. In: HACCP: Hazard Analysis and Critical Control Point Training Curriculum, 3rd ed. North Carolina Sea Grant, Raleigh, N.C.